Prophets of Deceit

Prophets of Deceit

A Study of the Techniques
of the American Agitator

LEO LÖWENTHAL
and
NORBERT GUTERMAN

VERSO

London • New York

This edition first published by Verso 2021
First published by The American Jewish Committee 1949
© Leo Löwenthal and Norbert Guterman 1949, 2021

1 3 5 7 9 10 8 6 4 2

Verso
UK: 6 Meard Street, London W1F 0EG
US: 20 Jay Street, Suite 1010, Brooklyn, NY 11201
versobooks.com

Verso is the imprint of New Left Books

ISBN-13: 978-1-78873-696-1
ISBN-13: 978-1-78873-697-8 (UK EBK)
ISBN-13: 978-1-78873-698-5 (US EBK)

British Library Cataloguing in Publication Data
A catalogue record for this book is available from the British Library

Library of Congress Cataloging-in-Publication Data
A catalog record for this book is available from the Library of Congress

Printed and bound by CPI Group (UK) Ltd, Croydon CR0 4YY

YEA, THEY ARE PROPHETS OF
THE DECEIT OF THEIR OWN HEART.

Jer. 23:26

Contents

Introduction to the Verso Edition: Psychoanalysis in Reverse

Alberto Toscano

Fascist potentials and potential fascists

In 1979, by which time he was the sole surviving member of the founding generation of the Frankfurt School (Adorno had died in 1969, Pollock in 1970, Horkheimer in 1973), Leo Löwenthal spoke to an interviewer about the role that the inquiry into latent authoritarianism had played in the Institute for Social Research's departure from Germany (first to Switzerland, then to the USA). As he recollected:

> In 1930, we began conducting surveys on the psychological and ideological behavior and modes of thinking among the progressive blue- and white-collar workers in Rheinland and Westfalen. As I always say ironically, we invented American methods, so to speak, because we didn't know them. On the one hand, we asked completely open questions: what the people think, how they vote, for example. But then we asked psychological projection questions: "Who are the great figures in history? Who should be master of the household?" Everything that was later identified in connection with authoritarian personality traits. . . . As we received the results—that was probably the beginning of 1931—our hearts leapt to our throats. For, on the ideological surface, these good Social Democrats and left-of-center voters were all very liberal

and republican. But on a deeper, psychological level, the majority were completely authoritarian, with admiration for Bismarck and strict upbringing of children and "the woman's place is in the home"—whatever. So it was really terrible, what all was revealed. Instead of proceeding with the study, we thought, for God's sake, what is going to happen in Germany? For, if that is the psychological make-up of the most progressive circles of the German population, is where, after all, resistance to the apparently unstoppable advance of National Socialism would have to be centered, then there would be no stopping it. And then, I think it was September 14, 1930, as 107 Nazi representatives were elected for the first time, we said to ourselves: it is not possible to remain in Germany.[1]

This rare example of how "social research helped the social researchers themselves,"[2] encapsulates a number of features of critical theory's confrontation with fascism, many of which shaped *Prophets of Deceit*, Löwenthal's 1949 collaboration with Norbert Guterman, one of the five volumes of the *Studies in Prejudice* which, under the general editorship of Max Horkheimer, the Institute jointly produced with the American Jewish Committee. The gap between class location and psychology, between "objectively" progressive interests and unconscious "subjective" attitudes was the space inhabited by the necessarily interdisciplinary and politically partisan (but not Party-based) inquiry that the Institute pushed ever since Horkheimer assumed its directorship. This inquiry developed over the temporal arc linking the impending rise of Nazism in the early 1930s to the postwar preoccupation with the persistence of fascist potentials in the very country that had helped to vanquish Hitlerism, provided the Institute with refuge and loudly advertised itself as the beacon of liberty.

The study Löwenthal references was part of the collective work that resulted in the Institute's most accomplished realization of the idea of critical social research, namely the 1936 *Studies on Authority and the Family*, whose theoretical framework was established in three long essays by Max Horkheimer, Herbert Marcuse and Erich Fromm. It was Fromm in particular who crystallized the notion of an authoritarian character marked by the "pleasure of obedience, submission, and the surrender of one's own personality," as well as "aggression against the defenseless and sympathy with the powerful."[3]

What particularly marked the *Studies* was the imperative to combine three materially and temporally distinct levels at which the potentials for authoritarianism were to be tackled: the sociopsychological one of the individual character; the socioeconomic level of the authoritarian tendencies intrinsic to capitalism and its crises; and, finally, an ideological level that encompassed the history of ideas and subjectivities. Approached through this multidimensional frame, authoritarianism was never a mere political event or a psychological disposition, but the offspring of a political-economic conjuncture and the cumulative product of bourgeois history and anthropology, as they reached a kind of terminal crisis of their own. Mindful of the presentism, as well as the mechanical analogies, that govern much contemporary thinking about fascism and its afterlives, it is worth underscoring the place of the *longue durée* in the critical theory of authoritarianism that *Prophets of Deceit* tries to embody and apply. The fact that Löwenthal and Guterman refer the reader to Horkheimer's 1936 essay on "Egoism and the Freedom Movement"—which traces a genealogy of bourgeois leadership and its authoritarian traits all the way to the Mediaeval "tribune of the Roman people" Cola di Rienzo—is testament to this. If, as Löwenthal stated in his (unpublished at the time) contribution to the Institute's *Studies*, "[p]eople of the present historical era have learned to view the world essentially from a perspective of domination and subordination,"[4] it is not sufficient simply to consider the functional requirements of capitalist reproduction, one must also inquire into the contributions to the latter of forms of life and thought that predate the current dispensation—namely the patriarchal family and the legitimations for authority articulated in the religion and metaphysics that accompanied capitalism's inception. Notwithstanding differences in method as well as in their respective conceptions of Marxism, it is worth noting that Guterman's signal contribution to the study of ideology, *La Conscience mystifiée* (Mystified Consciousness),[5] published in collaboration with Henri Lefebvre in 1936, also framed the analysis of contemporary fascism in terms of a history of fetishism that went back to the very origins of commodity exchange.

Prophets of Deceit is centrally concerned with the "potential fascist" (a title that had been toyed with for the most famous of the

Studies in Prejudice, The Authoritarian Personality) but like all the research projects and theses advanced in the ambit of the Institute for Social Research, it articulated this focus on individual psychology with a consideration of fascism's gestation in the *longue durée* of bourgeois anthropology and its catalyzation by capitalist crisis. In a 1950 essay reflecting on the place of psychology in the study of fascism, where he also briefly touched on the agitator's stereotyped repertoire, Horkheimer stressed the decisive place in the rise of fascism of the objective structure of social interest, as opposed to the individual psychology of the people. For him, masses were the object and not the subject of fascist rule, and their feelings a secondary (if significant) factor in the constitution of aggressive authoritarian regimes. Rather than a cumulative product of the authoritarian character, in the final analysis "fascism arose when the over-all economic situation required planned organisation and when leading forces turned the need of such planning into their own channels."[6] A few years prior, similar considerations—which find their most lapidary and controversial formulation in the dictum from Horkheimer's 1939 "Europe and the Jews": "whoever is not willing to talk about capitalism should also keep quiet about fascism"—also governed Horkheimer's comments on a draft of *Prophets*. As he wrote to Löwenthal on 29 July 1946:

> There are many more remarks I would like to make but the most important must simply wait until we can speak to each other. There is one thing which should not be omitted here: the agitators will probably be unleashed upon the people at a moment of economic depression. Therefore, it seems necessary to me to bring in the economic motive much more clearly than the notes indicate so far. We speak of the audience and the masses but masses are different. The audience of the agitator in time of war or prosperity is not the same as the audience in the period which immediately precedes a totalitarian uprising. The former is constituted largely of old women, cranks, asocial elements, etc. while the latter audiences which play a role in a fascist situation are much more rational. I remind you of the fact, so often observed by both of us, that the fascists in pre-fascist Germany were better informed about economic and diplomatic matters than the average non-fascist. I do not want to over-emphasize this point because your central theme is the psychology of agitation and I know very well

that the process of agitation tends to level the differences and to bring out the paranoid elements in each audience. However, we should not expose ourselves to the justified accusation that we ignore the role played by outright economic factors. There is also direct economic reasoning.[7]

Inasmuch as anti-fascist theories of fascism are always politically and ethically shadowed by the imperative of vigilance, the location and nature of fascist potentials— together with the relative weight of economic, political and psychological factors—remains an issue of abiding concern and dispute. Without papering over the important internal differences and shifts in work on fascism produced by the Institute's members in the 1930s and 1940s, it is particularly important when considering *Prophets* to recall its place within a broader collective effort to analyze authoritarian tendencies in the present. The *longue durée* of authoritarianism and its roots in bourgeois anthropology, as well as in structural and conjunctural features of capitalism, risks being relegated to the background, overpowered by the effects of recognition and resemblance that will strike any contemporary reader of Löwenthal and Guterman's book. The repertoire of the "lunatic fringe" of the 1930s and 40s is pretty mainstream fodder in 2021, while turns of phrase that populated the pamphlets and radio shows of these now-forgotten American agitators find uncanny echoes at the very summit of the capitalist state. In many ways, Donald Trump's tenure at the White House was definitive testament to the truth of Herbert Marcuse's observation in his 1970 preface to the second edition of *Prophets of Deceit*, where, with the Nixon presidency firmly in his sights, he wrote that "the demarcation line between the outsider agitator and the legitimate politician, between the extreme right and the center [is] being blurred (if not obliterated). Today, we recognize the essential features of the agitator as those of the political Establishment."[8] Around the same time, Adorno also stressed the need not to be misled by the apparent exceptionality and marginality that marked the Institute's agitator project. As he cautioned:

> the calculated influence of agitators on the "lunatic fringe" is by no means the only and probably not even the most important objective factor promoting a fascistically inclined mentality among the masses. This susceptibility reaches deep into the

structures of society itself and is generated by society before demagogues deliberately come to its aid. The opinions of demagogues are by no means as restricted to the lunatic fringe as one may at first, optimistically, suppose. They occur in considerable measure in the utterances of so-called "respectable" people, only not as succinctly and aggressively formulated.[9]

Intellectual co-workers

In distinct ways, Leo Löwenthal and Norbert Guterman are both exemplars of a kind of politically-oriented and collective intellectual work—threaded through institutes, journals, translations, editing, and so on—which is generally overshadowed by the mystique of authorship. Both born in 1900, they came of political and theoretical age in the tumultuous aftermath of World War 1.

Raised in a progressive Jewish family, though briefly serving as interpreter for the Foreign Legion in the war against the Red Army in 1919–20, Guterman emigrated from Poland to France in 1921, where he completed his studies in philosophy at the Sorbonne. It was there he met Georges Politzer and Pierre Morhange, with whom he would found the review *Philosophies*, where they were then joined by Henri Lefebvre, Paul Nizan, and Georges Friedmann. *Philosophies* was a pioneering experiment in contrasting the primacy of spiritualism within French philosophy, and in advancing a Marxist position in philosophy. In 1929, under the pseudonym "Albert Mesnil," Guterman would become the editorial secretary of the new journal *Revue Marxiste*. The *Revue* would receive from David Riazanov and the Marx-Engels Institute's journal, *Arkhiv K. Marksa i F. Engel's*, hitherto unpublished texts of Marx and Engels—among them sections of the 1844 *Economic-Philosophical Manuscripts*, which Guterman translated and prefaced for the *Revue*. In the late Summer of '29, due to internal disputes that pitted Guterman and Morhange against Nizan and Politzer, and the interference of the French Communist Party (an emissary from which was even punched by Guterman in an altercation over party funds), the journal was shuttered and Guterman expelled from the PCF, even though he remained adamant he had never joined (as he mused: "I was excluded even though I was never included. How can you exclude someone who doesn't belong?").[10] Having escaped a possible expulsion from France as a foreigner after the Communist newspaper *L'Humanité* published his name in response to the *Revue* affair, Guterman left for the United States in 1930, returning to Paris in 1932, where in 1933, alongside Morhange and Lefebvre, he founded the anti-fascist theoretical journal *Avant-Poste*. In its pages, he began the collaboration with Lefebvre that would find further expression in *La Conscience mystifiée*, as well as their pioneering edited selections from Marx (*Morceaux Choisis de Marx*, 1934) and Hegel (*Morceaux Choisis de Hegel*, 1939), and their edition of Lenin's notebooks on the *Science of Logic* (*Cahiers sur la dialectique de Hegel*, 1938).[11] Guterman would definitively leave for New York in 1933, where Lefebvre briefly joined him to work on *La Conscience*. There, he would collaborate assiduously, principally as a book reviewer and translator, with *The New Republic*, the *Partisan Review* and later the *Monthly Review*. Guterman became an associate of the Institute in exile in 1936. In 1941, Guterman penned a review of a number of volumes on propaganda for the final, English-language volume of the Institute's house journal the *Zeitschrift für Sozialforschung*.[12] In 1943, he was tasked by the Institute with writing an article in the *Partisan Review* to counter a series of articles published under the heading "The New Failure of Nerve" and written by Sydney Hook, John Dewey and Ernest Nagel, which Horkheimer and others felt were intended as an attack on their positions. Guterman's path was quite oblique, taking the form of a nuanced piece on Kierkegaard indicating how neither the variant of positivism associated with Hook et al. nor a radical subjectivism were adequate philosophical responses to the present crisis. In this context he presented a kind of ethical wartime warrant for critical theory:

> Any theory that comforts us through the implicit or explicit negation of the historical context in which our lives are caught, any theory that negates the reality of the struggle as though the full realization of man were possible in the immediate present, involves a degrading abandonment of lucidity. In our time, military virtue is part of the individual's self-realization, even though it exposes him to the risk of losing his own unique life ... the best fighters are not those who cultivate sacrifice as an end in itself but

those who even in the face of voluntary death preserve the conviction that a world is possible in which men will control history instead of being controlled by it.[13]

Guterman would go on to edit Horkheimer's *Eclipse of Reason* from lectures delivered in 1944, even drafting a (later discarded) preface.[14] He would also serve as the (beleaguered) translator of Adorno's co-authored book with Hans Eisler on film composition.[15] Horkheimer in particular seems to have appreciated Guterman's abilities: envisaging a relaunch of the *Zeitschrift* in 1946, he wrote to Löwenthal: "If you calculate that Guterman might devote at least part time to such an undertaking, we have, together with [Paul] Massing an editorial staff which is indeed unique in the world today."[16] Though affirming his primary authorship, Löwenthal himself spoke highly of the collaboration with Guterman. Writing to Horkheimer about *Prophets*, he observed:

> I have to say a word about the process of production. The notes are the result of common conversations between Guterman and me. As far as the ideas are concerned, I have contributed considerably more than he, but without him I could not have done so well. He deserves gratitude and credit for the work almost as much as I do. He took notes all the time while I spoke and he also took notes about his additions and later on he dictated them. I found just by my superficially going over your notes that some of the things to which you take exception are his formulations but also some of the points which you term excellent have to be credited to him. It is good team work. I do not know yet how to recompensate him adequately. I might write to you about this some other day because I have a vague idea.[17]

Löwenthal himself had joined the Institute in 1926, at the invitation of Horkheimer and Pollock, and would remain a core member until 1949. His principal theoretical contributions concerned the sociological and historical-materialist study of literature, as evidenced in his contribution to the first issue of the *Zeitschrift*, "Zur gesellschaftlichen Lage der Literatur" (On the Social Condition of Literature),[18] as well as articles on Ibsen and individualism, Conrad Ferdinand Meyer's and the upper middle classes,[19] and the ideological coordinates of Dostoyevsky's German reception.[20] Löwenthal's theoretical contributions to a Marxian sociology of literature were foreshadowed by his socialist activism as a student which saw him become 'Secretary General of the German Socialist Student League' around 1920, when he was a militant in the left wing of the Independent Social Democratic Party (USPD).[21] Prior to joining the Institute, Löwenthal, who hailed from an affluent and secular Jewish family though he briefly "kept a religious orthodox household,"[22] had been deeply involved in the "Jewish Renaissance" around the Jüdisches Lehrhaus in Frankfurt initiated by Franz Rosenzweig, and was especially close to the Orthodox Rabbi Nehemiah Anton Nobel (who had taught Rosenzweig).[23] It was around this period that Löwenthal published his first essay, "The Demonic,"[24] an ambitious if gnomic amalgam of Marxism, phenomenology, psychoanalysis and Jewish theology, praised by Bloch but harshly criticized by Kracauer and Rosenzweig. Also associated with the Lehrhaus was Erich Fromm, whose socialist politics Löwenthal shared[25] and whose psychoanalytic community, animated by Fromm's wife, he also participated in.[26] Löwenthal was already close friends with Siegfried Kracauer in his late teens, who introduced him to a very young Theodor Adorno. In his late reminiscences on the friendship with Adorno, Löwenthal would recall how, having taken up in 1923 his first paying position in an organization advocating for Jewish Refugees from Eastern Europe, "Oskar Wiesengrund told his son that Leo Lowenthal was not welcome in his house as long as he had something to do with Eastern European Jews."[27] In 1925, Löwenthal broke off association with the Zionist movement, with which he'd been involved through a Jewish newspaper he founded with Ernest Simon, the *Jüdisches Wochenblatt* (Jewish Weekly), when, as he put it: "I saw that the Zionist settlement policy would lead unavoidably to a horrible conflict with the Arabs, that an alliance was being made with the rich Arab landowners to drive out the poor Arabs."[28] Having joined the Institute in '26, Löwenthal would not just contribute his expertise in the sociology of literature, he would play an enduringly crucial role in the Frankfurt School's institutional life, not least through his editorship of the *Zeitschrift für Sozialforschung*, what Habermas called the Institute's "organizational core and ... intellectual center."[29] In the *Zeitschrift*, Löwenthal had particular responsibility for the review sections (where he would have edited Henri Lefebvre's sole contribution to the journal), but, as his correspondence with Horkheimer amply testifies, he was also intensely involved in the critically exacting and diplomatically arduous work of editing, and sometimes rejecting, pieces by members and associates of the Institute—most famously perhaps, the first version of Benjamin's Baudelaire essay, at Adorno's insistence. With the Institute's transplantation to the US, Löwenthal, thanks to his impressive organizational abilities and superior capacities for institutional and personal mediation, would take on an even more important role behind the scenes: coordinating the East (New York) and West Coast (Los Angeles) branches; dealing with publishers, universities, and state bodies (he himself being employed by the Office for War Information); and even overseeing the Institute's investments in suburban real estate in New York...[30] It was during the war that Löwenthal, along with other members of the Institute (above all Adorno, who had left Oxford for New York in 1938 to join Paul Lazarsfeld at the Princeton Radio Research project), began to engage in the communications research that would also inform *Prophets*—beginning with a sociological and ideological analysis of popular biographies, "The Triumph of Mass Idols."[31] As the septuagenarian Löwenthal would recount in a piece on "Adorno and his Critics," their US exile was also the context for continuing a working relation with Adorno that had begun with the latter's contribution of a long footnote on Sibelius to Löwenthal's 1937 analysis of the authoritarian tendencies in the works of Norwegian novelist Knut Hamsun. As he reminisced:

> Collaborative closeness is also documented by the first three theses on anti-Semitism that are incorporated in the *Dialectic of Enlightenment* and, above all, by our studies in the seductive and potentially dangerous devices of the American fascist agitator. This work culminated in my book *Prophets of Deceit*, to which Adorno anonymously contributed a draft of an introduction in addition to copious substantive comments and suggestions. Conversely, I had the privilege of participating in the original draft of the research plan for the famous *Authoritarian Personality*, on which Adorno was a senior author, and of contributing my own comments and suggestions on his chapters of this monumental work.[32]

The pied piper's formula

Prophets of Deceit had a rather long gestation, beginning at least with the "Research Project on Anti-Semitism" set out in the final 1941 volume of the *Zeitschrift*.[33] What eventually became Löwenthal and Guterman's book can be seen to develop problems outlined in Section IV of the project, preoccupied with "Types of Present-Day Antisemites"—among which the "Condottiere," the "Jew-baiter," and "Fascist-political" types all bear elements that the Institute would encounter in the American reactionary demagogues that were the object of its collective study. It is also worth noting that, aside from contributing to the drafting of the Institute's major theoretical statement on anti-Semitism, the "Elements" chapter in Horkheimer and Adorno's *Dialectic of Enlightenment*, Löwenthal was also a researcher—alongside Arkadij R. Gurland, Paul Massing, and Friedrich Pollock—in the vast unpublished study on "Anti-Semitism Among American Labor" that the Institute carried out in 1944–5. Löwenthal's written contribution to this project, the study "Images of Prejudice: Anti-Semitism Among U.S. Workers During World War II" is a striking pendant to *Prophets*, as well as an obvious prolongation, onto American soil, of the research on the latent authoritarianism of the German working class carried out in the 1930s.[34] In "Images," Löwenthal could test out many of the theses on the nexus between anti-Semitism and the conditions of social experience under late capitalism that he was developing alongside Horkheimer and Adorno. In particular, he framed the interview material—with its disturbing record of stereotyped hostility—in terms the way that anti-Semitism could operate among US workers as a perverted cognitive mapping of the capitalist totality and the disquiets it bodied forth.

In the persistent figure of the parasite, Löwenthal found evidence of how the "term *Jew* seems to function as expression of the notion that something is basically wrong with the status quo. 'Jew' is a perverted revolutionary concept, a perverted, critical, even nihilistic reaction to an existing social organisation"; "a blurred theoretical concept of social phenomena and their dynamics," grounded in "the facsimile of an experience."[35] Anticipating one of the insights in *Prophets*, Löwenthal also identified in anti-Semitic stereotypes an inverted, phobic projection of a utopian yearning, a "substitute

attack on social domination." For instance, he argued, "the accusation of anticollectivity [Jews as "aggressive," "superior," "arrogant,"
"clannish"] is yet another projection of the workers' repressed disappointment over the lack of genuine collectivity in contemporary
society."[36] For Löwenthal, this projective logic was also at work in
the fantasies of "specific forbidden Jewish enjoyments" and in the
conviction, widespread among US workers during the war (when
anti-Semitic attitudes seem to have spiked), that Jews had forged "a
sphere of independence in a world of interdependence, a sphere of
autarchy in world of mutual dependency, a sphere of license in a
world of restrictions."[37]

Where the study of anti-Semitism in US labor foregrounded the
fascist potentials evidenced in workers' attitudes towards and beliefs
about Jews, the agitator study homed in on potential fascists. Three
pilot studies were carried out to this end, one by Löwenthal on the
anti-Semitic pamphleteer George Allison Phelps, one by Paul
Massing on the pro-Nazi politician Joe McWilliams,[38] and one by
Adorno on Martin Luther Thomas, a Christian fascist demagogue.
When the radical journalist James Rorty (the philosopher Richard
Rorty's father) reported on the ongoing agitator study in the first
issue of *Commentary* in 1945, he underlined the manner in which
the Institute's content analysis revealed the fixed repertoire of
themes through which the demagogues cycled as they sought to
manipulate social anxieties into devoted allegiance.[39]

In his 1943 study on *The Psychological Technique of Martin Luther
Thomas' Radio Addresses* (posthumously published in 1975),[40]
Adorno had dealt with similar material under the heading of *devices*
or *tricks*—some of which directly overlap with the themes of *Prophets*,
for instance the "Great Little Man," "Communists and Bankers" (here
separated into "Reds" and "Plutocrats") or "Persecuted Innocence"
(which is incorporated in Löwenthal and Guterman's final theme, the
"Bullet-Proof Martyr"). Reflecting on the agitator project in a talk
from 1944, Adorno would note "the amazing stereotypy of all the
fascist propaganda material known to us."[41] It was Adorno himself
who, in a letter to Horkheimer, suggested *Pied Piper's Formula* as a
possible title for the volume that would become *The Prophets of
Deceit*.[42] The identification of the aspiring fascist leaders' themes or
techniques was not a mere methodological option; its finality was at

once political and pedagogical, namely the production of a popular handbook "which would help to expose the tricks used by fascist agitators and so disarm them and immunize the public against them."[43] Looking back on the Institute's collective efforts to cut a path through the welter of "astutely calculated absurdities" that make up fascist propaganda, Horkheimer and Adorno would continue to advance the idea of pamphlets for public use that could "vaccinate" the masses against the tricks and devices of agitation.[44]

Besides Adorno's study, Löwenthal could turn to one of his own earlier essays in the sociology of literature for a template applicable to the content analysis of authoritarian language, namely his 1937 *Zeitschrift* essay on Hamsun.[45] The ability to parse Hamsun's proto-authoritarian leanings through such thematic clusters as "Flight into Nature," "Fury," "The Vagabond," "Hero Worship," and so on, was itself a function of the undialectical stereotypy and anti-intellectualism of the Norwegian novelist's attitude and aesthetic. As Adorno had observed in his own agitator study, "theory is essentially taboo to the fascist. His realm is that of unrelated, opaque, isolated facts, or rather images of facts."[46] And while the dialectical critic task's is to lead this toxic picture-thinking back to the totality which it misrecognizes and distorts, it is also obliged to confront the modular instrumentality of the agitator's tricks.

The material for Löwenthal and Guterman's analysis consisted of pamphlets and transcribed speeches by a dozen or so "native fascists" (to cite the very positive review of the book in *The New York Times*),[47] produced between the early 1930s and the end of the World War. To dramatize their subject-matter, they began with a speech composed for them by the socialist literary critic Irving Howe out of a welter of statements made by the agitators—a conceit that partly echoes the fictional portrait of a proto-fascist petty-bourgeois that Guterman and Lefebvre produced under the heading "Candide 1934."[48] It is perhaps in their attention to the ideological and psychosocial functioning of the speech-form that Löwenthal and Guterman show their greatest debt to Max Horkheimer's formidable 1936 essay "Egoism and the Freedom Movement," which is explicitly if somewhat elusively presented as *Prophets'* "historical frame of reference." Exploring the vicissitudes of the bourgeois leadership of mass revolts all the way back to Cola di Rienzo's rise as a tribune of the people in late-Mediaeval Rome, Horkheimer had hypothesized that it was the contradiction between the bourgeoisie's reliance on mass action against feudal remnants and its overriding strategic objective and historical function, namely the imposition of its rationally administered class rule, that provided the clue to the often bewildering physiognomy of the bourgeois rebel or revolutionary. As he observed:

> While his actions conform directly to the interests of particular groups of owners, his behavior and pathos are always vibrant with the misery of the masses. Because he cannot offer them the real satisfaction of needs and must instead seek to win them over to a policy which stands in variance to their own interests, he can win his followers' allegiance only in part by rational arguments for his goals; an emotional belief in his genius, which inspires exultant enthusiasm, must be at least as strong as reason. The less the policy of the bourgeois leader coincides with the immediate interests of the masses, the more exclusively his greatness must fill the public consciousness, and the more his character must be magnified into a "personality." Formal greatness, greatness regardless of its content, is in general the fetish of the modern concept of history.[49]

There is no little irony in the fact that Horkheimer's tracing of bourgeois rhetoric back to the genre of the sermon, as practiced by Savonarola or Luther, would be used to analyze its degraded epigoni on the American far-right fringe, where the likes of Father Coughlin—a Roman Catholic anti-Semitic populist priest, and one of the subjects of *Prophets*—loomed large. According to Horkheimer:

> The popular address of modern times, which is half rational argumentation, half an irrational means of domination, belongs to the essence of bourgeois leadership, despite its long prehistory. ... The language of the sermon is democratic, it is addressed to all, but part of its message is that individuals and whole groups in principle remain outside as the wicked and the obdurate. ... How much the mass meeting in the bourgeois revolts must be understood as a psycho-physical influence, as a treatment or cure, can be seen even from its frequency and compulsory character. ... In these situations it is crucial to treat the soul of the people mechanically, as is shown by the value set on external format, the songs before and after the speech, the speaker's solemn appearance. The speech itself is not geared essentially to the rational forces of consciousness, but uses them only to evoke certain reactions.[50]

The agitators whose statements are mined and montaged by Löwenthal and Guterman are of course not bourgeois revolutionaries, or even rebels, in any but the most grotesque and degraded sense—they are indeed the very dregs at the end of the *longue durée* of bourgeois anthropology. Their voluble amalgam of authoritarianism and rebellion is something that preoccupied the Institute ever since Fromm had diagnosed it in his contribution to the *Studies on Authority and the Family*.[51] In his study on Martin Luther Thomas, Adorno had observed, in trying to capture the specificity of American revolutionary conservatism, that the "combination of an apparently rebellious or radical attitude, as in the sects, with authoritarian, ascetic, and repressive tendencies, parallels a familiar structure of the fascist mentality."[52] The amalgam of rebellious performance and despotic aura characteristic of the agitator stemmed from the fact that, unlike the reformist or revolutionary (bourgeois or otherwise), his aim is not to make the causes of social distress intelligible so that they may be transformed, but rather to exacerbate that distress and shape it into a channel of identification and control. As Löwenthal and Guterman put it, what the agitator "generalizes is not an intellectual perception; what he produces is not the intellectual awareness of the predicament but an aggravation of the emotion itself." In other words, a kind of *anti-cognitive mapping*, through which "[u]nder the guise of a protest against the oppressive situation, the agitator binds his audience to it."

Malaise and innuendo

The emotionally and intellectually paralyzing disorientation that marks life in late capitalism, beset by "depersonalization and permanent insecurity," is what Löwenthal and Guterman christen *malaise*, a kind of "eternal adolescent uneasiness" to which the agitator "gravitates ... like a fly to dung." The precondition for this malaise is a catastrophic impoverishment of the capacity for genuine experience, evidenced by the fact that "people have learned to live in patterns," and tend "to accept uncritically entire systems of opinions and attitudes, as if ideological tie-in sales were forced upon them," becoming "stereotyped appendages of this or that big cultural or political monopoly." Where fascism in power exploits "the connection between potential material poverty and real spiritual poverty"[53] at an industrial scale, the agitators of *Prophets* do so in what we could view as a more artisanal, if no less sinister fashion.

What the agitator performs, in his "act—something between a tragic recital and a clownish pantomime rather than a political speech," is a travesty of social change. The audience's malaise is reflected, teased, intensified, embellished, and ultimately turned towards a scapegoat or enemy, in a "call to the hunt." And, while, "[s]uffering from a kind of eternal restlessness, the agitator never seems to find a terminal and perfect image of the enemy," in a "striptease without end," he and his audience find "a temporary resting place" in their quest for a target in "the Jew, who confirms the fantastic fusion of ruthlessness and helplessness." What makes the agitator's act insidiously effective is the fact that he "does not confront his audience from the outside; he seems rather like someone arising from its midst to express its innermost thoughts." Especially in its conspiratorial register, agitation gains much of its force from the fact that it doesn't propose any kind of theory but rather, in thrilling, salacious or sadistic detail, appears merely to mirror or corroborate the listener's own (worst) instincts. As Löwenthal and Guterman astutely observe:

> the agitator seems to continue the work of the muckrakers by courageously revealing why the powers that rule the world wish to remain hidden. But by dealing, as it were, with the audience's notions at face value, by exaggerating to the point of the fantastic its suspicions that it is the toy of anonymous forces, and by pointing to mysterious individuals rather than analyzing social forces, the agitator in effect cheats his audience of its curiosity. Instead of diagnosing an illness, he explains it as the result of an evil spirit's viciousness.

This is just one of the ways in which agitation is, in Löwenthal's luminous phrase, a form of "psychoanalysis in reverse"; in other words, it comprises "more or less constantly manipulated devices to keep people in permanent psychic bondage, to increase and reinforce neurotic and even psychotic behavior culminating in perpetual dependency on a 'leader' or on institutions or products."[54] In dealing with the central function of anti-Semitism to the agitational repertoire, Löwenthal and Guterman apply the conception of "mimesis" or "mimicking" advanced in the fifth thesis of the "Elements of Anti-Semitism." Following the insight that powerlessness attracts violence all the way into the deep recesses of sociogenesis and psychogenesis, Horkheimer and Adorno reflect on how the "marks" left on the victims of fascism by violence "endlessly inflame violence"—drawing this back to the domain of a dialectically illuminated natural history:

> The chaotically regular flight reactions of the lower animals, the patterns of swarming crowds, the convulsive gestures of the tortured—all these express what wretched life can never quite control: the mimetic impulse. In the death throes of the creature, at the furthest extreme from freedom, freedom itself irresistibly shines forth as the thwarted destiny of matter. It is against this freedom that the idiosyncratic aversion, the purported motive of anti-Semitism, is ultimately directed. The psychic energy harnessed by political anti-Semitism is this rationalized idiosyncrasy. All the gesticulations devised by the Fuhrer and his followers are pretexts for giving way to the mimetic temptation without openly violating the reality principle—with honor, as it were. They detest the Jews and imitate them constantly.[55]

Parsing the anti-Semitic invective and insinuations of the American agitators, Löwenthal and Guterman provide a streamlined exemplification of the pattern of projection minutely anatomized in *Dialectic of Enlightenment*. As they write about the repeated references to Jewish whines, howls, yells, sneers, and so on:

> What the Jews are here implicitly blamed for is that they seem to challenge both the discipline of civilization, which prescribes restraint, and the suppression of the urge to display one's own emotion. They appear free to act out their passions and desires, their demands and fears, their sympathies and above all their antipathies. Once again, the Jews refuse to conform, this time on a deeper emotional level. They are portrayed as despicable and dangerous, for they insist on the right to be individuals. The agitator discredits such expressions of individualistic rebellion. This condemnation of Jewish expressiveness is accompanied by its caricaturing imitation.

An individuality is thereby projected into the stereotyped Jew, which the agitator's followers repress within themselves. This theme of the end or crisis of the individual is one that shadows all of the Institute's work on the *longue durée* and seemingly terminal crisis of bourgeois anthropology, from Horkheimer's chapter on "The Rise and Decline of the Individual" in *Eclipse of Reason*, to Adorno's own "hypothesis that the psychology of the contemporary anti-Semite in a way presupposes the end of psychology itself," and indeed to *Prophets* itself and its analysis of fascistic pseudo-communities as predicated on the "disintegration of individualism."[56] In his later years, Löwenthal himself noted that: "It was once a theoretical dream of our inner circle that, in addition to the social theme of authority, we would engage in a joint study of all aspects of the decay of the essence and concept of the individual in bourgeois society and its conversion to mere illusion and ideology."[57]

Especially in light of contemporary debates on the specificities of US fascisms, one cannot avoid noting that *Prophets*, like other work by the Institute on American anti-Semitism, fascist potentials and potential fascists, almost entirely neglects the place of anti-Black and anti-immigrant racism in the rhetoric or ideology of the agitators—thereby also failing to ask how projection and mimicking might differ and intersect when it comes to "Jews" and "Blacks" in the reactionary mindset.[58] At some points, as in the sixteenth theme, "Endogamic Community," Löwenthal and Guterman get frustratingly close to naming whiteness as a dominant theme in "native fascism." As they write:

> Just as with material goods, so the spiritual benefits of Americanism are to be enjoyed only by an endogamic elite of Christian Americans. The basic implication of the agitator's "defense" of American principles is that the human rights he proclaims should be transformed into a privilege. Even this doubtful privilege is nowhere defined clearly, except in contexts where its meaning comes down to the right to persecute minorities.

That anti-Semitism and anti-Black racism were, so to speak, co-constitutive of the agitator's performances and propaganda is testified by a recent discussion of Gerald L.K. Smith—one of Löwenthal and Guterman's agitators—in the context of an account of the history of the white supremacist Christian right in St. Louis, where Smith was one among the "voices that amplified the oscillating sense of entitlement and embattlement in the white resistance in the suburbs into extremist jeremiad." Among the ten-point code for Christian nationalists set out in Smith's journal, *The Cross and the Flag* (listed in *Prophets'* bibliography), was not just the struggle against an "organized campaign to substitute Jewish tradition for Christian tradition," or the end of immigration to safeguard "American jobs and American houses for... American citizens," but the fight against "mongrelization and all attempts being made to force the intermixture of the black and white races."[59]

In its brilliant efforts to decode the "secret psychological language," the "psychological Morse code tapped out by the agitator and picked up the followers," Löwenthal and Guterman—understandably preoccupied with diagnosing the pervasive presence and specificity of an anti-Semitism that the war against Nazism had pushed into the American underground, or even its unconscious—did not address the place of bare unapologetic anti-Black and anti-immigrant racism in the formation of the native fascist. Yet their study remains a vital model, especially when and where white supremacist, racist, anti-Semitic and fascist potentials lead a more covert or clandestine psychic and political life. This is the world of what, following this book's authors, we could call fascism as innuendo. As Löwenthal and Guterman write in the concluding "Dictionary of Agitation":

> In all his output the agitator engages in an essentially ambiguous activity. He never merely says: he always hints. His suggestions manage to slip through the nets of rational meaning, those nets that seem unable to contain so many contemporary utterances. To know what he is and what he says, we have to follow him into the underground of meaning, the unexpressed or half-expressed content of his hints, allusions, doubletalk.[60]

This too is anti-fascism—a painstaking, forensic journey into the underground of meaning.

Notes

1.   Leo Löwenthal, "'We Never Expected Such Fame': A Conversation with Mathias Greffrath, 1979," in *Critical Theory and Frankfurt Theorists:Lectures-Correspondence-Conversations* (Communication in Society, Vol. 4) (New Brunswick, NJ: Transaction Publishers, 1989), p. 246. The Institute's key study on the German worker was only published in German in 1980. See Erich Fromm, *The Working Class in Weimar Germany: A Psychological and Sociological Study* (Cambridge, MA: Harvard University Press, 1984).

2. Ibid., p. 247.
3. Erich Fromm, "Studies on Authority and the Family. Sociopsychological Dimensions," *Fromm Forum* 24 (2020), pp. 39 and 41.
4. Leo Löwenthal, "Toward a Psychology of Authoritarianism" (1934), in *False Prophets: Studies in Authoritarianism* (Communication in Society, Volume 3) (New York: Routledge, 2017), p. 286.
5. Norbert Guterman and Henri Lefebvre, *La Conscience mystifiée, suivi de* Henri Lefebvre, *La Conscience privée* (Paris: Syllepse, 1999).
6. Max Horkheimer, "The Lessons of Fascism," in *The Tensions that Cause Wars*, ed. Hadley Cantril (Urbana: University of Illinois Press, 1950), p. 223.
7. "The Correspondence of Leo Lowenthal with Max Horkheimer," *Critical Theory and Frankfurt Theorists: Lectures-Correspondence-Conversations*, p. 209. In his response, Löwenthal agreed that the "missing economic notes" (p. 211) posed a problem.
8. Löwenthal discusses the continued relevance of *Prophets* in *Critical Theory and Frankfurt Theorists*, p. 249. For the contemporary rediscovery of *Prophets of Deceit*, see Charles H. Clavey, "Donald Trump, Our Prophet of Deceit," *Boston Review*, 20 October 2020, bostonreview.net; Andreas Huyssen, "Behemoth Rises Again," *n+1*, 29 July 2019, nplusonemag.com; Scott McLemee, "Prophets of Deceit," *Inside Higher Ed*, 19 August 2009, insidehighered.com.
9. Theodor W. Adorno, "Scientific Experiences of a European Scholar in America," in *The Intellectual Migration*, ed. Donald Fleming and Bernard Bailyn (Cambridge, MA: Harvard University Press, 1969), pp. 364–5.
10. See Fred Bud Burkhard, "The 'Revue marxiste' Affair: French Marxism and Communism in Transition Between the Wars," *Historical Reflections / Réflexions Historiques* 20:1 (Winter 1994), pp. 141–64. See also "Norbert Guterman," *Le Maitron: Dictionnaire Biographique—Mouvement Ouvrier/Mouvement Social*, maitron.fr.
11. On Lefebvre and Guterman's collaboration see Michel Trebitsch, "Correspondances d'intellectuels. Le cas des lettres d'Henri Lefebvre à Norbert Guterman (1935–1947)," *Les Cahiers de l'IHTP* 20, *Sociabilités intellectuelles. Lieux, milieux, réseaux*, ed. Nicole Racine et Michel Trebitsch, March 1992.
12. Norbert Guterman, Review of *Propaganda Analysis* and other books, *Zeitschrift für Sozialforschung / Studies in Philosophy and Social Science* 9:1 (1941), pp. 160–6. Guterman would also reflect on propaganda in a review article published shortly before *Prophets*,

declaring: "It is an error to assume that the propagandist's primary aim is to gain the intellectual and moral adherence of his audience. The social function of totalitarian propaganda is of a quite different order—its primary objective is to serve as a herald of violence and a lubricant of the mechanisms of terror. It uses persuasion only as a superficial garb; this propaganda is not a perverted form of argumentation but an intensified form of blackmail, and its main argument is always the threat behind the argument. Propaganda conquers souls by first reducing them to passivity and then involving them in the practices of oppression." Norbert Guterman, "Four Books on Occupied France," *Commentary*, October 1948.

13.   Norbert Guterman, "Neither-Nor," *Partisan Review* 10:2 (March 1943), p. 142. Quoted in Thomas Wheatland, *The Frankfurt School in Exile* (Minneapolis: University of Minnesota Press, 2009), p. 129, which provides an excellent account of the "New Failure of Nerve" affair, and of the Institute's intellectual and institutional life in and around Columbia University. By way of anecdote, Wheatland also cites Edmund Wilson's observation on Guterman: "I have just thought of somebody else who ought to be a perfect model of an orthodox Marxist: Norbert Guterman. When I saw him some months ago, he told me that the trouble with Marxism was that it had too little instead of too much Hegelian Dialectic" (pp. 138–9).

14.   James Schmidt, "The 'Eclipse of Reason' and the End of the Frankfurt School in America," *New German Critique* 100 (Winter 2007), pp. 47–76.

15.   As an exasperated Guterman wrote to the editor of *Composing for Films*, Margaret Nicholson, in the wake of Adorno's innumerable interventions: "Now Dr. Adorno will be satisfied; there will be no other insertion; the edited manuscript will receive the author's final OK, & will go to the printer; the book will be chosen by the Book of the Month Club, translated into 72 foreign languages (including Sanscrit [*sic*]), and we will be happy forever after." Quoted in Sally Bick, "The Politics of Collaboration: *Composing for the Films* and Its Publication History," *German Studies Review* 33:1 (February 2010), pp. 148–9.

16.   Jack Jacobs, *The Frankfurt School, Jewish Lives, and Antisemitism*, (Cambridge: Cambridge University Press, 2015), p. 95. Löwenthal also wrote to Guterman, during the drafting of *Prophets*, that "Horkheimer has gone very carefully over your text and he wants you to know that in principle he agrees with almost everything and is in full harmony with your theoretical attitude" (p. 96).

17. Letter to Horkheimer, 2 August 1946, in *Critical Theory and Frankfurt Theorists*, p. 211.

18. Leo Löwenthal, "On Sociology of Literature" (1932), in *Literature and Mass Culture* (Communication in Society, Volume 1) (New Brunswick, NJ: Transaction Publishers, 1984), pp. 255–67.

19. Leo Löwenthal, "Conrad Ferdinand Mayer: An Apologia of the Upper Middle Class," *Telos* 45 (1980), pp. 97–113.

20. Leo Löwenthal, "The Reception of Dostoevski in Pre-World War I Germany," in *Literature and Mass Culture*, pp. 173–93.

21. Leo Löwenthal, *An Unmastered Past: The Autobiographical Reflections of Leo Lowenthal*, ed. and introd. Martin Jay (Berkeley: University of California Press, 1987) pp. 32–8.

22. *Critical Theory and Frankfurt Theorists*, p. 240. Guterman converted to Hassidic Judaism in his later years.

23. See Martin Jay, "Leo Löwenthal and the Jewish Renaissance," in *Splinters in Your Eye: Frankfurt School Provocations* (London: Verso, 2020), pp. 66–79. For intellectual and biographical overviews of Löwenthal, see also: Christoph Hesse, "Leo Löwenthal: Last Man Standing," in *The SAGE Handbook of Frankfurt School Critical Theory*, ed. Beverley Best, Werner Bonefeld and Chris O'Kane (London: SAGE, 2018), pp. 39–54; Martin Jay, "Introduction to a Festschrift for Leo Lowenthal on his Eightieth Birthday," in *Permanent Exiles: Essays on the Intellectual Migration from Germany to America* (New York: Columbia University Press, 1985), pp. 101–6; Leo Löwenthal, *An Unmastered Past*; as well as the interviews in *Critical Theory and Frankfurt Theorists*.

24. Leo Löwenthal, "The Demonic: Project for a Negative Philosophy of Religion," in *The Frankfurt School on Religion: Key Writings by the Major Thinkers*, ed. Eduardo Mendieta (London: Routledge, 2005), pp. 101–12.

25. Felix Weil, later an Institute member, and son of the grain merchant Hermann Weil, who bankrolled the Institute, belonged to the same student socialist association as Löwenthal. See "Ungrounded: Horkheimer and the Founding of the Frankfurt School," in *Splinters in Your Eye*, p. 7.

26. Martin Jay, "'In Psychoanalysis Nothing Is True but the Exaggerations': Freud and the Frankfurt School," in *Splinters in Your Eye*, p. 48.

27. "Recollections of Theodor W. Adorno" (1983), in *Critical Theory and Frankfurt Theorists*, p. 63.

28. Ibid., p. 240. This rupture took place in an article published under the pseudonym of "Hereticus," entitled "The Lessons of China" (with

reference to the Boxer Rebellion). There, Löwenthal wrote: "Zionism's borrowings from the arsenal of European diplomatic weapons were ill advised, that is to say, Zionism took out a larger loan that it had originally intended: for it engaged in European colonial policy against the Arabs" (p. 222).

29. Jürgen Habermas, "The Inimitable *Zeitschrift für Sozialforschung*: How Horkheimer Took Advantage of a Historically Oppressive Hour," *Telos* 45 (1980), p. 114.

30. Schmidt, "The 'Eclipse of Reason' and the End of the Frankfurt School in America," p. 52.

31. *Literature and Mass Culture*, pp. 211–46.

32. Leo Löwenthal, "Adorno and his Critics" (1978), in *Critical Theory and Frankfurt Theorists*, p. 50. It seems that shortly before Adorno's death, he fell out with Löwenthal over the latter's unmet request for a pension from the Institute. See Jay, "'The Hope That Earthly Horror Does Not Possess the Last Word': Max Horkheimer and *The Dialectical Imagination*," in *Splinters in Your Eye*, p. 22.

33. "Research Project on Anti-Semitism," *Studies in Philosophy and Social Science* 9:1 (1941), pp. 124–43.

34. For analysis and background on this project, see Catherine Collomp, "'Anti-Semitism among American Labor': A Study by the Refugee Scholars of the Frankfurt School of Sociology at the End of World War II," *Labor History* 52:4 (2011), pp. 417–39, and Mark P. Worrell, *Dialectic of Solidarity: Labor, Antisemitism, and the Frankfurt School* (Leiden: Brill, 2008).

35. Leo Löwenthal, "Images of Prejudice: Anti-Semitism Among U.S. Workers During World War II," in *False Prophets*, pp. 192–4. In another incisive formulation: "anti-Semitism among workers is thus a condensed, perverted, manipulated concept of all social conditions that they resent or reject" (p. 236).

36. Ibid., p. 209. This passage resonates with the one on Communists, intellectuals and bankers in the second thesis from the "Elements of Anti-Semitism," to which Löwenthal contributed: "The fantasy of the conspiracy of lascivious Jewish bankers who finance Bolshevism is a sign of innate powerlessness, the good life an emblem of happiness. These are joined by the image of the intellectual, who appears to enjoy in thought what the others deny themselves and is spared the sweat of toil and bodily strength. The banker and the intellectual, money and mind, the exponents of circulation, are the disowned wishful image of those mutilated by power, an image which power uses to perpetuate itself." Max Horkheimer and Theodor W. Adorno,

Dialectic of Enlightenment: Philosophical Fragments, ed. Gunzelin Schmid Noerr, trans. Edmund Jephcott (Stanford, CA: Stanford University Press, 2002), p. 141.

37. Ibid., p. 229.

38. On Paul Massing, whose 1949 study of pre-Nazi German anti-Semitism *Rehearsal for Destruction* was also a volume in the *Studies in Prejudice* series, see Mark P. Worrell, *"Es Kommt Die Nacht*: Paul Massing, the Frankfurt School, and the Question of Labor Authoritarianism during World War II," *Critical Sociology* 35:5 (2009), pp. 629–35.

39. James Rorty, "American Fuehrer in Dress Rehearsal," *Commentary* 1:1 (November 1945).

40. Theodor W. Adorno, *The Psychological Technique of Martin Luther Thomas' Radio Addresses* (Stanford, CA: Stanford University Press, 2002).

41. Theodor W. Adorno, "Anti-Semitism and Fascist Propaganda," in *The Stars Down to Earth and Other Essays on the Irrational in Culture* (London: Routledge, 1994), p. 226.

42. Jack Jacobs, *The Frankfurt School, Jewish Lives, and Antisemitism*, p. 96.

43. Rolf Wiggershaus, *The Frankfurt School: Its History, Theories, and Political Significance*, trans. Michael Robertson (Cambridge, MA: The MIT Press, 1994), p. 358. As Löwenthal recalled in his 1979 interview with Helmut Dubiel: "Horkheimer's dream, which was never fulfilled, was that each of these books in the series Studies in Prejudice should be rewritten in the form of small booklets in popular format for distribution in a given situation of anti-Semitic political outbreaks or the like here in America—namely, to teachers, students, politicians, that is, to so-called multiplicators. That was sort of the idea of a political-educational mass inoculation program, a 'fire brigade,' as the Americans say. Unfortunately, it never materialized. Dubiel: That's interesting, I didn't know that. I do remember the introduction to *The Authoritarian Personality*, in which the idea of a preventive democratic mass-education is formulated, but I considered that to be just a rhetorical ornament. Lowenthal: No, that was meant quite seriously. You're talking about a foreword by Max Horkheimer not only to *The Authoritarian Personality* but to all the volumes of Studies in Prejudice. We meant that quite seriously." *Critical Theory and Frankfurt Theorists*, p. 235.

44. Theodor W. Adorno and Max Horkheimer, "Vorurteil und Character," in *Gesammelte Schriften*, Vol. 9.2 (Frankfurt: Suhrkamp, 1997), pp. 360–73. Löwenthal and Guterman, in their closing lines, also borrow

from an epidemiological vocabulary, speaking of a "prophylaxis" against fascist agitation.

45. Leo Löwenthal, "Knut Hamsun," in *The Essential Frankfurt School Reader*, eds. Andrew Arato and Eike Gebhardt, introd. Paul Piccone (New York: Urizen Books, 1978), pp. 319–45. Löwenthal's dissection of Hamsun could be fruitfully compared with Guterman and Lefebvre's roughly contemporaneous engagement with Céline in *La Conscience mystifiée*, pp. 143–4.

46. *The Psychological Technique of Martin Luther Thomas' Radio Addresses*, pp. 104–5.

47. Carey McWilliams, "The Native Fascist," *New York Times*, 4 December 1949. For a somewhat more critical take, see Irwin Ross, "Prophets of Deceit, by Leo Lowenthal and Norbert Guterman," *Commentary*, March 1950. C. Wright Mills, who became a good friend of Löwenthal's, curiously observed in 1954 that *Prophets of Deceit* "ought to be read widely just now to understand something of what is involved in the Republican Party split" (presumably the opposition by the likes of Barry Goldwater to the Eisenhower administration's excessive liberalism). See "IBM Plus Reality Plus Humanism = Sociology," *The Politics of Truth: Selected Writings*, ed. John H. Summers (Oxford: Oxford University Press, 2008), p. 84.

48. *La Conscience mystifiée*, pp. 75–7.

49. Max Horkheimer, "Egoism and the Freedom Movement: On the Anthropology of the Bourgeois Era," *Telos* 54 (1982), p. 20. For an incisive critique of the limits of Horkheimer's argument, see Stathis Kouvélakis, *La critique défaite. Émergence et domestication de la Théorie critique: Horkheimer—Habermas—Honneth* (Paris: Éditions Amsterdam, 2019), pp. 109–20.

50. "Egoism and the Freedom Movement," pp. 31–4. Political speech as the mechanical manipulation of disaggregated masses is juxtaposed by Horkheimer to truly revolutionary situations in which the "speaker's goal then is for the masses to grasp the situation with their own consciousness; the action then follows from this as a rational consequence" (p. 34). An explicitly political observation follows from this: "The mass meeting is suitable for the purpose of exerting irrational influence; small groups of individuals with common interests are appropriate for discussions of theory, the analysis of a given historical situation, and the resulting considerations on the policy that should be followed. Movements striving to transcend the bourgeois order can therefore not use the mass meeting with the same exclusiveness and the same success" (p. 34).

51. Fromm, "Studies on Authority and the Family: Sociopsychological Dimensions."

52. *The Psychological Technique of Martin Luther Thomas' Radio Addresses*, p. 87.

53. "Terror's Dehumanizing Effects" (first published in *Commentary* in 1946), in *False Prophets*, pp. 183–4.

54. "Adorno and His Critics," p. 51. See also "Interview with Helmut Dubiel," in *Critical Theory and Frankfurt Theorists*, p. 234. The provocative link between the culture industry and fascist agitation advanced by Löwenthal here is more than a parallel or analogy, especially if we follow Adorno's observation according to which: "The mode of 'selling an idea' is not essentially different from the mode of selling a soap or soft drink. Sociopsychologically, the magical character of the word leader and therewith the *charisma* of the *Führer* is nothing but the spell of commercial slogans taken over by the agencies of immediate political power." *The Psychological Technique of Martin Luther Thomas' Radio Addresses*, pp. 40–1. American agitation also had a directly monetizable dimension—as noted in the sub-section of *Prophets* entitled "*The Money-Minded Martyr*," "American agitation is a racket as well as a political movement." "Racket" was an important concept for the Institute in exile, see Martin Jay, "Trump, Scorsese, and the Frankfrut School's Theory of Racket Society," *Los Angeles Review of Books*, 5 April 2020, lareviewofbooks.org.

55. *Dialectic of Enlightenment*, pp. 150–1.

56. Theodor W. Adorno, "Remarks on the Authoritarian Personality" (1958), cited in Peter E. Gordon, "The Authoritarian Personality Revisited: Reading Adorno in the Age of Trump," *boundary 2 online*, 15 June 2016, boundary2.org.

57. "Adorno and His Critics," p. 52. See also *Critical Theory and Frankfurt Theorists*, pp. 224 and 232. Guterman himself had explored the impasses of individuality and its ideologies in the context of capitalist crisis in his work with Lefebvre of the 1930s, including in a 1933 article for their journal *Avant-Poste*, "Individu et Classe."

58. For further reflections on this impasse, see Bruce Baum, "Decolonizing Critical Theory," *Constellations* 22:3 (2015), pp. 420–34.

59. Walter Johnson, *The Broken Heart of America: St. Louis and the Violent History of the United States* (New York: Basic Books, 2020), p. 329.

60. In his own agitator study, Adorno inimitably captures the sinister dimensions of this mode of communication between audience and

agitator: "Psychologically, what purposely remains unsaid is not only the knowledge which is too horrible to be stated frankly but also the horrible thing which one wants to commit oneself, which is not confessed even to oneself, and yet is expressed and even sanctioned by innuendo." *The Psychological Technique of Martin Luther Thomas' Radio Addresses*, p. 56. Comprehensive research into fascist innuendo would of course require attention not just to textually-encoded techniques, but to the media technologies and affective dimensions of agitational communication.

Foreword to the First Edition

Ideologies and ideological manifestations may be measured, or they may be understood as qualities, as meaningful structural units. Both techniques of content analysis lead the scientist to insights into the roots of social problems, in this case, of group prejudice and discrimination. This book by Leo Lowenthal and Norbert Guterman is confined to qualitative analysis. Not the frequency of the ideas, formulas, and devices to be found in agitational material, but the meaning of demagogy, of its techniques and appeals, its arguments and its personalities, is the theme.

Although the study employs many psychoanalytical concepts, in fact it is devoted not so much to the private physiognomy of the agitator as to the psychological content and significance of the agitator's behavior. It seeks to cast light on the inner, and often unconscious, mechanisms at which agitation is directed. But all this must be understood sociologically. Though the demagogue plays upon psychological predispositions with psychological weapons, the predispositions themselves and the aims striven for are socially created.

It is only the highly developed social situation that sets our demagogue apart from numerous predecessors back through the centuries and millennia. Demagogy makes its appearance whenever a democratic society is threatened with internal destruction. In a general sense, its function has always been the same: to lead the masses toward goals that run counter to their basic interests. And this function accounts for the irrationality of demagogy; the psychological techniques it employs have a definite social basis.

Today, under the conditions of a highly industrialized society, consumption is largely determined by production even in the field of ideologies. Attitudes and reactive behavior are often "manufactured." The people do not "choose" them freely but accept them under the pressure of power, real or imaginary. Study of the people themselves therefore does not suffice. The nature of the stimuli must be studied along with the reactions if we are to grasp the true significance of the phenomena of mass behavior. Otherwise, one might erroneously attribute to an underlying frame of public mind what may in fact be the product of calculated techniques of communication.

None of the specific techniques of agitation can be judged outside their political and social contexts. Their specific significance as a means of antidemocratic mass manipulation lies solely within the structural unity of the pattern this book seeks to formulate.

It is notable, for example, that the contemporary agitator, the expert propagandist who has assumed the role of leader, dwells incessantly on his own person. He portrays himself as both leader and common man. By suggesting that he too is a victim of sinister social forces, by displaying his own weakness as it were, he helps conceal from his followers the very possibility of independent thinking and autonomous decision. He sets the pattern for that most contemporary phenomenon, the deindividualized, incoherent, and fully malleable personality structure into which antidemocratic forces seek to transform man.

The content of present-day demagogy is obviously empty, accidental, and entirely subordinate to manipulative considerations. Our home-grown agitators, in the absence of an American tradition of nationalistic aggressiveness, created an artificial fusion with Italian and German fascist notions. They have also borrowed from certain forms of religious revivalism, without regard to any specific content, forms that exploit such rigid stereotypes as the distinction between the "damned" and the "saved." The modern American agitator has put these old-fashioned techniques to very good use.

"Good use?" the reader may well ask with some incredulity. American hatemongers are at present at a low point in influence and prestige. Even at the peak of their strength before the war, they failed to build a unified organization or to win substantial financial backing.

This is true, of course. But because the emphasis of the book is on the *meaning* of the phenomena under analysis, the agitator should be studied in the light of his *potential* effectiveness within the context of present-day society and its dynamics, rather than in terms of his immediate effectiveness. Although overt anti-Semitic agitation is at an ebb, it is important to study its content and techniques as examples of modern mass manipulation in its most sinister form.

This volume does not exaggerate the immediate importance of American demogogy, nor does it pretend to offer a photographic picture of the political realities of the day. Instead, it places under the microscope certain phenomena that may seem negligible at first sight, and by thus enlarging the most extreme and apparently unrealistic manifestations of antidemocratic behavior, it gains diagnostic insight into the latent threat against democracy.

Max Horkheimer

Foreword to the Second Edition

The agitator, "prophet of deceit," the demagogue who calls for change (or rather what he calls change), for housecleaning, eliminating, removing, returning or advancing to something better and purer, to the genuine American values, American freedom, American piety, American cleanliness—is he still playing a role in the political life of the nation? The man who expresses and exploits the deep-rooted malaise, the frustration and outright unhappiness of the underlying population, their real grievances, exploits them in order to sell himself as the savior and leader, as the one whom the people can trust and who will be different from all the other leaders, politicians, bosses, chiefs, senators, and representatives—is he still distinguishable from the respected, accepted, recognized leaders, politicians, and bosses when they step out of their offices and committee rooms, "go to the people," and "run" for election or reelection?

If we compare or contrast the agitator of the thirties and forties whom this book examines with the legitimate politicians of today, the shift in the target, tone, vocabulary seems slight. Where it goes beyond modifications of words, tones, tactics, the difference illuminates the road which this society has traveled within the last two decades. What has happened on this road is the introjection of the agitator into the legitimate political machine. In the terms of its legitimacy, and of its constituents, the agitator was an extremist (like the model set up in this book, an extremist on the far right), an outsider until and unless "he made it" and altered the machine in accordance with his goals and the interests backing his goals.

But as corporate capitalism streamlined and consolidated its organization of society, as the protection of its empire led to a costly and brutal war which required the mental and physical mobilization of the people, and as the dangerously spontaneous rebellion of the ghettos and of the young intelligentsia became a serious threat to the system, the demarcation line between the outsider agitator and the legitimate politician, between the extreme right and the center was being blurred (if not obliterated).

Today, we recognize some of the essential features of the agitator as those of the political Establishment. The social infrastructure, the main springs of agitation, the "background for seduction" are the same: exploitation of the prevailing frustration in ways which lead away from the roots of discontent and from its cure; a diffused appeal which is addressed to every American as "potential follower" since every American is confronted with political and economic forces which operate behind his back, forces which he rightly suspects without being able to master them; and, finally, the enemy (national, and within the nation) who is everywhere and who threatens every American, who infiltrates the party and the press, the office and the shop, the government and the union, the classroom and the bedroom. And if the "prophet of deceit" is an "advocate of social change" which really is no change because he suggests "the elimination of people rather than a change in political structure," so are the leaders of the established political parties on the campaign path: everything will be all right as soon as the old leaders go out and the new ones come in.

To be sure, this has always been the case, more or less. But precisely the "more or less" defines the structural tendency. For it is the structure of corporate capitalism which now is in blatant contradiction to its traditional economic and political institutions: free enterprise, free competition, free exchange of ideas, democracy. The contradiction is so striking that the Orwellian language of countersense becomes the everyday language, the normal universe of political discourse. And countersense or doubletalk is translated into action: striving for peace through bombing and burning; nonintervention not counting intervention in a dozen countries; assuring freedom of speech and assembly while beating and banning demonstrators and speakers. Countersense in word and action is indeed rational inasmuch as it protects the system and sustains its prosperity, but this rationality, itself irrational, demands the "normalization" of the irrational as political means, as method of integration. The psychological arsenal of the agitator is incorporated into that of the established power structure. Conservatism, perpetuating the powers that be, tends to assimilate the extreme right. The latter does not disappear; it is lavishly financed; some of its groups assume high respectability; others are crackpot organizations at the margins of society, but they all face the increasingly tough competition of the legitimate politicians and their media.

However, this transfer of the agitator from the outside to the inside, from the margins to the established order, requires certain changes in his arsenal. They express the administered solidarity, the identification of the ruled with the rulers, the "integration" which is so characteristic of the present stage of corporate capitalism. It necessitates a broadening of the appeal by excluding specific targets prevalent at the preceding stages of agitation, a modification of the image of the leader, and a shift from radical to conservative slogans. Anti-Semitism, which looms large in the documentation of this book, is not allowed to become part of the legitimate agitation, nor are other forms of racism (they reappear, only thinly veiled, in the reporting and propaganda against the Vietcong, North Koreans, etc.). Moreover, the legitimate politician does not "humiliate" his adherents, he does not impress on them their inferiority and his own superiority. On the contrary, the more chummy he talks, the more "common" he looks, the more he sells himself as "one of them," on the same level of discourse, sharing with them their needs, values, aspirations, the better his prospects, the greater his popularity.

Finally, the shift to conservative slogans. The enemy, indispensable factor of national unity and social cohesion, threatens at home. The radical youth, fifth column of the enemy abroad, defames our values, destroys our democratic process, soils our purity, defies our morality. What matters now is to preserve (or restore) that what we have had and what is. "Law and order" has become the shibboleth of freedom, and the competing leaders surpass each other in their promise that X will be more efficient in enforcing it than Y, Z, and all others. And this enforcement normalizes, and renders legitimate a good deal of the violence which the agitator illegitimately invokes: the police in several instances have become that paramilitary force of suppression which has been the agitator's dream. But legitimate force must not appear as violence. The language of countersense transfers the meaning of the word and makes it an attribute of those who protest and defend themselves against violence, while the language of the media continually works on the normalization of violence. "The verbal fury of the agitator is only a rehearsal of real fury"—does this proposition also foreshadow the realization of normalized violence on a larger scale?

The resources—individual and social—which are used by the agitator have not dried up, but they have been channeled into different forms of utilization; they have been normalized and recognized by the legitimate politicians. This difference in utilization between the traditional parties and the new challenger on the right draws the thin demarcation line between total suppression and democratic cohesion. It is only on the margin of the political establishment that the raw material of protofascist sentiment finds its voice. The contrast between the increasingly authoritarian establishment and the extreme rightist efforts to conquer it perhaps can be telescoped in the proposition that two of the three presidential candidates who campaigned in 1968 had "voters" whereas the third candidate had "followers." The follower has all but completely surrendered to the leader who promises an end to his frustration, while the voter still retains a demonstrable test of deliberation of decision. The fact that the third man did not succeed suggests that there is still time and space for intensifying and organizing the struggle against those forces and interests in the society which perpetuate the inhuman conditions for the rise of the prophets of deceit. The deep-rooted "general malaise," the unconscious and half-conscious knowledge that this universe of prosperity, comfort, and aggression is entirely unnecessary and irrational is described and analysed in this book, which was written about twenty years ago. The continued progress on the road to more prosperity, more comfort, and more aggression seems to go hand in hand with the progress of this malaise—a persistance which testifies to the actuality of this study.

Herbert Marcuse
La Jolla, California
August, 1969

Preface

Before and during the past war Americans were amazed to find that there existed in their midst a number of individuals who strikingly resembled the local Nazi *führers* of the 1920s in Germany. Most of them openly expressed admiration for Hitler and Mussolini, were rabidly anti-Semitic, and indulged in intensive vituperation of our national leaders. In addition, most of them headed small "movements" and published periodicals. They all made frequent political speeches, and some gave comfort and aid to our enemies.

It is this type of self-appointed popular spokesperson that is designated by the term agitator in the present study. No attempt has been made here to cover the history of political agitation in all its aspects or to analyze other forms of contemporary propagandistic manipulation of popular psychology, indigenous or imported.

The conventional image of the American agitator is that of an American copy of a foreign model. He is usually thought of as a crackpot whose appeals and goals derive neither from domestic conditions nor from native attitudes. Seen thus as a kind of foreign agent, the agitator has usually been fought by the method of exposure. His nefarious purposes and affiliations as well as the obvious internal inconsistencies in his statements have often been pointed out. Underlying this view of the agitator—and its attendant strategy of exposure—is the assumption that he can succeed in enlisting public support only through deception, his utterances serving merely to camouflage his true aims. Expose his tricks it is held, and you reduce him to helplessness.[1]

In this study of American agitation we have tried to demonstrate that the conventional image of the agitator is not a faithful portrait, that it differs from the picture that emerges from a careful study of his texts. These texts serve as the sole basis of the present study, but because we believe that the agitator often relies upon unconscious mechanisms to build instruments for manipulating his audience, we have tried to probe beneath the manifest content of his speeches and writings to disinter their latent content.

We have sought to extract what is common in the various agitational texts; on the whole, we have ignored the differences. From a mass of writings and speeches by this country's notorious agitators we have drawn the most significant characteristics of the different types of those who are sophisticated and intellectual in their approach as well as of those who are naive and primitive; of those who come from industrial areas and of those who come from rural areas. In the overwhelming majority of instances, the quotations used in this book can easily be found as recurrent themes in the agitational material.

The idea of studying agitation as a surface manifestation of deeper social and psychological currents was conceived by Max Horkheimer, director of the Institute of Social Research. The institute has conducted research along these lines since 1940 through pilot studies by Theodor W. Adorno, Leo Lowenthal, and Paul W. Massing. The present study, based partly upon these previous investigations, was undertaken in cooperation with the Department of Scientific Research of the American Jewish Committee, to whom the authors are indebted for continued encouragement and interest. Although they have drawn freely upon the earlier studies of the institute on the subject, especially that of Adorno, the authors take full responsibility for their interpretations and conclusions. Obviously, only a certain degree of probability can be claimed for conclusions about latent content. A merely textual analysis cannot determine with precision which of several possible meanings an audience might ascribe to a given theme. We recognize that our interpretations cannot claim to represent actual audience reactions. Rather, our purpose here has been to establish hypotheses on possible reactions. We believe that this approach may pave the way for an empirical exploration of the psychology of the agitator and for field work on his actual effects upon audiences. Methodologically, this study is frankly experimental; it touches a field that has been hardly explored.[2]

We wish to express our appreciation and thanks to associates and friends who were unsparing of their time and effort in helping us with this book. To Dr. Adorno, Professor Edward N. Barnhart of the University of California, Dr. Horkheimer, Dr. Paul Massing, Professors Paul F. Lazarsfeld, Robert K. Merton, and C. Wright Mills of Columbia University, and Professor Hans Speier of the Rand Corporation, who were kind enough to read the entire draft, we are deeply grateful for their comments and constructive criticism. Dr. Ernst Kris of the New School of Social Research, Dr. S. Kracauer, Miss Thelma Herman, Dr. Herta Herzog, and Joseph Klapper, gave us valuable suggestions on methodological and sociological problems.

In the selection of the representative agitators and the quoted texts, various organizations prominent in the task of combating anti-democratic propaganda have given us generous assistance. We wish to express special thanks to Leon Lewis of Los Angeles and to Miss Ellen Posner of the Library of Jewish Information in New York for their making source material available. Mrs. Edith Kriss of the Institute of Social Research showed exceptional devotion in the complicated and thankless task of organizing voluminous files of material. To Irving Howe we owe much for his help in preparing the final manuscript.

Leo Lowenthal
Norbert Guterman

Institute of Social Research
December, 1948

Notes

1. A pioneering exception is the study *The Fine Art of Propaganda* (edited by Alfred McClung Lee and Elizabeth Briant Lee, New York. 1939, and published under the auspices of the Institute for Propaganda Analysis). The authors sensed the need for a content analysis of agitational output and succeeded in isolating a number of central rhetorical devices used by the agitator. Another interesting study along these lines is "The Technique of Propaganda for Reaction: Gerald L. K. Smith's Radio Speeches" by Morris Janowitz *(Public Opinion Quarterly,* 1944, pp. 84–93).

2. Cf. Max Horkheimer, "Egoismus und Freiheitsbewegung." *Zeitschrift für Sozialforschung 5* (1936): 161–234. This study on the psychological background of various liberation movements in modern history has set the historical frame of reference for our book.

1

The Themes of Agitation

The Agitator Speaks

When will the plain, ordinary, sincere, sheeplike people of America awaken to the fact that their common affairs are being arranged and run for them by aliens, Communists, crackpots, refugees, renegades, Socialists, termites, and traitors? These alien enemies of America are like the parasitic insect which lays his egg inside the cocoon of a butterfly, devours the larvae and, when the cocoon opens, instead of a butterfly we find a pest, a parasite.

Oh, this is a clever scheme and if the American people don't get busy and fight it the whole vicious thing will be slipped over on you without your knowing what hit you. A comprehensive and carefully planned conspiracy, directed by a powerfully organized clique, and operating through official and semiofficial channels, has been in continuous existence since the days of Nimrod of Babylon, and is the ever lurking enemy of the people's liberty. Remember at all times that the tactics employed by these usurpers of Christian liberties will be to create horror and panic by exhibitions of maximum brutalities. (How would you like to have the bloodstream of your baby, or your son, or daughter, or wife polluted by dried blood collected from Jews, Negroes, and criminals?) It will be only ordinary sense at the first announcements of trouble for all householders to have several large receptacles for storing drinking water on their premises so that ravages of thirst may not add to the general ordeal.

Hitler and Hitlerism are the creatures of Jewry and Judaism. The merciless programs of abuse which certain Jews and their satellites work upon people who are not in full agreement with them create terrible reactions. I am not justifying the reactions and I am not condoning the reactions; I am merely explaining them. Have the Jews forgotten that the more they organize materially against their opponents, the more assaults will increase and the closer they are to persecution?

Remember, these Jews expect to show no mercy to Christians. What is to prevent Jewish gangsters from doing damage to synagogues on purpose so as to create apparent justification for retaliation—in which Christian Americans, who know too much and have displayed too much courage, would be picked up dead in or near synagogues?

We know what the stuffed shirts and reactionaries will say. They will say we are crackpots. They will say that this program will appeal only to the lunatic fringe. But surely it is not anti-Semitism to seek the truth. Or is it?

What's wrong? I'll tell you what is wrong. We have robbed man of his liberty. We have imprisoned him behind the iron bars of bureaucratic persecution. We have taunted the American businessman until he is afraid to sign his name to a pay check for fear he is violating some bureaucratic rule that will call for the surrender of a bond, the appearance before a committee, the persecution before some Washington board, or even imprisonment itself.

While we have dissipated and persecuted management, we have stood idly by and watched a gang of racketeers, radicals, and conspirators regiment our workers in the name of organized labor into a dues-paying conspiracy designed in Moscow to recruit workers for what they hope would become the American Red Revolution.

We are going to take this government out of the hands of these city-slickers and give it back to the people that still believe that 2 and 2 is 4, that God is in his heaven and the Bible is the Word. Down must come those who live in luxury, the laws that have protected the favored few, and those politicians who are disloyal to the voters!

Whenever a legislative body meets, liberties of the people are endangered by subtle and active interests. Lust for power, financial and political, is the ever-lurking enemy of the people's liberty. There is a deserved odium resting upon the word "liberal." Whether applied to Religion, Morals, or Politics, "Liberalism" is destructive of all fundamental values. In matters pertaining to Religion. Liberalism leads to Atheism. In Morals, it leads to Nudism. In Politics, it leads to Anarchy. In the framework of a democracy the great mass of decent people do not realize what is going on when their interests are betrayed. This is a day to return to the high road, to the main road that leads to the preservation of our democracy and to the traditions of our republic.

Alien-minded plutocrats roll in wealth, bathe in liquor, surround themselves with the seduced daughters of America, and cooperate in all schemes to build up pro-Communist and anti-Christian sentiment.

America, the vain—America, the proud—America, the nation of gluttons and spenders and drinkers. When Harry Hopkins got married, Mr. Baruch arranged the party. There were seven kinds of meat served—twenty-two kinds of food, and it had cost Barney Baruch $122 a plate; and they drank of the vintage of '26. You talk about the drunken orgies of history—we expect Capone to live like that, but as long as I am a Christian soul, I will not be governed by a man like that. That's what they do not want me to say. That's why I am such a bad man. Because I say what you all want to say and haven't got the guts to say.

We leaders are risking our lives to write a new page in American history. We propose without further ado, without equivocation, without any silly sentimentality sometimes known as Tolerance, to emasculate the debauchers within the social body and reestablish America on a basis where this spoliation can never again he repeated. I am attempting to speak one hundred times between the sixth of August and the fifteenth of September. This would be physically impossible for most men but thanks to the temperate and Christian life of my mother and father, I have been given a strong body and strong constitution. Even so, there will he nights that I will drop to the bed almost like a dead man, I will be so fatigued and exhausted. But I'll never throw mud at my opponent . . . I am led by the ethics and morals of Christ.

We are coming to the crossroads where we must decide whether we are going to preserve law and order and decency or whether we are going to be sold down the river to these Red traitors who are undermining America.

This meeting is not a lecture course, it is not an open forum . . . we are making history here today. This is a crusade. I don't know how we can carry on without money. All we want is money from enthusiastic friends.[1]

Background for Seduction

The agitator's harangue may appear simply as the raving of a maniac—and may be ignored as such. Yet speeches and articles that voice essentially the same ideas and are couched in similar language do attract steady audiences in this country, if, for the time being, only small ones. What are the social and psychological implications of such materials?

American agitation is in a fluid stage. Some agitators have occasionally come fairly close to the national political scene. Acting on the assumption that the United States was nearing a grave crisis, they have tried to build a mass movement—with most notable success during the years of the New Deal and shortly before U.S. entry into the war. But by and large this has been the exception.

Far more numerous are those less conspicuous agitators who are active locally and who, far from evoking the image of a leader worshipped by masses of followers, rather suggest a quack medicine salesperson. Their activity has many characteristics of a psychological racket: they play on vague fears or expectations of a radical change. Some of these agitators hardly seem to take their own ideas seriously, and it is likely that their aim is merely to make a living by publishing a paper or holding meetings.[2] What they give their admission-paying audience is a kind of act—something between a tragic recital and a clownish pantomime-rather than a political speech. Discussion of political topics invariably serves them as an occasion for vague and violent vituperation and often seemingly irrelevant personal abuse. The line between ambitious politician and small-time peddler of discontent is hard to draw, for there are many intermediary types. What is important, however, is that American agitation finds itself in a preliminary stage in which movement and racket may blend.

Whatever the differences among American agitators, they all belong to the same species. Even the unforewarned listener or reader is immediately struck by the unmistakable similarity of their content and tone. A careful examination of agitational speeches and writings shows that this similarity is not accidental but based on a unifying pattern—on certain recurrent motifs, *the constants of agitation.* Because these are not explicitly stated as such, the agitation analyst's first task is to isolate them. This, then, is the basic task of the present study: to discover the social and psychological strains of agitation by means of isolating and describing its fundamental themes.

As differentiated from propagandistic slogans, agitational themes directly reflect the audience's predispositions. The agitator does not confront his audience from the outside; he seems rather like someone arising from its midst to express its innermost thoughts. He works, so to speak, from inside the audience, stirring up what lies dormant there.

The themes are presented with a frivolous air. The agitator's statements are often ambiguous and unserious. It is difficult to pin him down to anything and he gives the impression that he is deliberately playacting. He seems to be trying to leave himself a margin of uncertainty, a possibility of retreat in case any of his improvisations fall flat. He does not commit himself, for he is willing, temporarily at least, to juggle his notions and test his powers. Moving in a twilight zone between the respectable and the forbidden, he is ready to use any device, from jokes to double-talk to wild extravagances.

This apparent unseriousness is, however, concerned with very serious matters. In his relationship to the audience the agitator tries to establish a tentative understanding that will lead to nothing less than seduction. There is a sort of unconscious complicity or collaboration between him and the listeners; as in cases of individual seduction, neither partner is entirely passive, and it is not always clear who initiates the seduction. In seduction there operates not only mistaken notions or errors of judgment that are the result of ruses but also, and predominantly, psychological factors that reflect the deep conscious and unconscious involvement of both parties. This relationship is present in all the themes of agitation.

When the serpent suggests to Eve that she eat the forbidden fruit, Eve knows that she would thereby be violating God's commandment. The serpent does not present an idea completely alien to her; he plays rather upon her latent desire to do the forbidden, which is, in turn, based on her inner rebellion against the commandment.

Working on the Audience

Agitation may be viewed as a specific type of public activity and the agitator as a specific type of "advocate of social change," a concept that will serve us as a convenient frame of reference.

The immediate cause of the activity of an "advocate of social change" is a social condition that a section of the population feels to be iniquitous or frustrating. This discontent he articulates by pointing out its presumed causes. He proposes to defeat the social groups held responsible for perpetuating the social condition that gives rise to discontent. Finally, he promotes a movement capable of achieving this objective, and he proposes himself as its leader.

Here, then, are the four general categories under which the output of any "advocate of social change" can be classified: Discontent; the Opponent; the Movement; and the Leader. Significant variations in the categories can be used to isolate subclasses; an especially useful division is to break down "advocate of social change" into "reformer" or "revolutionary," depending on whether the discontent is seen as circumscribed in area or as involving the whole social structure.

Unlike the usual advocate of social change, the agitator, while exploiting a state of discontent, does not try to define the nature of that discontent by means of rational concepts. Rather, he increases the audience members' disorientation by destroying all rational guideposts and by proposing that they instead adopt seemingly spontaneous modes of behavior. The opponent he singles out has no discernibly rational features. His movement is diffuse and vague, and he does not appeal to any well-defined social group. He lays claim to leadership not because he understands the situation better than others but because he has suffered more than they have. The general purpose of his activity, be it conscious or not, is to modify the spontaneous attitudes of his listeners so that they become passively receptive to his personal influence.

It is quite obvious that the agitator does not fit into the reformer type; his grievances are not circumscribed but, on the contrary, take in every area of social life. Nor does he address himself to any distinct social group, as does the reformer; except for the small minority he brands as enemies, every American is his potential follower.

Yet he does not fit into the revolutionary group, either. Although the discontent he articulates takes in all spheres of social life, he never suggests that in his view the causes of this discontent are inherent in and inseparable from the basic social setup. He refers vaguely to the inadequacies and iniquities of the existing social structure, but he does not hold it ultimately responsible for social ills, as does the revolutionary.

He always suggests that what is necessary is the elimination of people rather than a change in poitical structure. Whatever poitical changes may be involved in the process of getting rid of the enemy he sees as a means rather than an end. The enemy is represented as acting, so to speak, directly on his victims without the intermediary of a social form, such as capitalism is defined to be in socialist theory. For instance, although agitational literature contains frequent references to unemployment, one cannot find in it a discussion of the economic causes of unemployment. The agitator lays responsibility on an unvarying set of enemies, whose evil character or sheer malice is at the bottom of social maladjustment.

> Sometimes, these internationalists [a few international financiers] are not even interested in price or profit. They use their monopoly control to determine the living standards of peoples. They would rather see unemployment, closed factories and mines, and widespread poverty, if they might see the fulfillment of their own secret plans.[3]

Unlike the reformer or revolutionary the agitator makes no effort to trace social dissatisfaction to a clearly definable cause. The whole idea of objective cause tends to recede into the background, leaving only on one end the subjective feeling of dissatisfaction and on the other the personal enemy held responsible for it. As a result, his reference to an objective situation seems less the basis of a complaint than a vehicle for a complaint rooted in other, less visible causes.

This impression is confirmed when we observe with what facility the agitator picks up issues from current political discussions and uses them for his own purposes. Throughout the past sixteen years, despite the extraordinary changes witnessed in American life, the agitator kept grumbling and vituperating in the same basic tone. Unlike political parties, he never had to change his "general line." When unemployment was of general concern, he grumbled about that; when the government instituted public works to relieve unemployment, he joined those who inveighed against boondoggling.

Sensational news items supply him with occasions for branding the evil character of the enemy:

> The death of General George S. Patton, Jr., remains a mystery. He was a careful driver. He admonished all who drove for him to drive carefully.
>
> He was known to be wise and cautious in traffic. He was killed by a truck that charged into him from a side road.
>
> He opposed the Morgenthau Plan. He was against the liquidation of the German race merely because they were Germans. He refused to be dominated and bulldozed by revengeful Jews. He had promised to blow off the lid if he ever returned to the United States. Some people doubt if his death was an accident.[4]

His imagination does not shy away from obvious incongruities:

> Suppose—that the Third International had issued secret formulae and technical instructions to a handpicked personnel of the Communist Party in all countries . . .
>
> Do you remember a couple of years ago that a mysterious gas cloud of drifting death fell upon northern France and Belgium and floated across the channel and up the Thames even to London itself? . . .
>
> Do you know that even in Free America at the present moment, stark and violent Death waits upon the footsteps of men who know such facts and give them effectively to the public?[5]

It should by now be clear tht the agitator is neither a reformer nor a revolutionary. His complaints do refer to social reality but not in terms of rational concepts. When the reformer and revolutionary articulate the original complaint, they supplant predominating emotional by intellectual elements. The relationship between complaint and experience in agitation is rather indirect and nonexplicit.

The reformer and revolutionary generalize the audience's rudimentary attitudes into a heightened awareness of its predicament. The original complaints become sublimated and socialized. The direction and psychological effects of the agitator's activity are radically different. The energy spent by the reformer and revolutionary to lift the audience's ideas and emotions to a higher plane of awareness is used by the agitator to exaggerate and intensify the irrational elements in the original complaint.

The following incident illustrates the difference between the two approaches. In a crowded New York bus a woman complained loudly that she was choking, that she was pushed and squeezed by other passengers, and added that "something should be done about it." (*A typical inarticulate complaint.*) A second passenger observed: "Yes, it's terrible. The bus company should assign more busses to this route. If we did something about it, we might get results." (*The solution of a reformer or revolutionary. The inarticulate expression of the complainant is translated into an objective issue—in this case "the faulty organization of the transportation services that can be remedied by appropriate collective action.*") But then a third passenger angrily declared: "This has nothing to do with the bus company. It's all those foreigners who don't even speak good English. They should be sent back where they came from." (*The solution of the agitator who translates the original complaint not into an issue for action against an established authority but into the theme of the vicious foreigners.*)

In contradistinction to all other programs of social change, the explicit content of agitational material is in the last analysis incidental—it is like the manifest content of dreams. The primary function of the agitator's words is to release reactions of gratification or frustration whose total effect is to make the audience subservient to his personal leadership.

It is true that the agitator sometimes appears to introduce concepts that were not originally present in the audience's complaints. But these are not the result of an objective analysis. When the agitator denounces government bureaucrats for the privations of wartime rationing, he does so not because he has discovered any causal relationship between the two but rather because he knows that there is a potential resentment against bureaucrats for reasons that have nothing to do with rationing. The appearance of an intellectual distance between the agitator and the audience is deceptive: instead of opposing the "natural" current, the agitator lets himself be carried by it. He neglects to distinguish between the insignificant and the significant; no complaint, no resentment is too small for the agitator's attention. What he generalizes is not an intellectual perception; what he produces is not the intellectual awareness of the predicament but an aggravation of the emotion itself.

Instead of building an objective correlate of his audience's dissatisfaction, the agitator tends to present it through a fantastic and extraordinary image, which is an enlargement of the audience's own projections. The agitator's solutions may seem incongruous and morally shocking, but they are always facile, simple, and final, like daydreams. Instead of the specific effort the reformer and revolutionary demand, the agitator seems to require only the willingness to relinquish inhibitions. And instead of helping his followers to sublimate the original emotion, the agitator gives them permission to indulge in anticipatory fantasies in which they violently discharge those emotions against alleged enemies.

Sometimes this hostility takes on paranoiac overtones. The change of the shape of traffic lights in New York City, for instance, may inspire the following remarks:

> What a shock it must be to the descendants of the STAR OF DAVID to see *all* traffic signal lights in the Five Boroughs of Greater New York being changed, for the duration, from the full red and green circular light, about 6 inches in diameter, now to show a RED OR GREEN CROSS, for or against traffic. This change is made in the DIMOUT idea, but the use of the CROSS is the work of our Engineering Department of the N.Y. Police, so the Jews can be reminded that this is a Christian Nation.[6]

The reformer or revolutionary concentrates on an analysis of the situation and tends to ignore irrational or subconscious elements. But the agitator appeals primarily to irrational or subconscious elements at the expense of the rational and analytical.

Notes

1. The speech is a composite of actual statements made by American agitators. Except for the punctuation, everything—words, thoughts, appeals—is all theirs.
2. Compare the excellent study by J. V. Martin, "A Gentleman from Indiana," *Harper's Magazine*, (January 1947): 66.

3.   SJ, Sept. 8, 1941.
4.   CF, Feb., 1946.
5.   Pelley, *Official Despatch: Silver Shirts of America Are Mobilizing to Protect* YOUR *Life!*, p. 2.
6.   AID, June 15, 1942, p. 3.

2

Social Malaise

The first and most natural task that confronts a student of any movement of social change is to locate the cause of the movement in a specific condition of discontent. In most instances the solution of this problem presents no difficulties at all—in fact, the advocate of social change himself devotes a great part of his energy to articulating this cause. When we examine agitation, however we face an entirely different situation. That the agitator wants to exploit existing discontent is obvious enough; he seems always to be addressing people who are smarting under the harshest injustice and whose patience has been strained to the breaking point. But whenever the investigator scans the texts of agitation and, on the basis of experience in studying other kinds of social movements, tries to discover what is the discontent it articulates, he is consistently disappointed.

The difficulty is not that agitation fails to provide the investigator with answers but, rather, that it answers a question he did not ask: whenever he asks *what,* he is answered as if he had asked *who.* He finds numerous vituperative and indignant references to enemies, but nowhere can he find a clearly defined objective condition from which the agitator's audience presumably suffers. At best, agitation provides the investigator with contradictory or inconsistent references to such alleged conditions. Unless we decide that the agitator is simply a lunatic, we must assume that although a sense of discontent exists, he, unlike other advocates of social change, is either unable or unwilling to state it explicitly. Hence, the agitation analyst faces the task of himself explicating the state of discontent to which the agitator refers.

A Catalogue of Grievances

Even a cursory glance at agitational material shows that any attempt to analyze it by methods that help discover the purposes of the revolutionary or the reformer could lead only to an impasse. If we try to classify the agitator's complaints in terms of the simplest categories, we obtain approximately the following picture:

1. *Economic Grievances.* The agitator roams freely over every area of economic life. He may begin anywhere at all. Too much help is being extended to foreign nations. "If we have any money to offer for nothing, or to loan, or to give away, we had better give it to our own first. Of course, that is old fashioned."[1]

   Not only are foreigners taking our money, they also threaten our jobs. "People born in America have to commit suicide because they have nothing to eat while refugees get their jobs."[2]

   Behind such injustices stand "the International Bankers, who devised and control our money system, [and] are guilty of giving us unsound money."[3]

   Such situations constitute a danger to the American way of life, for "what is more likely to follow many years of Nudeal communistic confiscatory taxation, wool-less, metal-less, auto-less regimentation and planned scarcities than our finally becoming stripped by necessity to Nudism?"[4]

2. *Political Grievances.* International commitments by the United States government jeopardize political liberties. "Like Russia, the United States is suffering from the scourge of internationalism."[5] The American people are warned: "Be not duped by the internationalists who dwell amongst us."[6]

   Of course, it is only reasonable that "treaties and agreements . . . shall be reached with other nations, but . . . we want no world court and no world congress made up of a few Orientals and a few Russians and a few Europeans and a few British . . . to make laws for us to obey. . . ."[7]

   From within, this country is threatened by radicalism, which prepares strikes that are "dress rehearsals for a forthcoming general strike that is meant to paralyze the Nation. . . ."[8]

   We face both the danger of a "Soviet America . . . where . . . an Austrian-born Felix Frankfurter presides over an unending 'Moscow trial'. . . ."[9] and the rule of "tyrannical bureaucrats" who if they "could have their way completely" would institute a "dictatorship in America as merciless as anything on earth."[10]

3. *Cultural Grievances.* The agitator is greatly disturbed because the media of public information are in the hands of enemies of the nation. ". . . The Hollywood motion picture industry is being exploited by Russian Jewish Communists determined to inject their materialistic propaganda into the fresh young minds of our children."[11] Hollywood is "largely dominated by aliens who have appropriated to their own use the inventions and discoveries of native citizens and who now specialize in speculation, indecency and foreign propaganda."[12]

   "The American press will never be free" until control "is removed from racial, religious and economic pressure groups."[13]

4. *Moral Grievances.* The enemies of the agitator are notoriously lax in morals: they engage in luxury consumption, they are a "crowd of Marxists, refugees, left-wing internationalists who enjoy the cream of the country and want the rest of us to go on milkless, butterless, cheeseless days while they guzzle champagne."[14]

And what is most galling of all is that "we gentiles are suckers," for "while we were praying they had their hands in our pockets."[15]

Emotional Substratum

This list of diffuse complaints could be lengthened indefinitely; it should be sufficient to indicate that the grievances the agitator voices do not refer to any clearly delineated material or moral condition. The only constant elements discernible in this mass of grievances are references to certain emotions or emotional complexes. These may be roughly divided as follows.

Distrust

The agitator plays on his audience's suspicions of all social phenomena impinging on its life in ways it does not understand. Foreign refugees cash in on the "gullibility" of Americans, whom he warns not to be "duped" by internationalists. Strewn through the output of the agitator are such words as *hoax, corrupt, insincere, duped, manipulate.*

Dependence

The agitator seems to assume that he is addressing people who suffer from a sense of helplessness and passivity. He plays on the ambivalent nature of this complex, which on the one hand reflects a protest against manipulation and on the other hand a wish to be protected, to belong to a strong organization or be led by a strong leader.

Exclusion

The agitator suggests that there is an abundance of material and spiritual goods, but that the people do not get what they are entitled to. The American taxpayer's money is used to help everyone but him. "We feed foreigners,"[16] the agitator complains, while we neglect our own millions of unemployed.

Anxiety

This complex manifests itself in a general premonition of disasters to come, a prominent part of which seems to be the middle-class fear of a dislocation of its life by revolutionary action, and the middle-class suspicion that the moral mainstays of social life are being undermined. The agitator speaks of "the darkest hour in American history"[17] and graphically describes a pervasive sense of fear and insecurity:

> This afternoon America is caught in the throes of fear, apprehension and concern. Men are afraid . . . to vote, afraid not to vote. . . . Our population has been caught by the ague and chills of uncertainty. Unless these uncertainties can be removed, unless these fears can be destroyed, we shall never have prosperity again.[18]

Disillusionment

This complex is seen in such remarks as the agitator's characterization of politics as "make-believe, pretense, pretext, sham, fraud, deception, dishonesty, falsehood, hypocrisy."[19] In fact, "whenever a legislative body meets, liberties of the people are endangered by subtle and active interests."[20] Ideological slogans inspire resentment: "Democracy A Misnomer, A Trick Word Used by Jew and Communistic Internationalists to Confuse and Befuddle American Citizens."[21] Values and ideals are enemy weapons, covering up the machinations of sinister powers that, "taking advantage of the mass ignorance of our people, accomplish their purposes under the cloak of humanitarianism and justice."[22]

The Individual in Crisis

The analyst of agitation now faces the problem: Are these merely fleeting, insubstantial, purely accidental, and personal emotions blown up by the agitator into genuine complaints, or are they themselves a constant rooted in the social structure? The answer seems unavoidable: These feelings cannot be dismissed as either accidental or imposed, they are basic to modern society. Distrust, dependence, exclusion, anxiety, and disillusionment blend together to form a fundamental condition of modern life: malaise.

When we define the discontent utilized by agitation as malaise, we are, so to speak, on our own, for we cannot justify this definition by explicit references to agitational statements. It is a hypothesis, but it is a highly plausible one because its only alternative would be to see the maze of agitational statements as a lunatic product beyond analysis. Moreover, it helps to account for certain recurrent characteristics of agitation: its diffuseness, its pseudospontaneity, its flexibility in utilizing a variety of grievances, and its substitution of a personal enemy for an objective condition.

The agitator does not spin his grumblings out of thin air. The modern individual's sense of isolation, his so-called spiritual homelessness, his bewilderment in the face of the seemingly impersonal forces of which he feels himself a helpless victim, his weakening sense of values—all these motifs often recur in modern sociological writings. This malaise reflects the stresses imposed on the individual by the profound transformations taking place in our economic and social structure—the replacement of the class of small independent producers by gigantic industrial bureaucracies, the decay of the patriarchal family, the breakdown of primary personal ties between individuals in an increasingly mechanized world, the compartmentalization and atomization of group life, and the substitution of mass culture for traditional patterns.

These objective causes have been operating for a long time with steadily increasing intensity. They are ubiquitous and apparently permanent, yet they are difficult to grasp because they are only indirectly related to specific hardships or frustrations. Their accumulated psychological effect is something akin to a chronic disturbance, an habitual and not clearly defined malaise that seems to acquire a life of its own and that the victim cannot trace to any known source.

On the plane of immediate awareness, the malaise seems to originate in the individual's own depths and is experienced by him as an apparently isolated and purely psychic or spiritual crisis. It enhances his sense of antagonism toward the rest of the world. The groups in our society that are at present most susceptible to agitation seem to experience this malaise with particular acuteness, perhaps precisely because they do not confront social coercion in its more direct forms.

Although malaise actually reflects social reality, it also veils and distorts it. Malaise is neither an illusion of the audience nor a mere imposition by the agitator; it is a psychological symptom of an oppressive situation. The agitator does not try to diagnose the relationship of this symptom to the underlying social situation. Instead he tricks his audience into accepting the very situation that produced its malaise. Under the guise of a protest against the oppressive situation, the agitator binds his audience to it. Because this pseudoprotest never produces a genuine solution, it merely leads the audience to seek permanent relief from a permanent predicament by means of irrational outbursts. The agitator does not create the malaise, but he aggravates and fixates it because he bars the path to overcoming it.

Those afflicted by the malaise ascribe social evil not to an unjust or obsolete form of society or to a poor organization of an adequate society but, rather, to activities of individuals or groups motivated by innate impulses. For the agitator, these impulses are biological in nature, they function beyond and above history. Jews, for instance, are evil—a "fact" that the agitator simply takes for granted as an inherent condition that requires no explanation or development. Abstract intellectual theories do not seem to the masses as immediately "real" as their own emotional reactions. It is for this reason that the emotions expressed in agitation appear to function as an independent force, which exists prior to the articulation of any particular issue, is expressed by this articulation, and continues to exist after it.

Malaise can be compared to a skin disease. The patient who suffers from such a disease has an instinctive urge to scratch his skin. If he follows the orders of a competent doctor, he will refrain from scratching and seek a cure for the cause of his itch. But if he succumbs to his unreflective reaction, he will scratch all the more vigorously. This irrational exercise of self-violence will give him a certain kind of relief, but it will at the same time increase his need to scratch and will in no way cure his disease. The agitator says keep scratching.

The agitator exploits not primarily the feelings generated by specific hardships or frustrations, but more fundamentally those diffuse feelings of malaise that pervade all modern life. The malaise that is experienced as an internal psychic condition can, however, be explained only by the social process in its totality. Such an explanation, following the classical method of articulating causes of discontent in universal and verifiable terms and then proposing definite methods to remove them, is beyond the resources of the agitator.

Here the agitator turns to account what might appear his greatest disadvantage: his inability to relate the discontent to an obvious causal base. Although most other political movements promise a cure for a specific, and therefore limited, social ailment, the modern agitator, because he himself indirectly voices the malaise, can give the impression that he aims to cure some chronic, ultimate condition. And so, he insinuates, while others fumble with the symptoms, he attacks the very roots of the disease in that he voices the totality of modern feeling.

Because the malaise originates in the deepest layers of the individual psyche, it can appear to be an expression of frustrated spontaneity and essential spiritual needs. The agitator, implicitly working on this assumption, thus claims in effect that he represents the most general interests of society, while his opponents, who concern themselves with such limited, specific matters as housing or unemployment or wages, represent only selfish class interests. He can excoriate the others for their seemingly materialistic attitude because he, on the contrary, has at heart only the nation and the race.

He can thus identify himself with any symbol suggesting spiritual spontaneity and, by extension, with any symbol suggesting that he strives to gratify suppressed instinctual impulses. He can appear as the enemy of those unjust constraints of civilization that operate on a deeper, more intimate level than those imposed by social institutions, and he can represent himself as a romantic defender of ancient traditions that today are being trampled by modern industrialism.

This alleged spirituality is vague enough to include or exclude anything at all, to be dissociated from history and to be associated with the most primitive biological instincts. In its name the agitator can appeal to the Promethean energies of sacrifice and promise to satisfy the essential needs for participation in communal life, for spiritual security, spontaneity, sincerity, and independence. He can easily switch from money and unemployment to spiritual matters.

> There is something deeper, more substantial which has been removed from the foundation of our national life than the mere loss of money and loss of jobs. . . . Charity means seeking first the kingdom of God and His justice rather than seeking banks filled with gold.[23]

Malaise is a consequence of the depersonalization and permanent insecurity of modern life. Yet it has never been felt among people so strongly as in the past few decades. The inchoate protest, the sense of disenchantment, and the vague complaints and forebodings that are already perceptible in late-nineteenth-century art and literature have been diffused into general consciousness. There they function as a kind of vulgarized romanticism, a *Weltschmerz in perpetuum,* a sickly sense of disturbance that is subterranean but explosive. The intermittent and unexpected acts of violence on the part of the individual and the similar acts of violence to which whole nations can be brought are indices of this underground torment. Vaguely sensing that something has gone astray in modern life but also strongly convinced that he lacks the power to right whatever is wrong (even if it were possible to discover what is wrong), the individual lives in a sort of eternal adolescent uneasiness.

The agitator gravitates toward malaise like a fly to dung. He does not blink its existence as so many liberals do; he finds no comfort in the illusion that this is the best of all possible worlds. On the contrary, he grovels in it, he relishes it, he distorts and deepens and exaggerates the malaise to the point where it becomes almost a paranoiac relationship to the external world. Once the agitator's audience has been driven to this paranoiac point, it is ripe for his ministrations.

The prevalence of malaise in recent decades is reflected in growing doubt with relation to those universal beliefs that bound Western society together.[24] Religion, the central chord of Western society, is today often justified even by its most zealous defenders on grounds of expediency. Religion is proposed not as a transcendent revelation of the nature of man and the world, but as a means of weathering the storms of life, or of deepening one's spiritual experience, or of preserving social order, or of warding off anxiety. Its claim to acceptance is that it offers spiritual comfort. A similar development may be found in morality. There are today no commonly accepted—commonly accepted as a matter of course and beyond the need for discussion—moral values. Such a pragmatic maxim as "honesty is the best policy" is itself striking evidence of the disintegration of moral axioms. And much the same is also true for economic concepts; the businessman still believes in fair competition, but in his "dream life . . . the sure fix is replacing the open market."[25]

As a result, the old beliefs, even when preserved as ritualistic fetishes, have become so hollow that they cannot serve as spurs to conscience or internalized sources of authority. Now authority stands openly as a coercive force and against it is arrayed a phalanx of repressed impulses that storm the gates of the psyche seeking outlets of gratification.

When, for whatever reasons, direct expression of feelings is inhibited. they are projected through some apparently unrelated materials. We may accordingly assume that if the audience is not aware of the causes of the malaise, this is due not only to the inherent complexity of these causes but chiefly to unconscious inhibitions, which probably originate in a reluctance to struggle against seemingly superior forces. So the agitator sanctions immediate resentments and seemingly paves the way for the relief of the malaise through discharge of the audience's aggressive impulses, but simultaneously he perpetuates the malaise by blocking the way toward real understanding of its cause.

All such utilizations of malaise are possible only on condition that the audience does not become aware of its roots in modern society. The malaise remains in the background of agitation, the raw material of which is supplied by the audience's stereotyped projections of the malaise. Instead of trying to go back to their sources, to treat them as symptoms of a bad condition, the agitator treats them as needs that he promises to satisfy. He is therefore not burdened with the task of correcting the audience's inadequate ideas; on the contrary, he can let himself be carried along by its "natural" current.

Notes

1. CF, Feb. 1946. p. 710.
2. Phelps, Los Angeles, Dec. 23, 1940, radio.
3. CF, Oct., 1944, p. 454.
4. RTL, Mar. 27, 1942, p. 11.
5. DEF, Aug., 1939, p. 4.
6. Coughlin, Speech on March 26, 1939, reprinted in *Why Leave Our Own,* p. 161.
7. CF, Oct.–Nov., 1942, p. 8.
8. AP, Nov., 1945, p. 5.
9. Kamp, *Vote CIO . . . and Get a Soviet America,* p. 64.
10. CF, June 1942, p. 9.
11. Smith. *Letter,* "The Battle of Babylon," July, 1945, p. 2.
12. AP, Aug., 1944, p. 1.
13. SJ, Sept. 11, 1939, p. 13.
14. SJ, July 21, 1941, p. 11.
15. Charles White, New York, July 18, 1940, street corner.
16. Phelps, Los Angeles, July 27, 1940, radio.
17. Smith, Detroit, April 9, 1942, meeting.
18. Smith, *Why Is America Afraid?*
19. AP, Sept. 1944, p. 2.
20. SJ, Jan. 15, 1940, p. 19.
21. X, February 17, 1945, p. 1.
22. SJ, June 6, 1938, p. 5.
23. Coughlin, *Father Coughlin's Radio Discourses,* pp. 236–237.
24. Cf. Max Horkheimer, *Eclipse of Reason,* (New York: Oxford University Press, 1947).
25. C. Wright Mills, "The Competitive Personality," *Partisan Review* 13, no. 4 (1946): 436.

3

A Hostile World

The agitator articulates the themes of his writings and speeches as if they referred to specific and genuine issues arising from current social problems. He tries to appear as a bona fide advocate of social change, but in effect he merely manipulates and modifies those of the audience's feelings that reflect the malaise. He crystallizes and hardens these feelings and distorts the objective situation. In the themes related to discontent the audience's vague, inarticulate distrust becomes fixated as the stereotype of perpetual dupery; its sense of dependence serves to foster the belief that it is the object of a permanent conspiracy; its sense of exclusion is externalized into the image of forbidden fruits; its disillusionment is transformed into the complete renunciation of values and ideals; and its anxiety is both repressed and magnified into the perpetual expectation of apocalyptic doom.

Theme 1: The Eternal Dupes

Every form of persuasion implies an effort to convert or seduce and presupposes an initial intellectual or emotional distance between the speaker and the listener. The leader of a movement must first convince his audience that its ideas are inadequate for coping with the situation that produces its discontent. He cannot win adherents without in a sense humiliating them, that is, suggesting that they are inferior in knowledge, strength, or courage and that they need him more than he needs them.

In intellectual communication—for example, the activity of a teacher in relation to his students—the aim is to nullify the distance altogether. In the activity of a reformer or revolutionary, there is a similar tendency to decrease initial distances. The adherent's humiliation is at least in theory only temporary, for the leader always suggests that in the end the ignorant will become enlightened, the moderately informed citizen will acquire a higher social consciousness, and the timid follower will share in the leader's courage.

In agitation, this humiliation is permanent. In establishing the inferiority of his prospective followers, the agitator claims superior knowledge, which, he implies, he has obtained by virtue of his special position and abilities. The audience is inferior not because it is temporarily "unenlightened" but because it is composed of "dupes" and "suckers." Throughout his utterances there can be found many unflattering references to potential followers. The agitator speaks of striking workers as "just plain ordinary sincere sheeplike Americans."[1] When he refers to the "bemused" people taken in by the New Dealer's "hoax"[2] or of the "deluded innocents,"[3] his tone is relatively mild. It changes to worry when he speaks about the "gullibility of Americans"[4] and the "mass ignorance of our people" of which the "powers of anti-Christianity" take advantage.[5] When he deplores the fact that the "blind populace" is being led into the "horrible ditch of war" by blind leaders,[6] the agitator adopts a tone of regret. And when he calls his potential followers "sappy Gentiles"[7] or "dumb Americans,"[8] the agitator becomes stingingly indignant.

He intimates that the unenlightened condition of his audience is hopeless and permanent, is something the audience itself cannot remedy. He warns his audience that it needs his guidance in the bewildering situation in which it finds itself, but he offers it no way to escape its bewilderment by its own intellectual efforts. He enhances his listeners' sense of distrust by reminding them that they are ruled by "remote control" and that they are exposed to constant sinister manipulations. They are cheated all along the line, in rationing, in war, through the press and the movies.

He not only denounces Communist slogans as "catch-phrases to obtain power over . . . dupes"[9] but also brands preparedness against the Axis as a pretext for inflicting a hoax "on a long-suffering people in the name of and behind the cruel mask of 'defense.'"[10] Against such unscrupulous tactics, the "plain ordinary sincere sheeplike" people are helpless; they are always the victims, the eternal dupes.

The effectiveness of such frank and unflattering talk should not be underestimated. It must not be forgotten that the agitator banks on an audience composed of "dupes," people who bear the world a grudge because they feel it has cheated them, and who are therefore insecure, dependent, and bewildered. The agitator is referring to a common life experience. From childhood on, people are burdened by a repression of instinctual drives imposed on them by civilization in the name of its values. To live up to these values, they must constantly deny themselves and make sacrifices, for which the only solace is the promise that ultimately they will be rewarded. But in the lives of most people there occurs a moment, usually near middle age, when they realize that their dreams have remained and will remain unfulfilled. This realization gives way to a painful inner conflict, which may be resolved in several ways. The shock of disillusionment may be absorbed internally: the individual attributes responsibility to himself, to his real or imaginary inadequacies, lack of industriousness or thriftiness, inferior natural endowment, or even to insufficiently sincere adherence to the unfulfilled ideals. Or he seeks consolation in the promises of religion, transferring the realization of the ideals to the beyond. Or again he may draw some satisfaction from the fact of disillusionment itself, by becoming, as so many aging persons do, a "cynic," and flaunting that attitude with a kind of malicious pleasure. One way or another, the conflict or at least the acute awareness of it can be repressed, but the smooth operation of such repression depends upon the hold ideals or values have on the individual. In the past the values were unassailable, and if they were not realized, the fault was due to one's inadequacy. Today the hold of values is weakened, while the pressure of reality has grown greater. And precisely because values are now questioned, the fury of disillusionment can be turned against them.

The individual's growing belief that the values are fictitious adds the motive of humiliation to that of disillusionment. He has sacrificed his life, his "real" life, which comes to be defined precisely as the life denied by the ideal, for the sake of mere nothings. He is confirmed in such feelings by the everyday experience that ruthlessness and unscrupulous pursuit of material advantage are more profitable than rigid adherence to moral principles. All his life he has been a sucker, cheated by the values he accepted and those who preached them.

By calling his followers suckers and telling them they must follow him if they are no longer to be cheated, the agitator promises that he will take care of them and "think" for them. Those who chafe under an authority they distrust and whose motives they cannot understand, are now to be subjected to the promptings of an agitator who will sanction their spontaneous resentments and seem to gratify their deepest wishes.

The agitator thereby tends to destroy the common social rule that imposes optimistic stereotypes ("I feel fine"; Everything is OK") on human intercourse. In a society of independent producers this rule helped to smooth the mechanism of free competition by eliminating any possible intrusion of pity or self-pity. It also helped to preserve the sanctity of the individual by keeping his inner life concealed from his neighbor's curiosity. To pour out one's troubles in public was considered a mark of bad taste and vulgarity. Social life, of which the dominant image was the impersonal marketplace, was a neutral arena in which everyone was supposed to feel equally at ease. Unless he wanted to become an object of charity, the individual's intimate problems were not exposed to the group. The agitator breaks down these folkways; he seems to say, "let us be honest, let us admit we are disillusioned, ignorant and cheated." Such an invitation can only be welcomed by people who feel that they have always been "misunderstood." Hence, by reversing the optimistic stereotypes of liberal society, the agitator makes the feeling of acknowledged failure seem respectable.

Because in the eyes of the audience the whole world has become suspicious and estranged, it yearns for facile certainties and is ready to put its fate in the hands of someone who confirms it in its helplessness. "It is high time for Americans to get wise," says the agitator.[11] Yet those who have got wise to all the tricks are just the ones who are deceived by the most primitive ruse. The investment swindler knows that his easiest victims are to be found among those who have learned to distrust respectable banking establishments. Even while he tells his listeners that they are a group of fools, the agitator lays claim to their confidence—for how could someone who warns and insults them possibly want to cheat them? His bad manners become a guaranty of his sincerity. They can trust him, for he does not flatter them, and because they are unable by themselves to "pierce the sham of propaganda,"[12] their only possible course of action is to join his movement. "Better find out whom you can trust—now."[13]

On the one hand the agitator brands his followers as suckers, harping on the suffering they have endured in their unsuccessful lives and thereby satisfying their latent masochism. On the other hand, he transforms this very humiliation into something to be proud of, a mark of the new elite he will eventually elevate. By projecting the responsibility for it on an unscrupulous and immoral enemy, he offers his followers a means of warding off in advance all future humiliations. The humiliation is simultaneously deepened and surrounded by a halo.

While the agitator thus frees the audience from its burdensome obligation of understanding its plight, he gives it a feeling that it is at last facing the true facts of existence. Yes, they are suckers, but now they know it. And what is more, they do not have to be inhibited about their intellectual inferiority; they can admit it openly; their leader encourages them to do so. Ordinarily intellectual inferiority results in exclusion from the company of the successful, but in the relationship between agitator and audience, this is reversed: the agitator seems to be especially interested in the little man who has not made the grade. Though he does not give his listeners the feeling of having attained intellectual insight or of being accepted as demarcated individuals, he does make it possible for them to feel at ease in their common inferiority.

Theme 2: Conspiracy

The dupe is pictured not merely as cheated but as cheated systematically, consistently, and perpetually. Nor is his inability to overcome his bewilderment and helplessness surprising, for he is the victim of a *"comprehensive and carefully-planned political conspiracy."*[14]

In nurturing the idea of a permanent conspiracy directed against the eternal dupes, the agitator plays upon and enlarges the tendency among people who suffer from a sense of failure to ascribe their misfortunes to secret enemy machinations. The dismissed employee, the jilted lover, the disgruntled soldier deprived of a promotion, the student who fails an examination, the small grocer driven out of business by a chain competitor—any of these may be inclined to blame mysterious persecutors motivated by obscure grudges. However, the tendency of frustrated people to imagine themselves the targets of powerful enemies need not necessarily lead to paranoia. Often enough such suspicions are not devoid of objective justification in a world where the individual's sphere of action is increasingly restricted by anonymous social forces. Our daily existence actually is influenced by tremendous developments whose causes are difficult to grasp. Hence many people are anxious to learn what is happening behind the scenes.

When the agitator tells his listeners that they are "pushed" or "kicked" around and are victimized by bankers and bureaucrats, he exploits feelings that they already have. Such stereotypes as "Wall Street machinations," "monopolist conspiracies," or "international spies" are present, however, not as well-defined ideas but as tentative suspicions about the meaning of complex phenomena. As inadequate reflections of reality, they might serve as starting points for analysis of the economic and political situations.

The agitator proceeds in exactly the opposite way. He refers to popular stereotypes only to encourage the vague resentments they reflect. He uses them not as springboards for analysis but rather as "analyses" themselves—the world is complicated because there are groups whose purpose it is to make it complicated. On a social scale he stirs his audience to reactions similar to those of paranoia on an individual scale, and his primary means of doing this is by indefinitely extending the concept of conspiracy.

Where others might speak of the ultimate implications of a political program, he sees a deliberate plot: the New Deal is nothing but "good Marxian sabotage to break down the existing order."[15] British War Relief is "sponsored by same internationalists who got us into World War I."[16] The B'nai Brith is "a worldwide spy and pressure system"[17] that has "unlimited funds" and "maintains its own Gestapo."[18] Economic crises are contrived by "a small but powerful, well-organized and well-financed minority."[19] Even such a trivial occurrence as a polemical attack on a senator is sufficient for the agitator to evoke a "secret society" for "smearing of individual members of the senate."[20] Phrases like the "Hidden Hand"[21] or "International Invisible Government"[22] appear in his writings and speeches again and again.

Any organization the agitator conceives as hostile to his aims he includes in the conspiracy. He speaks of it as seeking "to destroy . . . the American way of life,"[23] and calls on "all Christians to stand together" because a conspiracy is afoot "to ruin the Church."[24] Similarly, "class hatred is created by lies and *conflicting explanations,* all helping to create *confusion* and to conceal *the real authors* of the devilish plans for the destruction of Christian or Western civilization."[25]

This inflation of the notion of conspiracy not only serves as a diversion from attempts to investigate social processes but also blurs the identity of the groups designated as conspirators. The very stereotypes that once referred more or less definitely to social oligarchies now refer to gigantic but undefined secret international plots. The term *octopus,* once used by Frank Norris in a novel about railroad magnates, now becomes diffused into the "international invisible government."[26]

In this transformation of a circumscribed group of magnates into mysterious invisible rulers, the process of blurring reality by encouraging paranoiac tendencies is clearly evident. As compensation, the idea of conspiracy acquires a sensational and thrilling connotation, and all the problems of modern life are centered in a comfortingly simple, if vague and mysterious, cause. This systematization of conspiracies into one grandiose plot is declared by the agitator to be "obvious even to a dullard," for

> all this step-by-step bungling—this amazing unity of deception, internal sabotage, and gross incompetence in the leaders of Britain, France

and even of the United States—is not an accident. It is, rather, indicative of a central directing influence—a World Government group."[27]

There is no telling how far this conspiracy may extend. In fact, it has been going on since time immemorial.

> The doctrine of ruling by force from hidden sources, and this secret group, ruled over Babylon of Nimrod, Egypt, Babylon of Nebuchadnezzar, Medio-Persia, Greece and Rome. And this same secret society became the Jacobins of the French Revolution and placed Napoleon in power in Europe and when Russia and then England overthrew him (see Dumas' works), they moved into Germany where they became known as Communists, from whence they overthrew Russia, and produced the bastard children, Fascism and Nazism.[28]

These fantastic images seem, first of all, to satisfy the audience's craving for an explanation of its sufferings. In that sense the agitator seems to continue the work of the muckrakers by courageously revealing why the powers that rule the world wish to remain hidden. But by dealing, as it were, with the audience's notions at their face value, by exaggerating to the point of the fantastic its suspicions that it is the toy of anonymous forces, and by pointing to mysterious individuals rather than analyzing social forces, the agitator in effect cheats his audience of its curiosity. Instead of diagnosing an illness, he explains it as the result of an evil spirit's viciousness, for the conspirators are not pictured as motivated by any rational purpose but, rather, by a gratuitous will to destruction:

> My informant tells me that the bloodless revolution is being brought about through a planned policy of destructionism—a destructionism which pretends to alleviate suffering, poverty, unemployment and hunger . . . a destructionism which eventually aims at bankrupting the nation and thereby bringing about repudiation of debts and the overthrow of government.[29]

And this conspiracy is directed at the very vitals of the people—in fact, if the people are to survive, they must act immediately to destroy this conspiracy, for "the intriguers have taken us so far down their alley that we have lost our time honored powers of resistance. More than a palliative is needed at this critical juncture."[30]

Here we see how the paranoiac brooding and the projection of conspiracies end with suggestions for acts of violence. Because the very term *conspiracy* has connotations of illegality and treason, the conspirators are pictured as acting in lawless fashion and with complete impunity. This implies that existing laws and institutions cannot cope with them and that extraordinary measures are needed.

Theme 3: Forbidden Fruit

If the agitator's audience is composed of eternal dupes who have always been the prey of an ubiquitous conspiracy, the agitator will presumably emphasize all the good things of life that the "others" enjoy but the audience does not. Here, as in almost all other themes, it might appear that the agitator is following the beaten track of revolutionaries, by advocating redistribution of social wealth.

Actually, he manages to steer clear of such explosive implication. True, he refers to the alleged good life led by those he calls the enemies. But he associates enjoyment of private pleasure with vice and luxurious excess. He is eloquent in describing the carefree existence of "alien-minded plutocrats" who "roll in wealth, bathe in liquor, surround themselves with the seduced daughters of America."[31] But he is equally eloquent in denouncing indulgence in materialistic pleasures: "America, the vain—America, the proud—America, the nation of gluttons and spenders and drinkers. A nation whose population has deserted the church and in many instances, debauched the home."[32]

The debauch of "alien-minded plutocrats" is condemned in the following moral reflections: "Drunkenness became just a humorous, though effective way of getting relaxation. Adultery became just a method of showing sincerity of affection and a usual part of comradeship between good friends of opposite sex."[33]

The agitator evokes a bizarre vision of oversized, luxurious homes, where alcohol flows and swimming pools abound. Children play in nurseries while adults revel in game rooms, nightclubs, racetracks, and bedrooms. "The sweet and simple things of life" are "discarded, absent, forgotten."[34] This perverse and adulterous life is branded as un-American, characteristic of foreigners and refugees who squander fabulous fortunes when they are not busy stealing jobs from Americans. "With hundreds of thousands of Jews running away from war bringing wealth here and making themselves obnoxious in 'hot spots' and vice resorts with their lavish spending."[35]

Such a way of life is also un-Christian, enjoyed by "Oriental erotics" of whom American Christians are the "unwary hosts."[36] These "erotics" debauch "youth for the purpose of wrecking Gentile morale."[37] Uncannily and scarily, "all this is being done by an invisible power. Rape and the evasion of income taxes plays a big part in all this."[38]

The very presence of material comfort is viewed with suspicion and implicitly condemned by the agitator. Among the accusations leveled against President Roosevelt is the fact that he was "born in the lap of luxury" and "never made a payroll in his life."[39] Often the agitator whets the appetite of his followers with detailed descriptions of the luxuries of the enemy while arousing their moral disgust at such corrupt practices.

When Harry Hopkins got married, Baruch gave a party for the "Palace Guard" at the Carlton Hotel, where you need $100.00 before you can rent a room; and pay $2 before you can order a cup of coffee. But Mr. Baruch arranged the party, and they were all there: Harry Hopkins, the bride, Mr. Nelson, Mr. Henderson. There were seven kinds of meat served—twenty-two kinds of food, and it had cost Barney Baruch $122 a plate; and they drank of the vintage of '26. Now, I am no connoisseur of champagne. McCullough of the Post-Dispatch says it is $20.00 a quart—and if I had a quart of that I might get a good story in the Post-Dispatch tomorrow. [Laughter.] But there isn't any more of that, I understand, now because of the war with France. There was $2000 served of that drink. There was precious perfume at $40 a tiny vial to each woman there. You talk about the drunken orgies of history—we expect Capone to live like that, but as long as I am a Christian soul, I will not be governed by a man like that.[40]

Even while the agitator seems to be furiously voicing the claims of his audience for a greater share of social wealth, he is actually suppressing their claims. Even while he offers, he actually denies enjoyment of the good things of life. Enjoyment of wealth means debauch and vice—hence wealth is a forbidden fruit. Moreover, the agitator portrays it in such fantastic terms that the common man cannot even dream of acquiring it but must content himself with the "sweet and simple things of life."

Rather than offering suggestions for a greater utilization of productive facilities or a more just distribution of the social product, the agitator encourages resentment against the excesses of luxury. Appealing to puritanical attitudes the agitator condemns indulgence not in order to propose the elimination of poverty but, rather, to exasperate his followers' feelings of envy while simultaneously arousing their sense of guilt at being envious. He activates revolutionary sentiment but directs it against the caricature he has himself drawn of human aspirations for pleasure. The violent language in which he castigates those who enjoy the "cream" of this country while the rest go "milkless" is thus ultimately directed against the audience's own desires. Even when the agitator denounces the "society world of snobbery and fraud" and shouts "Down must come those who live in luxury!"[41] he is not proposing to the audience a way for it to increase its share of wealth and pleasure. When the golden calf is destroyed and its worshippers dispersed, his followers may still expect nothing for themselves—they have been taught by the agitator to distrust their own aspirations to comfort. The image of abundance is dangled before them but is never accessible. All that can result for the follower is an inner exacerbation of his resentments. If the agitator cannot promise his adherents a greater share of the good things of life, he can suggest that the good life consists in something else, the gratification of repressed impulses; and that if they are obedient to him they will be offered the luxurious sinners as sacrificial prey.

Theme 4: Disaffection

An important aspect of the malaise is a growing sense of disillusionment with ideals, values, and institutions. The agitator skilfully works on this disillusionment by simultaneously damning and praising the accepted ideologists. On the one hand, he likes to give the impression that, like most other advocates of social change, he is against certain social conditions because they violate universally accepted values. On the other hand, he often concurs in and reinforces his audience's suspicion about those values.

He speaks as a champion of democracy and Christianity and protests that he is "merely defending the Bill of Rights."[42] He invokes the "Christian doctrine of human liberty"[43] and extols "American individualism" and "free enterprise."[44] He is the guardian of "the Bible, the Christian Faith, American institutions and the Constitution."[45]

Yet, when confronted with his audience's moral confusion, he implies that he shares neither the conservative's total acceptance of existing values and institutions nor the "naive idealism of the liberals."[46] He knows that the "two-party system is a sham"[47] and "democracy" a "trick word."[48] "In fact, justice matters more than democracy."[49] And "Liberaliam—in politics—leads to Anarchy."[50]

It can of course be maintained that the first group of statements is merely camouflage for the second. To some extent this is probably true, but it is hardly likely that the audience is fooled into taking the agitator for a sincere champion of democracy. It is much more likely that the agitator who utilizes democratic stereotypes is quite aware that his words ring hollow: he does not intend to be taken literally. In view of his known sympathy for European fascism, the agitator's use of democratic phrases serves to create the impression that the difference between fascism and democracy is not as important as it is made out to be—or more accurately, that it is not at all what really matters. The agitator constantly seeks to blur this difference. In reality, he declares, he is "no more a fascist than Abraham Lincoln and Teddie Roosevelt";[51] he is called one merely because he is one of the "individualists who still believe in Constitutional government."[52] To muddy the waters further, he hurls the accusation of fascism against those who have come to symbolize opposition to fascism. He consistently denounces the New Deal as an effort to introduce totalitarianism into the United States, and declare that "Roosevelt got his technique from Hitler and the Jews."[53]

In bandying the two antithetical concepts of democracy and fascism in such a way that the clear distinction between them is obliterated, the agitator seems to act on the premise that his audience's loyalties are uncertain. He therefore seems bent not on concealing but on flaunting his cynicism, the effect of which is to sanction and fixate his audience's disillusionment. It is characteristic of the agitator's whole approach that he confirms his adherents' disillusionment by both his affirmations and negations, for in the way they are expressed by him both bar any possible surmounting of the disillusionment. In the way he points to the traditional as the great ideal, the agitator discourages a serious critique of existing values; in the way he debunks existing values, he makes impossible any sincere attempt to realize them more effectively in practice.

This dual assault on the value system, which runs like a thread through agitational material, is, so to speak, the one occasion when the agitator comes to grips with opposing arguments. It is part of his general desecration of the idea of truth as such. Underlying the agitator's rejection of those values by which it is possible to distinguish democracy from its opposite is the implication that in the present world, where the masses are eternal dupes and the victims of a perennial conspiracy, everything must give way to the urge for self-survival. The distinction between truth and lies is accordingly inconsequential; both are neutral means to be used according to their helpfulness to his cause.

That the agitator's preachments profoundly contradict ideals such as democracy, equality, and justice, that are commonly held to be universal does not seem to bother him, for he capitalizes on the general sense of disillusionment among his adherents by articulating their suspicion that the enemy's ideals are mere camouflage for social coercion. Instead of sifting the valuable aspects of the ideal from the way it may be misused, he junks both. All that is left then for him—and this is what he takes great pains to imply to his audience—is an idealless use of force against the troublemaking enemy. His doctrine thus consists in drawing the ultimate consequences of a totally amoral opportunism, as discussed below.

Unseriousness

The agitator's ambiguous approach to values is often revealed in an undercurrent of unseriousness in his statements, the effect of which is to dismiss ideals as mere bunk, hogwash, lies. Take his attitude toward the law, for example. There are too many laws and regulations behind which are hidden "the gossamers of un-Americanism."[54] What is more, "any '*law*' is alien fodder to Anglo-Saxons."[55] As against "inspired" laws he champions "individualism."[56] Yet the agitator simultaneously poses as a champion of legality, denouncing the "rulings" of the New Deal as "illegal."

These apparently conflicting views are synthesized in statements that express more fundamentally the agitator's genuine attitude toward law:

> Will the United States be required to remunerate Jews for their losses in a war with Hitler's Germany, a war that the Jews, themselves, promoted? Would it not be nearer to equity, nearer to measure for measure if the Jews were required to compensate non-interventionists and political "isolationists" for their loss of life and treasure?[57]

What is serious in these statements is their very lack of seriousness. Going beyond the revelation that law can be a cloak for brute force, the agitator shows here that brute force need hardly be clothed at all, for instead of being discarded as a sham, legality is now exploited as a blatant gesture of defiance. Behind such statements is the outlook that led the Nazi regime to "fine" the German Jews $400,000,000 when a Polish Jew killed a German embassy clerk in Paris. That a legal justification was given to such a step was not primarily, as it might seem, a concession to hypocrisy or prejudice; on the contrary, it was simply a means of emphasizing the complete arbitrariness of the operation.

Transformation of meaning

The agitator twists the meaning of basic ideals in such a way that he infuses them with his own content. He celebrates "the instrument of the American ballot, which instrument makes all men equal in the affairs of their government"[58] while simultaneously calling for extralegal measures: "I am talking about cleaning America. Let me tell you how to do it. General Franco found one way."[59]

The agitator transforms democracy from a system that guarantees minority rights into one that merely affirms the privileged status of the majority. Persecution of minorities is thus within the rights of the majority and any attempt to limit the exercise of this "right" is interpreted as persecution of the majority by the minority. Such an interpretation of democracy results in its negation: "Do the Jews clamor for democracy only because a democracy is too weak to resist their encroachments? . . . If it is, then a lot of us will want to be done with democracy."[60]

The agitator submits religion to the same kind of treatment. He stresses the particularistic connotations of religion by suggesting that Christianity is an exclusive creed, a kind of tribal fetish, endowed with primitive attributes of clannishness and violence. He denounces "the false premise that all, and particularly Jews, are 'brothers'—to the Christian. . . . The Jew, religious or otherwise, is today as always against Christ, therefore *not* a 'brother.' ABC stuff!"[61]

In the presence of demonic powers, the foremost feature of Christianity is "a militant routing of evil in high places by humble followers of Christ."[62] The church thus becomes a tabloid version of *ecclesia militans*. The agitator suggests that "for America to pray" and "for America to fight" are the same thing,[63] and he does not hesitate to recommend putting "prayers across . . . at the point of a gun"[64] or building "barricades to protect the principles of the Prince of Peace."[65] The agitator thus appears as a policeman of virtue, a sergeant defending the ideal, a corporal fighting for truth. "Unite in dropping prayer-bombs upon the camp of the enemy"[66] and exercise justice as a member of a "Social Justice platoon."[67]

This transformation of values into their opposites receives its final twist when the agitator declares: "If Smith is America's No. 1 Fascist (anti-Semite) as Judeo-Reds proclaim, then, according to New Testament, Christ must be World's greatest Anti-Semite!"[68]

Anti-Universality

The agitator explicitly rejects the ideal of universality. This rejection is evidenced, for instance, in his attitude toward tolerance, which he brands as "silly sentimentality"[69] and "non-Christian,"[70] as contrary to self-interest and a weakness that must be eradicated for the sake of survival.

TOLERANCE—A numerous group of alien and native rascals shout "tolerance" but with their own foul tongues, they would lap up the blood of their own critics.[71]

As though realizing that tolerance is a cultural luxury for those in power who may preach and violate it with equal impunity, and that it reflects the social weakness of those out of power, the agitator uses the caption "None but the Strong Can be Magnanimous."[72] He implies that tolerance is opposed to truth, and when involking the concept of truth, he almost always associates it with violence. He claims that he is persecuted and threatened with death if he dares speak the truth, and then directly identifies it with the application of force: "The Cross and The Flag' speaks the truth. We have arrived at the hour when we must have more two-fisted talking and real action."[73]

Truth is further equated with intolerance in anti-Semitism: "When telling the truth about Jewish organizations or leaders is punished as a crime by our courts—what becomes of the four freedoms of the Gentile majority in the USA?"[74]

The agitator applies a similar technique to the concepts of the brotherhood, humanitarianism, universal justice: all are shown to be contrary to the crudest requirements of self-interest. "'Racial equality,' 'social equality,' and 'natural equality' are absurd concepts, either in biology or common sense, and nobody knows this better than Jews who are ballyhooing such concepts."[75]

Through these three devices—unseriousness, transformation of values, and negation of universalism—the agitator tries to convince his audience that ideals and values are merely misleading advertising slogans, used to defraud the dupes.

Theme 5: Charade of Doom

The possibility of total disaster is invoked by many advocates of social change as a contrast to their solutions. The reformer or revolutionary helps his audience visualize this possibility as a definite obstacle to be removed (capitalist society or antiunion employers or nationalism); although he evokes visions of catastrophe and, to some extent, exploits existing fears, he summons the audience to work toward an achievable utopia rather than to flee from imminent danger.

In agitation, however, the positive alternative to the threat of disaster is either totally lacking or suggested only in the vaguest form as a return to "the good old days." The agitator presents the threatening chaos as unavoidable and inexorable. By elaborating present dangers—and in our time he has abundant material to draw upon—he may seem bent on making his audience realize the urgency of the situation. In fact he achieves the opposite by associating these dangers with trivial ideas or grotesque fantasies. Just as through the theme of disaffection he cheats his audience out of intellectual curiosity, so does he cheat it out of fear as a possible stimulus to organized social thought and action.

Through the exploitation of the fear of impending chaos, the agitator succeeds in appearing as a radical who will have no truck with mere fragmentary reforms while he simultaneously steers his adherents wide of any suggestion of a basic social reorganization. He equates the threat to profits with the impending chaos:

> If we lose this fight, if the American worker bends his knee to Lewis, Browder, and Stalin, in the Middlewest tonight, this will be just the beginning. Then comes the destruction of profits. When profits go, wages go; when wages go, jobs go. Then comes chaos, revolution, confiscation, and the breakdown of our beautiful, free American system.[76]

The postwar strikes are interpreted as "a pretext for ushering in a new political and social order in the image of Karl Marx, Leon Trotsky, Prof. Harold J. Laski and the House of Rothschild."[77]

In the above passages the agitator embroiders on the usual conservative stereotypes. He goes further in playing on the middle-class fear of revolution, as associated with material discomfort and confiscation of private property:

> CIO and radical AF of L unions . . . can, and will, when "Der Tag" (sometime prior to 1941) is decided upon by the Hidden Hand, plunge cities into darkness, shut off water, gas, phone, telegraph, radio, food, and transportation generally, so that in terror imposed by fear, thirst, and starvation, the weakkneed NEW DEAL politicians, businessmen, and labor leaders in most large cities are expected to surrender to Anti-Christ dictatorship.[78]

Where the agitator diverges from the conservative politician, however, is in tying the threat of chaos not only to such relatively serious matters as strikes but also to circumstantial minor causes of discontent, such as food or tire shortages, which he represents as the deliberate work of liberals and radicals. The revolution is imminent whether or not there are strikes. War taxation is not merely a burden but a conspiracy to strip us down to the point of hunger and starvation and bankruptcy where our taxes will cost us our homes."[79]

In thrusting before his audience the terrors of the impending doom, the agitator often paints it in terms of sexual connotations:

> After all, what is more likely to follow many years of Nudeal com-munistic confiscatory taxation, wool-less, metal-less, auto-less regi-mentation and planned scarcities than our finally becoming stripped by necessity to Nudism.[80]

> The world is moving rapidly toward chaos, which will mean revolu-tion, waves of sadism, murder, rape, incest, conflagration, atom bomb conflicts, annihilation of whole populations.[81]

It may be conjectured that by his references to rape, incest, and plunder, the agitator evokes sadistic fantasies that add a connotation of promise to the warning: his followers may vaguely hope that when the deluge comes they, too, may be allowed to perform the acts that are attributed to the enemy.

The fear of specific dangers, such as the threat of inflation or war, is drowned in gloating visions of universal chaos: "We approach our day of doom under the guidance of the most incompetent and Satanic array of rascals ever assembled by any government in the history of the world."[82]

Fear is no longer used as a psychological signal pointing to the exis-tence of specific dangers; like the Conspiracy it becomes ubiquitous and eternal.

> History follows same pattern for Satan uses same tactics, and same kind of people. . . . Under Satanic guidance all activities of man are being forced into roads leading to chaos and destruction.[83]

Whatever associations the audience may have had with concretely experienced causes of apprehension are dissolved by the blaring alarum of threatening catastrophe. Confronted with such an inexorable fate, the audience can feel only complete impotence.

> No matter to what extent the Roosevelt dynasty betrays the common man in America, or what atrocious crimes it commits, or how low it sinks in ethics, morals and common decency, nothing will be done about it now and probably nothing can be done. The disease must run its course, the cycle must complete itself.[84]

The audience's unpleasurable reactions are here offset by the fact that its subordinate social role is vindicated by being placed in a historical perspective: individual and personal failures are subsumed under the national, international or even cosmic failure. Though the agitator's adherent has lost the dignity of a man participating in constructive activities on his own initiative, he is compensated by a kind of tragic dignity that raises his insignificant personal defeat to the status of an historical event.

By being spread over a larger surface, the original fear becomes thinner, less urgent and compelling, but it acquires an enhanced imaginative reality. Fear is transformed into a morbid nihilistic expectation, perhaps even hope, of total destruction.

The actual reasons for despair are utilized to indulge in a charade of despair, and as though to emphasize this, the agitator does not hesitate to introduce motifs of outright grotesqueness in his prophecies. He spices real threats with the vision of a deadly onslaught on the human race planned by celestial and earthly powers:

> Already restricted crop production due to Internationalists' schemes plus storms, floods, attacks by insects, etc., this year points to what may be expected in years 1943, 1944, and 1945, in which scientists say we will be plagued with the coldest summers and winters in history.[85]

As a consequence of this piling of mock horrors onto real ones, the listeners are encouraged to follow the path of least resistance intellectually. To understand the causes of their frustrations they need no longer cope with such complicated problems as tax laws, unions, governmental policies, the organization of the credit system, etc. All these bewildering matters have been reduced to a common denominator: they are nothing but various aspects of the essentially ruthless setup of the world, symptoms of one big, horrid overwhelming, superhuman or subhuman elemental phenomenon. Inability to meet resourcefully a bread-and-butter situation may produce a feeling of inferiority, but such a feeling is out of place when one is faced with a dilemma arising from cosmic causes. What else can one do but leave the understanding of such a confrontation to the available spiritual elite?

This conscious reliance on the wisdom of the great is probably furthered by unconscious regressive tendencies. The explanation of everyday mischances in terms of uncanny world catastrophes revitalizes and reinforces the heritage of infantile anxieties. The unconscious finds in the agitator's interpretations a replica of its own primitive reactions to the outside world; the listener plays the role of the little child responding to the warning that bogeys may come for him.

Something that is feared on one level of personality is often desired on another. This seems especially true for the peculiarly fascinating experience of catastrophe. The gospel of doom relieves the individual of responsibility for struggling with his problems; one cannot resist an erupting volcano. The agitator's listeners are told in effect that between their limited capacities and the tremendous forces that threaten them there is an ineradicable disproportion. As a result, everything goes. A man involved in catastrophe feels justified in departing from established moral codes if it, means saving his life. The idea of catastrophe contains a welcome stimulus to the listeners' destructive instinctual urges.

It is not difficult for the agitator's adherents to take the further step of projecting disaster onto the imaginary enemy. This is a process akin to that unconscious transference that permits the average man to assume that accidents or sudden fatalities are more likely to strike some unknown man rather than him. Thus the agitator offers his followers, who either are or believe themselves persecuted, a method of relieving their feeling of social inferiority by indulging in fantasies in which other people—those they envy or dislike—suffer annihilation.

The agitator expresses the unconscious wish of the dissatisfied to drag all other persons down to their own level of insignificance. Since "we" are down and out and have no chance to escape catastrophe, "we" do not want anyone else to be spared this fate. Freed from the inhibitions of conscience by the agitator's evocation of inevitable doom, his listeners can give gratifying play to fantasies arising from repressed destructive impulses. Because the agitator has used actual threats of catastrophe to construct a fantasy-threat that bars positive satisfactions to his adherents, they seem driven to seek the compensation of gratifying the death instinct: "The whole world will go down with us." For the unconscious, the threatened apocalypse, which might have been the stimulus to action to ward off social dangers, here becomes the "solution" itself.

Notes

1.   CF, Feb., 1948, p. 714.
2.   Smith, New York, Oct. 20, 1936, meeting.
3.   Sanctuary, *The New Deal is Marxian Sabotage*, p. 1.
4.   SJ, Dec. 8, 1941, p. 15.
5.   SJ, June 6, 1938, p. 5.
6.   SJ, Sept. 15, 1941, p. 3.
7.   LIB, Mar. 21, 1940, p. 9.

8.   AID, Jan. 27, 1941, p. 3.
9.   Sanctuary, *The New Deal is Marxian Sabotage*, p. 1.
10. Mote, Cleveland, July 2, 1942, meeting.
11. SJ, July 21, 1941, p. 11.
12. SJ, Nov. 17, 1941, p. 9.
13. AID, July 3, 1938, p. 1.
14. Mote, *Testimony before the U.S. Senate Committee on Military Affairs*, June 30, 1941, p. 6.
15. Sanctuary, *The New Deal is Marxian Sabotage*, p. 1.
16. AID, Nov. 18, 1940, p. 3.
17. AID, Apr. 28, 1941, p. 4.
18. Kamp, *Native Nazi Purge Plot*, p. 56.
19. AP, June, 1945, p. 3.
20. CF, June, 1942, p. 4.
21. Hudson, passim.
22. Winrod, passim.
23. Kamp, *Native Nazi Purge Plot*, p. 6.
24. Smith, Detroit, May 11, 1943, meeting.
25. Sanctuary, *The New Deal is Marxian Sabotage*, p. 2.
26. DEF, Feb., 1941, p. 7.
27. SJ, Nov. 17, 1941, p. 9.
28. DEF, Mar., 1939, p. 13.
29. SJ, June 6, 1938, p. 5.
30. Sanctuary, *Tearing Away the Veils*, p. 47.
31. Smith. *Letter*, "Kill Him! Kill Him! Kill Him!" Aug., 1945, p. 2.
32. CF, Aug., 1942, p. 12.
33. Phelps, *An Appeal to Americans*, pp. 15, 16.
34. Phelps, *An Appeal to Americans*, p. 16.
35. AID, Jan. 6, 1941, p. 3.
36. CF, Aug., 1945, p. 609.
37. LIB, May 7, 1940, p. 12.
38. Phelps, Los Angeles, Aug. 4, 1940, radio.
39. Pelley, *What You Should Know About The Pelley Publications*, p. 2.
40. Smith, St. Louis, March 25, 1944, meeting.
41. Phelps, Los Angeles, Aug. 18, 1940 and Oct. 1, 1940, radio.
42. CF, July, 1942, p. 12.
43. SJ, Mar. 4, 1940, p. 19.
44. Kamp, *Famine in America*, p. 50.
45. DEF, Jan., 1940, p. 14.
46. Smith, Detroit, Mar. 22, 1943, meeting.
47. Smith, Detroit, Mar. 19, 1943, meeting.
48. X, Feb. 17, 1945, p. 1.
49. Coughlin, Speech on March 26, 1939, reprinted in *Why Leave Our Own*, p. 161.
50. DEF, Sept. 1935.
51. Smith, New York, Oct. 20, 1936, meeting.
52. Kamp, *With Lotions of Love . . .*, p. 4.
53. AP, Oct., 1945, p. 13.

54. SJ, Jan. 15, 1940, p. 19.
55. AP, Nov. 1945, p. 12.
56. Kamp, *Famine in America*, p. 50.
57. AP, Jan., 1945, p. 11.
58. Smith, "The Next President of the United States," radio address, p. 4.
59. McWilliams, New York, July 29, 1940, street corner.
60. AP, Jan., 1945, p. 11.
61. AID, May 5, 1941, p. 1.
62. AID, July 17, 1939, p. 3.
63. Smith, "The Next President of the United States," radio address, p. 4.
64. quoted in: A. B. Magil, *The Truth about Father Coughlin,* New York, no date, p. 14 (date of lecture referred to: January 22, 1934.)
65. Coughlin, Speech on March 26, 1939, reprinted in *Why Leave Our Own,* p. 161.
66. DEF, Feb., 1940, p. 4.
67. SJ, June 13, 1938, p. 3.
68. AID, Sept. 19, 1945, p. 4.
69. LIB, Oct. 14, 1933, p. 11.
70. Phelps, *An Appeal to Americans,* p. 16.
71. AP, Aug., 1944, p. 1.
72. LIB, Dec. 23, 1933, p. 8.
73. CF, May, 1942, p. 16.
74. PTB, Jan., 1943, p. 4.
75. AP, Apr., 1945, p. 14.
76. Smith, *Mice or Men,* radio address in 1939, p. 4.
77. AP, Nov., 1945, p. 5.
78. AID, July 3, 1938, p. 1.
79. Smith, Detroit, Feb. 7, 1943, meeting.
80. RTL, Mar. 27, 1942, p. 11.
81. CF, Feb., 1946, p. 702.
82. DEF, Nov., 1941, p. 30.
83. AID, June 2, 1942, p. 3.
84. AP, Jan., 1945, p. 3.
85. AID, July 1, 1942, p. 1.

4

The Ruthless Enemy

Like all advocates of social change, the agitator finds the enemy responsible for his followers' sufferings. But although in other movements defeat of the enemy is a means to an end (a new society or a reformed society of one sort or another), in agitation it is an end in itself. The enemy is conceived not as a group that stands in the way of achieving a certain objective but as a superoppressor, a quasi-biological archdevil of absolute evil and destructiveness. He is irreconcilable, an alien body in society that has no useful productive function. Not even in theory is he amenable to persuasion. There is no bridge that the enemy can cross for repentance. He is there forever, evil for the sake of evil.

The agitator finds the raw material for such a portrait in the existing stereotypes of hostility. His targets are innumerable. After naming them as the "communists," "the Nazis, the Fascists and the Japs," "the (so-called) Friends of Democracy," "the Internationalists," "the New Deal Bureaucrats," "Walter Winchell," and "Communist and pro-Communist journals," he remarks that "the above list does not include all of our enemies. We could name one hundred more classifications of foes, but the ones listed indicate the type of opposition we face. WE ARE PROUD OF OUR ENEMIES. IT IS AN HONOR TO BE HATED BY SUCH PERSONS AND ORGANIZATIONS."[1] However, the agitator makes an effort to integrate the diffuse hostilities of his audience into a definite image, which we shall now try to define.

For purposes of analysis, the agitator's portrait of the enemy is divided into three parts: the political appearance, the psychological substratum, and the pseudoreality reference, the Jew. Chapters 4, 5, and 6 discuss each of these versions.

Theme 6: The Reds

The agitator makes use of all the familiar antiradical stereotypes. He speaks of the "beast of Bolshevism, the desecrator of the divine, the killer of Christians,"[2] and warns his audience that:

> like a Bubonic plague, Bolshevism moves across the face of the earth, burning churches, slaughtering the ministers of God, ridiculing the things we hold sacred, referring to religion as the opiate of the people, breeding discontent.[3]

Yet the agitator's position as one who wishes to produce the impression of being the most vocal enemy of revolution is not without ambiguity, for the radicals are not merely his enemies, they are also his competitors. Like them he aims at enlisting mass support, and like them he promises not the partial palliatives of the reformist but a definitive solution of the problems that harass his audience.

The agitator must therefore establish the inferiority and unreliability of his radical rivals while simultaneously reassuring the earth's mighty that the passion aroused by his invective will not be turned against them. That is why his denunciations of communism are so virulent: he must show that he hates the enemies of private property more than do its wealthiest exponents.

Whenever he can, the agitator uses the language and ideas of what is currently respectable to show that he is a loyal and trustworthy citizen. No better example of this can be seen than in the way he seizes on the prevalent fear of communism to twist it for his own purposes. Many of his statements about the "reds" are indistinguishable from what a bona fide conservative, or even liberal, might say about communism. But when they are examined in the context of the agitator's total output, they are seen as utilized by him in a unique approach. This approach is marked by three features.

1. *For the agitator, the revolution may come tomorrow:* He never discusses or analyzes the particular stage of development at which the radical movement may be at any given time; he makes no effort to distinguish between various kinds of radical movements, revolutionary or reformist, extreme or mild; he does not differentiate between the different tactics used by these radical movements. All are lumped together into an undifferentiated revolutionary threat. This threat is not located in any specific movement or event or possible development; it is simply reduced to the danger of immediate revolutionary violence.

His imagery of communism is drawn from civil war situations, violent seizure of power by armed minorities amidst an orgy of blood and violence. In fact, the revolution may happen any minute:

> Only hope is for Congress to awaken in time. Present Judeo-Red inspired-directed-financed strikes are part of Bolshevik revolutionary technique to sabotage our economy and facilitate *Reign of Terror* coincident with outbreak of World War III.[4]

The agitator's concept of communism is infinitely extendable. Adopting the air of someone "in the know," the agitator tells his listeners that groups holding actual political or economic power are linked to communism. At the same time its threat is used to satisfy a craving for fantastic and gruesome stories. The agitator suggests a principle of systematization for an almost paranoiac state of mind: "Confusion out of mouths of columnists, ambassadors, bishops, courts, politicians, yet same RED THREAD tieing all together."[5]

The extent of this danger can be seen when it is realized that "with Communists drinking tea in the White House and 2,850 of them on the payroll of the United States . . . the time has come for America to wake up and act."[6] Under such circumstances, suggests the agitator, it seems almost impossible to expect the government to act, and no other way is available but the spontaneous rising of the people.

2. *He blurs the specific nature of the communist threat by identifying it with general forebodings of impending doom:* Behind communism are "international outfits," and whether they plan a revolution or a world union, the same force is at work: "Certain international outfits attempting to rob us of our national sovereignty, promote us into supergovernment, or make us part of an international Communist revolution, or take us back into the British Empire."[7]

The agitator blurs the distinction between communism and other ideologies distasteful to him by denying the very reality of communism: "There is no 'Communism' in the world and none is intended now or at any time in the future. It is a vast dupery."[8] It is as though "front" organizations are the dupes of communism, and communism itself is also a "front" for something else. This stigmatization of communism as a kind of dupery divests it of any ideological significance and extends its meaning to the point where it is completely vague. For the agitator, such an extension is a powerful device: it enables him to suggest that communism is merely a label to conceal sordid activities, and that consequently anyone whom the agitator considers sordid may be called a communist.

3. *He associates the communists with the Jews:* "Those who support...
Communism will not escape our opposition even though they seek sanctuary under the banner of their advertised race or religion and cry aloud that they are the objects of unjust attack."[9]

The identification of the communist with the Jew is well known, but the use to which this identification is put by the agitator is not. When the agitator describes communists as Jews, he transforms them from a group of people who might presumably be converted to his side into a group forever irreconcilable.

He also introduces the connotation that the enemy is weak. To fight Stalin may be a formidable job, but once his advisers are identified as those Jews who "seek sanctuary under the banner of their race or religion," they are easy prey. The very fact that they complain of being "the objects of unjust attacks" shows this to be true. In this way the communist bogey is tremendously inflated only to be debunked, and the fears whipped up by references to its power are unmasked as ridiculous. The communist leadership is entirely Jewish: "Who Are the Leaders in Communism—JEWS? Can you name even one Irishman, Dutchman, Italian, Greek, or a German who are big Communist leaders?"[10] And for this very reason communism is weak:

> The weak point of the Communist Party lies in its almost 100% Jewish leadership. There are a few 'Gentile-fronts'—Foster, Browder, etc.—but from Comintern Representative down to local leader practically all authority and responsibility is in the hands of the Jews.[11]

The communist who had been portrayed as a wolf turns out in the end to be a disguised Jewish sheep who must be mercilessly punished by the other sheep as a means of exorcising their fears.

Theme 7: The Plutocrats

The agitator denounces both the radicals and those who are denounced by the radicals. It might be supposed that the primary purpose of his attacks on the wealthy is to reassure his followers of his radicalism. But closer scrutiny of agitational texts shows this purpose to be only an incidental part of a wider scheme.

Superficially, such attacks remind the audience of liberal and populist polemics against big business monopolies. In their private

lives these financiers engage in terrible debauchery; in their public
lives they are conspirators gratifying their lust for power. They cause
war: "No one who is without an understanding of money and banking can have the slightest knowledge of what this European war is
about."[12] They "have been waxing fat on the money of sucker stockholders."[13] This country is divided between "the billionaire bankers
and their crowd on one side and the bulk of the American people
on the other."[14]

Hence it might appear that the agitator adopts the ideas and language
of the communists. In explaining the causes of the recent war, he seems
to echo their declaration that it was provoked by imperialism:

> The battle of Singapore is a battle for Kuhn, Loeb and Company and
> J. P. Morgan Company. . . . Hundreds of thousands of American and
> English boys, possibly, will sacrifice their lives to save Malaya—and
> incidentally to preserve the investments from which profits are
> wrenched from the natives of Malaya to swell the purses of interna-
> tional bankers.[15]

But this debunking is only preparatory to a subtle, almost imperceptible
twist: the attention of the audience is concentrated not on capitalism
but on the bankers.

For all his articulation of spontaneous motives of anger, the agitator is remarkably consistent in avoiding any specific references to
giant trusts in manufacture, transportation, and public utilities. But
the agitator does attack the leading industries of communication; he
seems to feel that they are his most immediate competitors. "You go
to double feature shows and what you see is propaganda. About the
only time you ever get any real meat is when you hear Gerald Smith."[16]
When he does occasionally mention industrial enterprises, such as
"mining facilities," he hastens to add that these are controlled by a "few
international financiers" who insist on "laying down their own rules of
production."[17] When enumerating his targets, he places "special interest, feudal lords, slave owners and imperialists" beside "international
bankers," but he always manages to suggest that the main enemy is the
"system of finance":

> They want an imperialistic combination which will exploit the whole
> world, its natural resources and its people, and ultimately make of all
> people imperialistic slaves to be taxed and killed in battle, at will, for
> the preservation of their system of finance and imperialistic greed.[18]

In sermonizing thus against "Mammon," the agitator seems to be exploiting traditional associations: Christ casting the money changers from the Temple. But his real motives are modern, even ultramodern, and he seems quite aware of this. He indicates this when he says:

> Let us be realists and recognize that our destiny is confined to our America. It is not woven with the destinies of the empires abroad. By fighting for them we are fighting for neither peace nor democracy, but for the perpetuation of an obsolete financial slavery operated and controlled by the Sassoons, the Montefiores, the Rothschilds, the Samuels.[19]

The key word in this quotation is "obsolete." Using the old populist image of the banker who manipulates gold, the agitator seems quite oblivious of the fact that in recent decades banks and industrial capital have merged into gigantic combines, but in fact he encourages the ruling powers to weed out from their ranks useless survivals of earlier decades: domination must be streamlined to be strengthened. The banker, here as almost everywhere else in agitation, identified with the Jew, is the symbol of outmoded methods of indirect domination. The banker is also an attractive target for the agitator's audience, which tends to seek personifications of the anonymous causes of financial loss.

The agitator is here following the stereotype that identifies economic power with financial power. Now that the banker or financier, an habitual object of hatred, has lost much of the power he had in the nineteenth century, this hatred can be more openly expressed. When the Nazis distinguished between productive and predatory capital, which they stigmatized as Jewish, they effectively exploited the distinction between economic and financial power.

To the audience the financier is especially hateful because he seems to enjoy life and luxury without holding, as does the industrialist, any actual commanding power. The omnipotent banker seems also to be identified with—to be, in fact, an enlarged symbol of—the middleman, who, in the eyes of the audience, is often responsible for economic processes that actually occur in the sphere of production. The middleman, like the banker, is thought of as particularly predatory; the industrialist is conceived as the apostle of initiative, ingenuity, and efficiency.

As though worried that his audience might misunderstand his intentions and extend his attack on the bankers to the groups he wishes to spare, the agitator hastens to add that "if the time has arrived for us to issue a democratic disclaimer against international banking, we will not accept in its stead international Communism."[20] In fact, he is opposed to capitalism only because he wants to destroy communism, which "can not be eliminated until capitalism with its usurious money system is removed, lock, stock and barrel, from our social lives."[21] Here again the phrase "with its usurious money system" indicates how strategically obsolete his characterization of capitalism is.

On an agitational plane, he is committed to a fight on two fronts: against communism and against "usurious" capitalism. He avoids the strategic drawbacks of such a fight by a bold imaginative construction: the identification of communism with capitalism. The exponents of revolution are equated with the exponents of plutocratic exploitation. At the same time, the agitator shows how much he hates the capitalists when he calls them communists. That there are obvious logical objections to the notion of a capitalistic group plotting the destruction of the system from which its profits are derived does not bother the agitator. He has several theories at hand to explain this phenomenon. In one of them, communism is represented as a tool of financial interests that aim to establish fascism:

> Communism—Special bait dangled before a large segment of the population that has been frustrated economically by international bankers but which, nevertheless, is promoted by international bankers to create a revolutionary background for the establishment of the Servile State, i.e., Fascism or Nazism.[22]

A variant theory is that communism and capitalism are both weapons in the hands of a third party: "Unrepentant capitalism and conniving Communism—the right and left hands of internationalist imperialism—have littered our fair land with un-American activities."[23]

But the agitator's preferred method of establishing the connection between capitalism and communism is by suggesting that "atheistic Communism" was "originally spawned in Jewish capitalism and Jewish intellectualism."[24] The most striking formulation of this theory traces all modern isms back to a common Jewish ancestor:

> One must remove the causes to get rid of recurring effects . . . we are concerned with liquidating the causes which created the concept of Hitlerism in the minds of men. These causes run back from Stalin to Lenin; from Lenin to Marx; from Marx to the Rothschilds; from

the Rothschilds to the Bank of England; from the Bank of England to the pack of usurers who transubstantiated a vice into a virtue in the sixteenth century.[25]

Here we see the essential purposes of the amalgamation of communism and capitalism: by being thrown together, they cancel each other's ideological and functional characteristics and can be made to appear a tool of a racial enemy—the Jew. Furthermore, the joint disavowal of "unrepentant" capitalism and communism suggests the possibility of a third system to replace them:

> An objective analysis shows that the German people could not have hoped to free their homes, churches, schools and institutions from the Red menace, without also breaking through the web of Jewish Capitalism which had been created around them. Necessity is the mother of Invention, so they established an economic system peculiarly their own, divorced from the international Jewish banking fraternity. *This fact sent a chill over the internationalists.*[26]

It is perhaps this very incongruity, amounting almost to uncanniness, of the idea of the "communist banker" that attracts the audience as a simple explanation of bewildering real situations. The agitator's attack on the banker who enjoys life seems to play up to the audience's resentments of the banker's enjoyments of the "forbidden fruit." And because the agitator's articulation of malaise contains a strong undercurrent of appeals to violence, the destruction of the "communist banker" seems, in anticipation at least, great fun to his audience.

The uncanniness of this combination of bankers and communists suggests a psychoanalytical interpretation. The banker who enjoys the forbidden fruit and preaches abstinence to others, who rolls in gold while he wants others to be thrifty, is a father image, object of ambivalent Oedipal emotions. The unnatural "marriage" of banker and communist seems "natural" to the unconscious, which in a sense considers every marriage forbidden because the mother grants the father sexual rights denied to the child. In this case, the marriage is particularly scandalous. The agitator's theory of communism "spawned" by capitalism or of the Jew who begets both, suggests that their marriage is incestuous. The banker and communist who enjoy one another and deprive the helpless child in the name of the incest taboo are hypocrites of the worst sort.

In the process of agitation the attachment to the father becomes diverted to the agitator himself functioning as a substitute father image who reminds his listeners of the incestuous marriage and confirms the scandalousness of incestuous relationships. At the same time he mobilizes resentment against both parents who deny sexual gratification to the follower and force him to look for it elsewhere, in a community of "brothers." These psychoanalytical connotations of the image of the communist banker are in accord with its political function of suggesting the inevitability of a fascist solution: psychoanalytically fascism has been viewed as a revolt of the "brothers" against parental authority.

We may then sum up agitation material on the theme of the plutocrat in the following propositions:

- When the agitator attacks capitalism, he rails not against social institution, but a group of evil individuals.
- These individuals he identifies as manipulative financiers, thereby appealing to the political emotions of an outlived era, usually the populist era in which the banker was seen as the great enemy.
- By identifying the banker as the enemy and by restricting his denunciations to finance, the agitator leaves free from attack the crucial area of modern capitalist production.
- The agitator reconciles his denunciations of communism and capitalism by constructing the "communist banker," the Jew, who utilizes both communism and "usurious" capitalism for his own ends.

Theme 8: The Corrupt Government

When the agitator criticizes the government, he behaves like any other spokesman for a party out of office, but he differs from the reformer in the verbal violence of his attacks. And unlike the revolutionary, he limits his denunciations to the personnel of the government; he does not attack its basic structure.

The New Deal proved to be a particularly convenient target for the agitator. By denouncing governmental agencies, he could pose as an enemy of regimentation:

> Those men who are sent to Washington to protect the welfare of their friends and neighbors, to follow the orders of the common masses for whom they have agreed to be servants, then fail to work for the welfare of their friends and neighbors, and to carry out their orders, should be punished as all traitors and breakers of faith should be punished.[27]

The agitator hints that he cannot expose the "vast bloc of lawless usurpers" who "have moved into positions of power"[28] as vigorously as he would wish. "You know today we cannot use free speech in America...."

A man gets up here to talk Americanism and they have a hundred lights on him. . . . Sure, an American can't talk today."[29] But the agitator is able to talk boldly about not surrendering "my Americanism to Samuel Dickstein or anyone else"[30] precisely because he knows that a liberal-minded administration will continue to grant him the opportunity to voice his opinions.

When the Nazis denounced the German Republic for its inability to cope with economic problems and its failure to break the *diktat* of Versailles, they benefited from a condition of acute crisis in which the breakdown of liberal government had become apparent to the masses. Much the same thing was true of the situation in which the Italian Fascists seized power. In both countries, moreover, there had been powerful socialist movements that for several decades had persuaded masses of people, especially the workers, that the governments were not "theirs" but were instruments of their exploiters. Both the Nazis and the Fascists capitalized on this general suspicion of established government by derailing the attitudes of "class consciousness" off the socialist tracks.

The situation in the United States is somewhat different. Here there is no long-established antigovernmental or anticapitalist tradition that the agitator can exploit. The influence of the various radical groups is and has been negligible, and even the populist rebellion, whose tradition the agitator tries at many points to utilize, was mainly against specific abuses of various financial groupings rather than against the government as such. In the United States there is no prevalent feeling among the masses that the government is not "theirs." Whatever complaints the bulk of the American people may have are formulated in terms of remedying a specific situation ("bureaucrats," "the trusts," "anti-labor Congressmen." "socialistic New Dealers"). Such complaints do not, however, constitute a rejection of the social or political status quo. For the agitator this is a very considerable handicap and as a result he must exercise a certain amount of care in the way he denounces the government. He stresses that Washington is the arena of a perpetual struggle for power between the forces of disintegration and national unity: "Washington is full of tricksters with whom it is very difficult for some of our most patriotic representatives to cope."[31]

Portraying the administration as influenced by agents of financial interests, the agitator suggests that it only pretends to represent the people as a whole: "The President, thereupon, appointed a committee to investigate the rubber situation, headed by Bernard Baruch, who for years has been known as a 'Wall Street fixer.' Someone has well said—Why should we appoint the Devil to investigate Hell?"[32]

But no matter how severe his denunciations of individual members of the government, he praises the nation's "capable executives" or "foremost business executives and managers" and urges them to "resist the aggressions of political bureaucrats."[33] He suggests that the social forces that hold actual economic power in this country do not exercise the influence they should, while the influence of the "tyrannical bureaucrats" in the government is "out of all proportion to the influence they exert among the people."[34]

The agitator is interested in suggesting, however, that at least as now practiced, representative government in this country is a sham, and that the actual rulers are secret groups. In this respect he benefits from a widespread present-day feeling that major decisions do not originate with the elected representatives but with lobbies catering to special interests. The audience may thus believe that he is revealing the true state of affairs by naming the groups he dislikes as the manipulators of the government. "We have a set of bureaucrats in power in Washington who are working for certain foreign monopolies and certain banking interests when they should be working for the people of the United States."[35] He confirms suspicions that "big financiers get tips of contracts before they are given out by the government, enabling them to buy stocks."[36]

The administration is accused of aiming at the confiscation of all privately owned property and the agitator is "amazed at the lack of courage exhibited in America by its foremost business executives and managers to resist the aggressions of political bureaucrats and revolutionists in Washington."[37] Such seemingly trivial remarks serve in effect to glorify the direct rule of economic power groups at the expense of representative government.

The agitator can play on the inchoate suspicions of his audience that vague impersonal and irresistible powers determine the destiny of the nation. He fans the traditional American distrust of bureaucracy and centralization and interprets the New Deal's attempts to regulate big business as the first steps in the establishment of a dictatorship:

> Roosevelt State Capitalism is not to be pursued under constitutional forms. The wealth is *not* to be supervised by capable executives of the people who have created it individually, that high and low may profit. These Americans, victims of Reaction in government, are

simply to relinquish their massed increments into the hands of a perpetual political oligarchy whose fiat is to be unalterable and whose omnipotence is sacrosanct.[38]

Such criticism directed against individuals who supposedly insinuate themselves into high posts, can have wide popular appeal: the listener is free to apply the stigma of vicious abuse of power to every official who is for any reason whatever an object of his resentment. The agitator's attacks further a preexisting ambivalent attitude toward institutionalized authority. Officials are pilloried while at the same time respect for authority is maintained by the eulogy of established institutions.

Theme 9: The Foreigner

In the agitator's portrait of the enemy, foreignness is a prominent trait. The plutocrat or banker is "international"; the administration is dominated by "international monopolies." Because foreign encirclement would hardly seem a plausible danger to the United States, the agitator warns against the dangers of foreign entanglements. And he finds a replica of the Nazi motif of living space in the immigrant population. He denounces plans to let new immigrants enter this country:

> Once landed on our shores, they would immediately start muscling Americans out of their jobs and their businesses. These "pioneers" would not develop new farms, mines, and enterprises, as did our forefathers. They haven't the intestinal stamina to pioneer; they would take, by their gold-usury-squeeze methods, what has been built by Americans.[39]

In the above portrait the alien seems to be a dangerous competitor, a predatory element associated with "international" bankers, but he is simultaneously associated with communism:

> From the four corners of this earth, foreigners came to our country to monopolize our resources. They are wolves in sheep's clothing, wise in the ways of propaganda and crime . . . the countries across the seas have sent crafty propagandists, who are destroying everything through subversive agitation.[40]

As against this banker-communist foreigner, the agitator evokes the image of the "good old days" when aliens with "their foreign isms were not busy working among the American people."[41] The alien is thus connected with the disturbing aspects of contemporary life, while the nostalgic image of the "good old days" suggests a pristine and uncontaminated era of security.

Overshadowing such immediate political implications is the agitator's stress on the foreigner's intrinsic differences from the native. Because he is endowed with immutable characteristics, the foreigner is essentially unassimilable. Aliens not only are responsible for "atheism, mental and moral decay, vulgarity, communism, imperialism... intolerance, snobbery, treason, treachery, dishonesty"[42] but they bring with them asocial characteristics that no amount of exposure to clean American air can purge:

> When he [the foreigner] comes to American or grows up in America, he carries the cheating, double dealing, ugly spirit of some Asiatics and Europeans in his heart and nourishes that ugly spirit by reflecting it in his social, political, fraternal and business affairs.[43]

While stressing how much of a danger aliens are because they "cleverly" divide "the American people . . . into groups,"[44] the agitator identifies them with Jews, a device that reassures those among his listeners who may themselves be among the millions of foreign-born or descendants of foreign-born that he intends no harm against them. The concept of the foreigner is narrowed down to those who "inevitably bear a characteristic racial stamp."[45] The agitator declares that "we don't care whether you come from Italy or Czechoslovakia . . . from Ireland or Wyoming. . . . Are you Christian and are you Aryan?"[46]

We see here an interesting development of the agitator's stereotype of the foreigner: from a specific external political threat to the country's economy, the foreigner is transformed into the perennial stranger characterized by irreducible qualities of foreignness. When the agitator arouses fear of communism, resentment against the government, and envy of financiers, he is largely referring to the audience's conscious experience; but when he arouses hostility against the stranger, the agitator seems to be reaching for a deeper layer of the psyche. In the agitational image of the enemy, the foreigner tends to be transformed from a specific dangerous but tangible power into an uncanny, irreconcilable extrahuman or subhuman being. This role of the foreigner in the agitator's total image of the enemy is explicitly seen in his references to the refugee.

The Refugee

For the agitator, the refugee is the most fearsome version of the foreigner. The very weakness, the very plight of the refugees is an argument against them for "*they fled from the wrath of the treacherously outraged peoples of those nations,* as they may one day flee as well from the wrath of a finally aroused populace in America."[47] The refugee becomes identified with the parasite who seeks dupes to do his dirty work.

> A "Refugee" is a member of the male sex who comes boo-hooing to the United States because he's "too cowardly" to fight like "real men" do, in Europe. He would establish himself in business or profession while the "real men" fight for HIS liberty.[48]

The refugee not only refuses to do dirty work but threatens the economic security of native Americans:

> According to the admission of our State Department, 580,000 Refugees had been admitted to the United States up to January, 1944, mostly on temporary permits. These Refugees have swarmed into positions formerly held by American professional men now absent on account of the war and constitute a serious threat of postwar unemployment for native Americans. . . .
>
> If there are hungry to be fed abroad, let the spirit of Christ stimulate us to export our surpluses instead of destroying them. It is not necessary or desirable that Refugees be brought to America to be fed.[49]

And the final identification of the refugee with the image of the enemy is made when he is depicted by the agitator as both a plutocrat-banker and a parasite who will end up on the relief rolls:

> But it is reliably reported that comparatively few of the Jewish refugees are agriculturists. By far the greater number of them are city dwellers, and small independent merchants—ranging from peddlers to store keepers and bankers. These newcomers, therefore, would not seek colonies in the rural areas but hope to concentrate in our already crowded cities; and since many of them are already penniless, would go on the relief rolls almost upon their arrival.[50]

The agitator endows refugees with characteristics that make them seem distasteful creatures, untouchables whom one avoids as if it were a social commandment to shun them. His picture of the refugee thus becomes a miniature version of the Nazis' notion of the subrace, and his evidence for such an unflattering portrait ranges from the refugee's alleged spiritual corruption to his most superficial mannerisms of behavior.

Ultimately, the refugee is identified with the ancient figure of the outcast, a man cursed by the gods, an exile who does not deserve a better fate. As such he raises a variety of ambivalent feelings among those who are subject to the agitator's appeal. The refugee seems an ideal model for irreconcilability: he has no home, he is accepted neither where he came from nor where he comes to. The refugee and the outcast become symbols of vague unconscious urges, of the repressed contents of the psyche, which, mankind has learned in the course of its history, must be censured and condemned as the price for social and cultural survival. The outcast serves to exorcise the fears as well as the temptations of self-righteous individuals. The hatred for the refugee seems thus a rejection of one's inner potential of freedom.

We may further develop this hypothesis by examining the implications of the fact that the refugee is called a "beggar."[51] One reacts ambivalently to the beggar: his humiliation is gratifying on a subconscious level, while at the same time it produces a feeling of conscious guilt. Once this ambivalence is lifted by the agitator's assurance that contempt for the beggar is not only a respectable but a necessary reaction, he can become a legitimate object of fury and spite. His suffering becomes a valid punishment for the fact that he has suffered at all.

The refugee's homelessness becomes the psychological equivalent of the audience's repressed instincts. Such an equation prepares for a release of banned instincts against banned people; a psychological bridge is constructed between the need of a resentment against repression and the resentment against a people without a country. He who has no home does not deserve one.

Notes

1. CF, June, 1942, p. 2.
2. Phelps, Los Angeles, August 13, 1941, radio.
3. Smith, *Americans! "Stop, Look, Listen,"* radio address, p. 1.
4. AID, Sept. 25, 1945, p. 2.
5. AID, May 5, 1941, p. 4.
6. Smith. *"Labor on the Cross,"* radio address, p. 1.
7. Smith, Detroit, Mar. 22, 1943, meeting.
8. Sanctuary. *The New Deal is Marxian Sabotage*, p. 1.
9. SJ, April 13, 1942.
10. X, Feb. 27, 1948, p. 4.
11. CF, Mar., 1947, p. 913.
12. Mote, *Testimony before the Committee on Military Affairs*, p. 8.
13. Phelps, *An American's History of Hollywood*, p. 5.

14.   RC, Oct. 6, 1941, p. 3.
15.   SJ, Jan. 19, 1942, p. 5.
16.   Smith, Detroit, Mar. 19, 1943, meeting.
17.   SJ, Sept. 8, 1941, p. 11.
18.   Smith, *The Hoop of Steel,* 1942, p. 22.
19.   Coughlin, Speech on Feb. 5, 1939, reprinted in *Why Leave Our Own,* p. 73.
20.   Coughlin, Speech on Feb. 19, 1939, reprinted in *Why Leave Our Own,* p. 93.
21.   SJ, June 10, 1940, p. 6.
22.   AP, Aug., 1944, p. 1.
23.   SJ, Feb. 20, 1939, p. 20.
24.   SDEF, May, 1940, p. 5.
25.   SJ, Dec. 22, 1941, p. 4.
26.   DEF, Jan., 1939, p. 6.
27.   Phelps, Los Angeles, March 30, 1941, radio.
28.   LIB, Apr. 7, 1938, p. 8.
29.   White, New York, July 18, 1940, street corner.
30.   CF, Dec., 1944, p. 486.
31.   Phelps, Los Angeles, July 20, 1941, radio.
32.   CF, Aug., 1942, p. 9.
33.   Mote, *Testimony,* etc., p. 3.
34.   CF, June, 1942, p. 9.
35.   CF. Aug., 1942, p. 15.
36.   Phelps, Los Angeles, Oct. 20, 1940, radio.
37.   Mote, *Testimony Before the Committee on Military Affairs,* pp. 2 & 3.
38.   RC, Mar. 10, 1941, p. 6.
39.   LIB, Nov. 28, 1940, p. 12.
40.   Phelps, Los Angeles, July 27, 1940, radio.
41.   Phelps, Los Angeles, July 30, 1941, radio.
42.   Phelps, Los Angeles, July 28, 1941, radio.
43.   Phelps, Los Angeles, August 4, 1941, radio.
44.   Phelps, Los Angeles, Aug. 14, 1940, radio.
45.   SJ, Nov. 24, 1941, p. 14.
46.   McWilliams, New York, July 13, 1940, street corner.
47.   LIB, Sept. 28, 1939, p. 10.
48.   X, April 28, 1945, p. 2.
49.   CF. Oct., 1944, pp. 455–456.
50.   SJ, Nov., 28, 1938, p. 8.
51.   Phelps, Los Angeles, July 28, 1941, radio.

5

The Helpless Enemy

The agitator faces a problem: As he frightens his followers with the specter of a ruthless enemy, must he not reassure them that the enemy can actually be defeated?

Most social movements recognize that at the time of their formation they are weaker than their enemy, a situation that is presumably to be changed by the movement's becoming stronger than its opponents. But in agitation there is no need to weaken the enemy, only to unmask his inherent weakness. His strength is based not on actual power or might, but on tricks and deception.

The agitator so constructs his enemy themes that the political attributes of the enemy lead directly and unobtrusively into psychological attributes. In the latter he continues the process of dehumanization already begun in the political portrait, and then twists this dehumanization into helplessness. A low animal, a parasite, a bug is inhuman and therefore undeserving of sympathy; it is helpless and therefore easy to destroy. By portraying the enemy as a criminal, a degenerate, a low animal, a bug, the agitator stirs deep layers of hatred and frustration in his listeners; their itch to violence becomes unbearable, and their hatred of this unspeakable enemy overflows. The agitator steps into the muddy pool of the malaise in order to channelize it into a stream of hate.

Theme 10: Creatures of the Underworld

Criminals

The agitator speaks of his opponents as "down-right villains"[1] or as "hoodlums."[2] The president is "supported mainly by gangsters and racketeers"[3] and is "the kind of stooge the Overseas Gang required to work their program of spoliation through the Congress."[4] Referring to plans for unification of Allied efforts during the war, the agitator finds that "it smells like that page in history which gives account of the attempt on the part of Benedict Arnold to put our troops under the command of a foreign power."[5] He is constantly discovering "widespread suspicion" created by "traitors of both alien and domestic breed" and learns that even Republican leaders are perhaps "only traitors in disguise."[6]

But the enemy is more than a mere traitor, or villain, or hoodlum; he is a murderer. Without naming names, the agitator makes it clear that he holds the enemy responsible for a good many unexplained deaths:

> Christ warned all posterity that the Jews were then and to be "Satan's Chosen People" and that compromise with them spells destruction. Because Christ's warnings have not been heeded by those calling themselves Christians, wars alone, created by "Satan's Chosen People," just the past 25 years, have liquidated over 50,000,000 Christians! To bring this close to home, another recent opponent of NUDEAL, Colorado's *Sen. Alva Adams*, died of a sudden attack, making 19 dead Congressmen so far this year—3 times the death rate of England in 1940 their year of worst blitzkriegs![7]

Such remarks are not isolated: the agitator exploits the conspiracy device to suggest to his audience that accidents and natural events are diabolic plots of the enemy. He sees a sinister significance in the fact that Senator Lundeen was "killed in an airplane accident . . . on his way home to address a rally of people who were protesting any premature entrance into the war";[8] he suggests that this and other deaths reveal the enemy's determination to achieve his ends by any means whatsoever—"if you hew to the line and let the chips fall where they may, anything can happen."[9]

It is noteworthy that in playing up such stories the agitator makes no reference to law-enforcement agencies. The enemy is not only identified with the criminal underworld but is shown as operating with impunity; murder remains unpunished, even uninvestigated. The agitator's harping on the enemy's terrorism might suggest to the audience that political murder is a natural expedient. The enemy gets away with murder, but this works both ways: the potential victim of today can become the executioner of tomorrow.

And so murder and persecution are in the air, ubiquitous, unrelenting, ever-threatening. The enemy is dragged down from the remote realm of power politics, revolutionary theory, and stock exchange manipulations to the vulgar level of the underworld. But these very denunciations of the agitator imply that his audience, until today the victim of this criminal horde, will tomorrow participate in a collective hunt of revenge. The enemy is offered as legitimate quarry. Because the enemy commits such criminal deeds with impunity, can the agitator's followers feel any squeamishness about the methods to be used in retaliation? There is nothing left but for the followers to take the law into their own hands, and the agitator himself will:

> treat personally with John L. Lewis, Robert M. LaFollette, and Samuel Dickstein, as three treasonable and surreptitious disrupters . . . to arrest them as soon as possible with Silvershirt backing, and after presenting due evidence of their traitorous activities to a Silvershirt jury, to confine them upon conviction in a Federal penitentiary for the remainder of the lives.[10]

Degenerates

The enemy is a ruthless criminal and constitutionally inferior. Because he is abnormal, he must be isolated and removed. He is foreign not only because he belongs to another nation or race but also because he is organically incapable of behaving according to norm: "We want neither your physical nor your mental diseases which cause your peoples to engage, incessantly, in mass murder and devilish destruction."[11]

In the description of the enemy, perversion and hysteria are closely connected with destructiveness.

> Why are Winchell's reactions pathological? Why does he rant and rave and become hysterical? Why is he fanatically determined to destroy the reputations of others? . . . [He] is an ego-maniac. . . . He is abnormally sex-conscious . . . a confirmed neurotic . . . and definitely psychopathic.[12]

The enemy, those "Socialists, Communists or psychopathic radicals," is "howling about Fascism in America."[13] "In all his career, Adolph Hitler did not approach the insolence of this minority in the number and grossness of their lies, in the perverse and stubborn nature of their wickedness."[14]

That such epithets of degeneracy are vague does not at all impair their usefulness. For one thing, they arouse distrust of everything the enemy says or does, but more important, they suggest the conclusion that the insane enemy must be isolated. Nor can there be any pity for the insane once their sickness has been designated as socially poisonous.

Here again the agitator's appeal is based on an ambivalent approach to the alleged characteristics of the enemy; the very piling up of the enemy's horrible characteristics implies to his followers the possibility that, in such a situation of extreme social dangers, they too will be able to be released from their inhibitions. By diagnosing the enemy in terms of a syndrome of hysteria, perversion, and insatiable hatred, the agitator stigmatizes the enemy with the disease he is encouraging among his followers.

Low Animals

A criminal or psychopath, however dangerous, may still retain human features, and law and custom provide procedures for handling them. But the agitator breaks this last tenuous link between the enemy and humankind by transforming him into a low animal. Likening the enemy to a vicious animal is more than a metaphor of abuse because the agitator's use of this metaphor is so persistent, so overwhelming, that in effect it usurps the place of its object in the perception of the audience. Like a poet whose inspiration is controlled by his ultimate purpose, the agitator confines himself in his imagery; his animals are of the "unrespectable" kind, rodents, reptiles, insects, and germs. He speaks of "criminal alien rats, and other forms of rodents,"[15] of the "Bolshevik rat's nest."[16] He states expressly that whatever other form the enemies may take is a disguise; in reality they are "poisonous, subversive vipers, regardless of the name they take on."[17] He calls for energetic, ruthless action against the enemy on the ground that "we dare not play with the poisonous venom of a reptile."[18] But it is when evoking insects or bacteria that he is most eloquent:

> Like a cloud of grasshoppers, like vermin in the closet, like white ants in the cellar, like termites in the furniture, a million propagandists have moved in upon us.[19]

He develops a metaphor in great detail:

> These alien enemies of America are like the parasitic insect which lays his egg inside the cocoon of a butterfly, devours the larva and, when the cocoon opens, instead of a butterfly we find a pest, a parasite.[20]

In these foregoing examples the human connotations of terms like *propagandists* or *alien enemies* are literally buried under the mass of insects.

A favorite animal of the agitator's is the termite. In ridiculing one of his pet targets, former Foreign Commissar Litvinov, the agitator refers to him as "The Termite Lit-Val-Hin-Max-Graf-Buch-Har-Stein."[21] The "enemies of America" are seen as "working like termites right here in

America on the pillars of our social, economic, religious, and political life."[22] These "termites have overrun the subway, the theatres, Coney Island, the Lower East Side, Flatbush, the Bronx, Newark."[23]

The microorganism seems to combine all the vicious enemy qualities in the highest degree. It is ubiquitous, close, deadly, insidious; it invites the idea of extermination; and most important, it is invisible to the naked eye. The agitator expert is required to detect its presence: "The propaganda of the alienisms is seeping through the bloodstreams of our national life like a deadly germ."[24] The danger of contamination is too great to leave anyone time to discuss this diagnosis:

> It only takes one venereal germ to destroy the body of a clean young man. It only requires one communist, well placed, to destroy a home, a mill, a factory, a school, or a section of the government.[25]

The terrifying implications of a threat of epidemic are so vivid that the mere accumulation of appropriate terms may suffice to produce the desired associations:

> Disease: Since B#243 quoted THE JEWISH PRESS 9-27-40 that *Polish Jews are typhus carriers*, predicting that such brought into Germany would spread that disease and help destroy Hitler. . . .
> The Jewish NY TIMES 11-20-39 quoted special cable from Berlin that Warsaw's ghetto was put under armed guards segregation due to "*Jews* were making profits from the need of the Polish population; furthermore, they were *dangerous carriers* of sickness and pestilence." This is borne out by Board of Health WPA project in 1934–35 in New York City to determine the relation between rats and *typhus fever cases*. . . .
> Since hundreds of thousands of such "refugee" Jews have flooded our large cities during NUDEAL (aided and abetted thereby regardless of immigration laws), and since THE JEWISH PRESS boasts that such Jews taken into Germany will cause typhus epidemics, what a danger exists in our midst![26]

Because the enemy is a terrifyingly dangerous insect or germ, he must be exterminated ruthlessly: "What the average Gentile means to say is: 'It's going to take violence to rid the nation of the Locust Swarm, and the sooner we get it over with, the happier for the nation.'"[27] Indeed, people "are tired of the millions of alien Jews flocking like locusts to our country de-housing and de-jobbing native Americans."[28]

Lest this agitational emphasis on low animals seem a mere fantastic aberration, it should be pointed out that European agitation indulged—and with all too evident effectiveness—in similar characterizations of its enemy. According to an eyewitness account, peasants recruited from the native population of Nazi-occupied countries to help in mass murders were given an intensive training course that lasted only a few hours, and that consisted in the study of pictures representing Jews as repulsive small beasts. (Cf. Ludwig Hirszfeld, *Historja Jednego Zycia* [Warsaw, 1947], ch. 18.) Similarly, in posters that were widely used by the Nazis to disseminate anti-Semitism Jews are pictorially distorted to such an extent that the spectator must actually make an effort of the imagination to rediscover the human form in what appears to be some strange sort of bug. (Cf. Jacques Polonski, *La Presse, la propagande et l'opinion publique sous l'occupation* [Paris, 1946], p. 108.)

How is this extraordinary content of agitation to be accounted for?

The agitator dehumanizes the enemy on several levels: the enemy seems to the agitator to be a foreigner who comes from suspect geographical regions; he is a criminal who inhabits reprehensible moral regions; and he is a degenerate who derives from disgusting biological regions. To these evocations of the enemy image, the audience responds by experiencing a threat to its livelihood from the invading strangers; a threat to its emotional balance by the specter of the ubiquitous criminal whose crime it finds simultaneously repulsive and seductive; and a threat to its human status from the feared and filthy subhuman creature.

Various degrees of aversion to small animals are well known in psychiatric and everyday observations. Clinical experience indicates that there is a certain connection between extreme detestation of small animals and feelings of unconscious ambivalence toward childhood sexual development. Psychoanalysts have tried to show this ambivalence projected through parasitophobia in two ways: (1) the victim of parasitophobia longs for that phase in infancy in which the child, like a parasite, clings to and desires the mother, while (2) through his rejection of the parasite he expresses his subsequent revulsion from this attachment by means of the sadism into which his longing receded after being subjected to serious genital shocks and disappointments. In the parasitophobia the longing is still present but has been repressed by sadism; the longing continues its subterranean existence while the sadism is manifestly dominant.

The agitator's tirades against vermin provide a rationalization for the release of sadistic impulses against the dirty enemies. The gesture with which a person violently eradicates vermin and the mixture of repulsion and pleasure he may draw from this act, can serve as a vicarious rehearsal for the lust to annihilate more substantial enemies.

The frustrated person (and we must always bear in mind that agitation is aimed at the frustrated) cannot tolerate the lack of frustration that he sees or imagines he sees in other people. Hence he yearns for ceaseless acts of destruction against the vermin as foreigners and against the foreigners as vermin. What agitation tries ultimately to achieve here is to distort and corrupt the very process of the audience's vision and audition. The audience must be conditioned to see the enemy as an animal and to hear the enemy making animal sounds.

There is another aspect of response that the agitator's stress on low animals finds in his audience. Swarms of insects, vermin, and rats seem to be a particularly appropriate vehicle for projection by the masses of their unconscious realization that they are nothing, in many instances, but a mere mass. In violently eradicating the hated vermin, the sadomasochistic person tries symbolically to separate himself from the crowd and confirm his individuality.

Theme 11: Call to the Hunt

The agitator has shown that the wolf in sheep's clothing is actually a sheep in wolf's clothing. But an enemy overtly designated as helpless would cease to be an urgent menace and would not be a satisfactory object for the projection of resentments and fears. The agitator therefore simultaneously dangles both notions before his audience: his enemy is both strong and weak. He reconciles the apparent contradiction by indirectly suggesting that the enemy disguises his weakness by daring to be dangerous: weakness and strength blend in arrogance.

Weakness is inherent in the notion of the enemy as a stranger, an outlaw, a psychopath, and a low animal. None of these images suggests genuine danger. As for the enemy conceived as a germ or scourge, he can be dangerous only if moral taboos or humane considerations hamper efficient antisepsis.

Lacking any solid social support, despised and hated by the people, the enemy has never been able to seize and hold power, has never dared emerge undisguised into daylight. In fact, the enemy is aware of his weakness. He hides like a rat "in alley ways and other dark holes";[29] he lurks "in the shadows of anonymity"[30] and even cultivates "a passion for anonymity."[31] He hatches his plots while traveling "in a special train with the shades drawn."[32]

When he dares come into the open somewhat, the enemy's weapon is manipulation of public opinion. He controls the media of mass communication and operates "among the so-called intellectuals, professional people, school teachers, preachers, student groups."[33] As a trickster, a shady character, an impostor without real strength, the enemy is thus the antithesis of the hard-working, puritanical, and self-restrained entrepreneur who adheres to social convention and rules of moderation and has nothing to hide from the public. But the enemy, nowhere nearly as solid a character, has nothing but his wits at his disposal; he is a dealer in words, in mere ideas, in articles, in speeches. Shut his mouth by force, and he collapses.

The agitator buttresses his suggestion that the enemy is fundamentally weak by linking the various kinds of enemies together in such a way that those who are merely targets of contempt take the edge off, so to speak, those who might symbolize danger. This amalgam of enemies is effected by a verbal device: cumulative enumerations of various enemies. The agitator speaks of "aliens, Communists, crackpots, refugees, renegades, Socialists, termites and traitors."[34] All the doctrines he attacks hardly differ in substance: "Bolshevism ... regardless of whether it is called New Dealism, Communism, Liberalism, Rooseveltism, Social Democracy or Judaism."[35]

No group has any genuine independent existence, and all are pretty much alike. The very fact that the agitator can speak in one breath of "this radicalism, this racketeering, this sabotage . . . Nazi spies, communist agents"[36] or of "these dictators, these czars, these fascists, these Nazis, these communists, these gangs"[37] may suggest that there is no need to be cautious in attacking any of them. In these enumerations the underlying motive becomes apparent when refugees are linked with crackpots, termites, and traitors. Such combinations deserve not only moral indignation but also contempt. Such an enemy is morally and mentally debased, an "unspeakable gang of alien scalawags. Communist fellow travelers, revolutionary Jews, third generation frustrates, mongrel misfits, and hypocritical humbugs."[38]

The agitator seems occasionally to express surprise at finding such characters together: "an amazing conglomeration of cunning Communists, befuddled fellow-travelers, Utopian dreamers, and revolutionary visionaries, in most every key post of consequence."[39]

By this amalgamation of the various stereotypes of the enemy, the nature of the audience's hostile emotion is transformed. The agitator

supplants individual prejudice by mass prejudice. Individual prejudice is an attitude charged with emotional valuations and embodying
idiosyncracies. Stubborn, even irrational clinging to idiosyncrasies
or prejudices is popularly interpreted as a kind of individualism. But
when the agitator amalgamates the various hostile stereotypes of
the enemy, the individualistic kind of prejudice gives way to a cold,
abstract, standardized fury that is closer to the paranoiac's destructive rage than to the passion of hatred. The enemy is hated with an
emotional intensity that can be aroused only by a human being, and
treated with a cold pitilessness that can be mobilized only against an
inanimate object: "The Jewish Menace has now reached a stage that
it can only be dealt with INTERNATIONALLY in the same way that
Cancer, Malaria and Leprosy are dealt with and quite calmly at that
and without any bloodshed."[40]

While the international financiers, the House of Morgan, Stalin, the
Jewish refugees, the Communist, and the fellow traveler are equated
and are the objects of the same fury, its immediate target is in this case
the weakest group, the Jews. We need not assume that the agitator's
followers are completely deceived by the demagogy that attributes
dangerous traits to the helpless victim. They may be dimly aware that
the object of their fury is really innocent of the charge used as a pretext
for attacking it, but precisely because a weak target is singled out, they
may remember their own deep-rooted fears of meeting the same fate
as the victim-enemy.[41] The enemy's weaknesses come to symbolize
the audience's own futile and abortive protest against oppression. In
offering members of the audience a quarry to be hunted, the agitator
provides them with an effective method of relief: they are to vent their
resentment on some helpless victim. Once the various hostile impulses
against different enemies have been amalgamated by the agitator,
reduced as it were to a uniform gaseous state, they exert equal pressure
on all points and tend to break through at the weakest point. Where
that is everyone knows.

The act of the frustrated little man who impotently vents his fury
on his child or wife is reproduced on a social scale. The individual
perpetrator of such an act may realize its irrationality and may feel
consciously guilty, but on the social level the concentration of fury on
stereotypes of weakness acquires a new connotation. By identifying the
victim of persecution with the dangerous persecutor, the agitator sanctions and rationalizes an act of cowardice and impotence and makes it

appear as an act of courage and wisdom. At the same time he relieves his followers from one of their basic fears: the fear of being pushed to the bottom of the social ladder. They are offered a group that deserves a fate worse than their own, a group of underprivileged people that they, the manipulated, can manipulate and humiliate with impunity. This transformation of the enemy from a dangerous persecutor into the persecuted quarry is the essence of the enemy theme in agitation.

But it is not a replacement of the persecutor by the quarry; in the image of the enemy the two coexist. Hostility against the quarry can be effectively aroused only when the audience half believes it to be dangerous; the hunt is always conceived as an act of self-defense. In this way the followers are reminded that although they are an elite today, they are in constant danger, and can retain their privileged status only by faithfully following the leader in the constant hunt of the enemy. Not even extermination of the enemy removes the danger he represents; he has to be killed again and again, killed only to be revived once more so that he may fulfill his function indefinitely.

Lumping-Together Device

It is this image of an organically weak and unassimilable enemy that emerges as the result of the lumping together of the various enemy types. In the very process that blurs the distinctions between all the enemy groups, the Jew alone becomes more sharply delineated. From the outset he is present in all the versions of the enemy as their invisible essence, and when the agitator enumerates his various "vicious foes," it is always the Jew who stands out as the most conspicuous, tangible, and accessible target. Consider, for example, the following list:

> the Judaeo-Maxists, Anglophiles, International bankers, radio commentators, Hollywood, Anti-Defamation League, Anti-Nazi League, Friends of Democracy, Rhodes scholars, *PM, Daily Worker, Chicago Sun, The New Masses, The Nation* and *The New Republic*.[42]

Aside from the fact that communism, liberalism, and anti-Nazism are elsewhere represented as Jewish activities, the only group that emerges as clearly identified here is "the Judaeo-Marxists," the Jews. The implication apparently is that an Anglophile, communist, or liberal is recognized through his being a Jew or being associated with Jews; and that to *be* a Jew is equivalent to belonging to a group or organization that the agitator considers pernicious.

Likewise in the list "HIDDEN HAND agencies—Communist Party, CIO, AFL, Federal Council of Churches, Jews, et al.,"[43] the apparently non-Jewish terms only help to throw a more glaring light on the Jews. A member of any of the enumerated organizations is not recognizable as such and may leave it any time, but a Jew must always remain a Jew whether he wishes to or not.

> As Lindbergh said in Des Moines this week, sooner or later the American people are going to be looking for a few flocks of scapegoats. And it's not going to be the Irish, the Spaniards, the Egyptians, or the Hottentots who'll be called to that accounting.[44]

Indeed, the very idea that any group other than the Jews could be a scapegoat is almost comical. The agitator knows very well that he need not be more explicit. But he does not rely on merely existing anti-Jewish stereotypes; he also helps to refurbish them and develop new ones. Reduction of the formidable persecutor to a helpless creature is supplemented by a converse process, to be discussed in the following chapter, in which this helpless creature is endowed with the qualities he must have if he is to serve the agitator's political and psychological purposes.

In singling out the Jews, the agitator need not necessarily resort to explicit "lumping together." He speaks as though he knew that the tendency to single out the Jew as the source of all their troubles is latent in his listeners, and that the very mention of a Jewish name suffices to push all other "enemies" into the background. The procedure is illustrated in a speech made by an agitator who begins by depicting himself as the target of persecution by the powers that be and the communists.[45] It seems that as a result of an insulting remark he made about President Roosevelt,

> orders came down from Washington—I was nineteen years old at that time—orders came down from Washington calling for my arrest. I was imprisoned and indicted by a Federal Grand Jury on charges of threatening the life of the President.

This incident was followed by various tribulations, involving communist activities in the army and the "New-Deal-dominated War Department." His opposition to communism, he went on, made him appear suspect, and he was not allowed to go to the front:

> I immediately volunteered for the D-Day invasion of Europe saying that I wanted to do anything and everything that any other soldier

> had to do in this war to demonstrate that I was a true American and
> a loyal soldier—and a loyal soldier saying that I had volunteered for
> overseas service; that I loved America and I was a Christian and if
> I was guilty of anything wrong. I told them to call me up before an
> investigating board and examine my record and my life.
>
> So I was turned over to one Major Goldstein [laughter] in the psycho-
> neuropathic ward of the station hospital for observation [laughter].

During the speaker's recital of the sufferings inflicted upon him as a
result of insulting remarks, the audience kept quiet as though impressed
by this tale of persecuted innocence. Mention of a Jewish name produced laughter—a relief of tension.

The discovery of the Jew among the conspirators has subconsciously
been expected all the time; the preceding list of enemies is revealed as
a joke, and the Jew is its point. This point is enhanced by the association of the Jew with mental disease, for the suggestion is that not the
persecuted hero but the Jew is the real psychopath.

The relief expressed by the laughter is also caused by the realization
that there is a simple method of "cleaning up" this "whole bad, smelly
mess of persecution."[46] All that is needed is to crush those psychopathic
Jews. Behind these horrors there is a man whose name has been made
so comical that pronouncing it dispels all fears. The humiliated followers
thus become the humiliators, and act out their sense of superiority over
their enemy.

The laughter seems to foreshadow the pleasure of the anticipated
hunt. The suggestion is that the followers are laughing only because
they are generous—they should hit, and hit hard, instead of laughing.
Like the cat, they play with the mouse.

Pattern of Obsession

The persistence with which the agitator builds his fantasy image of the
enemy stems from a paranoiac conception of his relationship to the
world. In any event, the agitator is the least restrained of all figures in
public political life. Without inhibition or even the suggestion that he
is in any way exaggerating, he can assert that "I read a pamphlet not
long ago that said that 67 per cent of the House of Representatives were
Jewish. I read a pamphlet that said it and it guaranteed the truth of it,
put out by a publisher here in New York. And the Senate is somewhat
the same, only a little less, about 59 per cent."[47] Or he can ask with
regard to the wartime evacuation of London: "Did you read about

the wholesale evacuation of London, ostensibly to get women and children away from the terrible Nazi bombers—that haven't arrived at this writing? *Are Jewish refugees in the evacuated homes now, we wonder?*"[48] And when the agitator is asked by the Library of Congress for copies of his publications, he is again on his guard; he suspects that it is one of the "tricks . . . used to trap Christian Americans. . . ."[49] To complete our citations of the paranoiac character of agitational material. we find the agitator discoursing on "why Mussolini turned against the Jews": "One factor compelling immediate action was the question of hygiene. Syphilis in a virulent form is highly prevalent among the natives of Abyssinia. Mussolini resolved to combat both miscegenation and disease. Much to his surprise, he encountered considerable opposition in Italy. He discovered that it came primarily from Jewish sources."[50]

Such paranoiac delusions as are found in the above statements are in reality the projections of hatred. The persecutor always represents some of the features of the person who suffers from the paranoiac delusion. As Freud puts it, the man who thinks "I hate him" twists the thought into a defensive projection: "He hates me." (Cf. Sigmund Freud, *Psychoanalytic Notes upon an Autobiographical Account of a Case of Paranoia,* in *Collected Papers,* vol. 3.) By indulging in this projection, the paranoiac relieves himself of part of his fear of self-destruction. The agitator, by directing his audience's fears onto the image of the enemy, similarly relieves it of some of its fears. But just as the paranoiac finds only temporary relief by fixating the blame on a particular target, so the most the agitator can offer to his audience is a palliative for, rather than a cure of, its fears.

And so he, together with his followers, continues to search. It is this search, rather than any actual object of the search, that seems to characterize the relationship between agitator and audience. Behind one enemy there always lurks another. Suffering from a kind of eternal restlessness, the agitator never seems able to find a terminal and perfect image of the enemy; each version leads to another, each destruction of the enemy's disguise to the renewed discovery that he has still another disguise. It is like a striptease without end.

Agitator and audience seem, however, to find a temporary resting place in their hunt for target of their accumulated resentment. Here at last the "real" enemy seems to have been found: the Jew, who confirms the fantastic fusion of ruthlessness and helplessness.

Notes

1. Smith, Detroit, Mar. 22, 1943, meeting.
2. SJ, Oct. 9, 1939, p. 4.
3. Maloney, New York, July 25, 1940, street corner.
4. Pelley, *What You Should Know About The Pelley Publications*, p. 2.
5. CF, Nov., 1944, p. 466.
6. AP, Sept., 1944, pp. 3 & 4.
7. AID, Dec. 3, 1941, p. 2.
8. Smith, Detroit, Mar. 19, 1943, meeting.
9. Smith, Detroit, Mar. 19, 1943, meeting.
10. LIB, Mar. 28, 1938.
11. Phelps, *An Appeal to Americans*, p. 10.
12. Kamp, *With Lotions of Love* . . . pp. 47–48.
13. DEF, Mar., 1937, Lewis Valentine Ulrey in, p. 19.
14. AP, June, 1945, p. 3.
15. Phelps, Los Angeles, Aug. 27, 1940, radio.
16. RC, Dec. 8, 1941, p. 4.
17. X, Feb. 24, 1945, p. 2.
18. Smith, "Mice or Men," radio address, p. 3.
19. Smith, *"The Next President of the United States"* p. 2.
20. Smith, *"Dictatorship Contes With War,"* radio address, p. 1.
21. Sanctuary, *Litvinoff, Foreign Commissar of the U.S.S.R.,* p. 3.
22. Phelps, Los Angeles, Aug. 6, 1941, radio.
23. AP, Aug., 1944, p. 16.
24. CF, Aug., 1942, p. 13.
25. Smith, *"Americans! Stop, Look, Listen,"* ibid, p. 2.
26. AID, Dec. 30, 1940, p. 1.
27. LIB, Mar. 28, 1938.
28. X, Feb. 13, 1948, p. 2.
29. Phelps, Los Angeles, Sept. 8, 1940, radio.
30. Smith, *"Mice or Men,"* radio address, p. 3.
31. Kamp, *Famine in America*, p. 49.
32. AP, Feb., 1944, p. 6.
33. Smith, *"Mice or Men,"* ibid, p. 1.
34. AP, June, 1945, p. 6.
35. LIB, Mar. 28, 1940, p. 11.
36. Smith, *"Labor on the Cross,"* radio address, p. 4.
37. Smith, Detroit, Mar. 19, 1943, meeting.
38. AP, Sept., 1944, p. 10.
39. Kamp, *How To Win The War,* p. 3.
40. *Women's Voice,* Letter by H. H. Beamish in, Mar. 27, 1947, p. 13.
41. The French historian Mathiez quotes the following excerpt from an official police report written after the execution of twelve persons at the beginning of the Terror: "I must tell you that such executions have the greatest political effects, but the most considerable of them is the appeasement of popular resentment. The wife who lost her husband, the father who lost his son, the merchant who has no trade, the worker who pays everything so dearly that

his wages amount to almost nothing, perhaps resign themselves to their own sufferings only when they see people more unfortunate than themselves and when they think these people are their enemies." A. Mathiez, *La revolution française, Paris* (1928).

42. AP, Oct., 1945, p. 15.
43. AID, May 22, 1939, p. 2.
44. RC, Sept. 22, 1941, p. 2.
45. Lawrence Asman at a Smith meeting, Cleveland, Apr. 4, 1946.
46. Smith, Cleveland, Apr. 4, 1946, meeting.
47. White, New York, July 18, 1940, street corner.
48. LIB, Oct. 7, 1939, p. 5.
49. AID, June 23, 1942, p. 4.
50. SJ, Mar. 27, 1939, p. 11.

6

The Enemy as Jew

The American agitator denounces communists, plutocrats, and refugees without qualification, but he insists on distinguishing between "international" and "American," atheistic and religious, "good" and "bad" Jews. To believe him, his feelings toward the Jews are quite friendly, and he is attacking only so-called organized Jewry. The functional characteristics of the enemy, which he sometimes explains as consequences of racial characteristics, he at other times sees as the cause of racial characteristics. Communist or plutocrat lead to the Jew, but the Jew seemingly leads back to the communist or plutocrat.

The American agitator's failure to develop an explicit and complete anti-Semitic program may be due to the political immaturity of American agitation or to the opprobrium attached in this country to public expressions of anti-Semitism. Whatever the reason, indirect approaches to anti-Semitism actually help the agitator; he can pose as an objective student who is not obsessed by hatred and who should therefore not be denounced as a fanatic. Anti-Semitism, he says, is "one of the mysteries of the centuries"[1] and he merely wonders "if the entire matter of preservation of the Jewish community as a separate and peculiar community should not be given study?"[2]

He can build up a certain suspense: his listeners know that anti-Semitic themes will come but they are not always sure how the agitator will put them across. The agitator can also imply that his reserve in discussing such matters is due to the power of the forces opposing him, but because he always manages to put across his anti-Semitic bias, he suggests that he has succeeded in defying the power of the opposition.

In this chapter no attempt is made to develop a theory of anti-Semitism. We are here concerned only with the stereotypes of the Jew as they appear in agitational material and the way in which the agitator develops and transforms those stereotypes into a logically self-contradictory but psychologically consistent image of the Jew, who appears both as weak and strong, victim of persecution and persecutor, endowed with unchangeable racial characteristics and irrepressible individualism.

Theme 12: The Victim

The Jew is Persecuted

The theme of the persecuted Jew appears in many variations: sometimes he is pictured as a tool or victim of providence; sometimes the severity or existence of persecution is denied; and sometimes the agitator even implies that the Jews stage pogroms against themselves. Whatever the variation, however, the agitator succeeds in keeping his audience constantly aware of the so-called Jewish problem. It matters little whether he denies being an anti-Semite or pretends to explain or even deplore it; in each case he manages to suggest that anti-Semitism is a fundamental and relevant category in the discussion of public issues.

The agitator characterizes persecution of Jews as a kind of natural phenomenon:

> They were thrown out of every country that got a hold of them . . . Mussolini came in and they were thrown out . . . Mr. Hitler came along and he threw them out. . . they were thrown out of Poland . . . they were thrown out of Norway . . . France had to throw them out. France is throwing them out.[3]

The agitator is apparently aware of the public revulsion against the Nazi acts of violence. To counteract the possible effects of it, he absolves fascist leaders from all responsibility:

> We cannot let ourselves be hoaxed into believing that these refugees have fled from the wrath of Franco in Spain, or from the wrath of Hitler when they left Moravia, or Slovakia, or now from Poland. No! *They fled from the wrath of the treacherously outraged peoples of those nations,* as they may one day flee as well from the wrath of a finally aroused populace in America.[4]

Before the spectacle of Jewish misery, the agitator eschews any display of emotion and instead urges his audience to study the question "objectively." He seems to refute the notion that he appeals primarily to passions, and presents the audience with a systematic survey of Jewish history preceded by the following remarks:

> Recurring persecutions and expulsion of the Jews have marked the history of every age and country since the fall of Jerusalem. . . .

As background for current reading about the Jews—particularly the war mongering of their international financialists and political policymakers [we present the following survey].⁵

Although the explanation is here purely secular, and the fall of Jerusalem is associated with the intrigues of international bankers, the overall purpose of this "background for current reading" is to impress upon the reader the permanent and inevitable character of Jewish persecutions. The personality and motives of the persecutor recede into the background; the Nazi attack on the Jews is a problem that concerns only the Jews, who, because they are destined to suffer, cannot be defended by any earthly power. By summoning them to seek refuge only in spirituality, the agitator drives home the idea of their absolute defenselessness, and he underscores the precariousness of this refuge by comparing it to a bomb shelter:

> If there was ever an occasion for Jewry to abandon its materialism, now is the acceptable day. Until there is a deep spiritual reawakening in the hearts of Jewish leaders, there will be perpetuated the story of Egypt in America and every other nation—a story which will chronicle the worst sufferings of God's once chosen people. Perchance the rich can flee—for a time. But the poor, innocent, misled little Jew will remain, as he always does, to bear the plagues of persecution. . . . Have the Jews forgotten that the more they organize materially against their opponents, the more assaults will increase and the closer they are to persecution? There is no security for Jews except in the bomb shelter of spirituality.⁶

The Jew is not Persecuted

One of the major devices by which the agitator develops his theme of the Jew as victim is often to deny the very existence of persecution. "The persecutions of which the Jews in Germany complained were in reality no persecutions at all,"⁷ for even if there were one or two difficulties in Germany, nonetheless "synagogues are open on Saturday the same as usual and rabbis receive their pay without molestation."⁸

Toward such matters the agitator is eager to be as unimpassioned and cautious as possible. One must not be too hasty in accepting news reports: "No one in this country knows the exact truth about German treatment of the Jews except that its severity has been greatly exaggerated."⁹ For the fact is that though "the wails of the rabbis about the persecuted Polish Jews clutter up the press. . . we can dry our sympathetic tears; the sob stories are not true!"¹⁰ The agitator is not taken in by mere newspaper reports; he reasons dispassionately: "At present there are three and a half million Jews in Poland and they would not be there if there had been any 'persecution.'"[11]

What does the agitator achieve psychologically by thus flouting the historical evidence of persecution of Jews? For one thing, because the Jewish complaints are branded as exaggerated, the Jews are established as professional complainers who take advantage of the gentiles' kindheartedness. At the same time, the persecutions are reduced to something quite ordinary, normal, and legal, routine activities of a modern state. Here the agitator implies that the term *persecution* does not really apply to the Jews, for the Jews are not quite normal human beings anyway. One does not speak of a termite's or a parasite's rights when it is exterminated. Such creatures cannot be said to be persecuted; they are simply destroyed.

True, the Jews groan and lament, but they are still alive: "On all sides we hear of the 'terrible German pogroms,' *but we have yet to hear of a single Jew killed in one under the Hitler regime.*"[12] In fact, hints the agitator, it is not unlikely that Jewish complaints are merely a stratagem to conceal aggressions against Christians: "All this hue and cry about Hitler's persecution was smokescreen to hide the disappearance— mostly to USA is my guess—of millions of Jews in Europe."[13]

And so what appears to others as an attack on a defenseless group becomes a struggle between the forces of order and a cunning enemy whose demand for rights is merely a pretext for securing unfair advantages. Only the suckers can pity Jews, only those who allow their pity to make them the victims of the Jews. One must suppress one's altruistic impulse in relation to them as one suppresses it when witnessing the arrest of a criminal. The impunity with which actual persecution of the Jews is denied seems to imply that whoever joins the hunt of the Jews need not fear punishment or moral disapproval, for, says the agitator, the persecuted are really the persecutors.

Anti-Semitism Disavowed

The agitator's repudiations of anti-Semitism, or even direct assertions of pro-Semitic feelings—"I am a friend of the Jews"[14]—are variations of the rhetorical figure of apophasis (mention of something while denying intention to mention it). The form, sometimes the mere tone, of such statements belies their presumed content. The audience always knows, for the agitator manages to insert an anti-Semitic insinuation in the very midst of his disclaimer. For example: "*Liberation* has never deliberately dealt in rancors. It has picked no quarrel with the Jew as individual but strictly what his race represents in the mass."[15] Whether the individual is blamed for the group or the group for the individual, the effect is the same.

The existence of anti-Jewish animosity is justified by innuendo: the Jews are behind both capitalism and communism. The same ambiguity is developed in the guise of careful definitions:

> Neither Father Coughlin nor *Social Justice* is anti-Semitic. . . in the sense that it is opposed to any individual Jew, to any religious Jew, to any group of Jews.

> We are opposed, however, to having atheistic Jews *impose their code of life upon our political structure, our social structure, our economic structure and our national structure.*[16]

Such formulations actually define the anti-Semitic tactics: the Jew must always be attacked on some pretext; the fact that the Jew is persecuted must be exploited politically. If despite all the agitator's sincere efforts to the contrary anti-Semitism still flourishes, it is not his fault. He even promises to defend the Jews, and takes this opportunity to outline a program of action for the anti-Semitic extremists:

> Will I ever assail Jewry in general? Ridiculous!

> If and when the day should come when the anti-Semite radicals will grow strong enough as a result of the depression and Communist aggression to rise against the Jews, I will be in the front ranks of the Cohens, the Franklins, the Issermans, the Wises, the Bambergs and the other sons of Israel fighting in their defense.[17]

Although these denials afford the agitator an additional opportunity to keep the so-called Jewish problem alive in the minds of his audience, they are especially helpful in the dissociation of anti-Jewish action from anti-Jewish sentiment. Even those who do not harbor any anti-Semitic feelings must be mobilized for the hunt, or at least neutralized. It is as though the agitator were aware of the fundamental difference between the kind of "bona fide" suburban anti-Semitism, which is not usually associated with a conscious political purpose, and totalitarian anti-Semitism, in which the Jew is primarily an object of political manipulation. An anti-Semite of the traditional type may recognize that at least some Jews are good citizens, although he would not care to meet them socially. What the agitator aims at is to impress upon his audience the need to persecute all Jews, the "good" and the "bad," a distinction he does not take very seriously in any case. And by developing the idea of collective responsibility of the Jews, he provides the rationalization for this attitude.

All Are Guilty

The agitator professes to be so opposed to anti-Semitism that he often gives the Jews advice on how to combat it. "Why don't the Jews who want peace and quiet repudiate such character assassins as Walter Winchell?"[18] Or he addresses himself directly to Jewish religious leaders: "The evil doers in their own midst must be cried out against by the rabbis."[19]

By suggesting that the "bad" Jews are able to engage in their destructive activities because they enjoy the passive support of the "good" ones, he smuggles in the notion of collective responsibility.

> I say to the good Jews of America, be not indulgent with the irreligious, atheistic Jews and Gentiles. . . be not lenient with your high financiers, and politicians who assisted at the birth of the only political social and economic system in all civilization that adopted atheism as its religion, internationalism as its patriotism and slavery as its liberty.[20]

The agitator does not run any risk of being misunderstood in his timeworn distinction between the good and bad Jews. Jewish solidarity and Jewish collective responsibility are treated as so self-evident that the very idea that some "good" Jews might escape the wrath of the aroused gentiles appears as ridiculous. As though to make this clear, the agitator playfully refers to a fictitious central Jewish organization that could correct any Jewish transgressors:

> FOR THEIR OWN PROTECTION I sincerely wish that the General Jewish Council would take some of their incorrigible children to the woodshed. A few lightning flashes properly aimed and a few thunder claps efficaciously yelled would do much to rectify the barometer of class hatred. . . .[21]

The agitator's seemingly casual reference to racial tensions as "class hatred" serves to intimate that all Jews belong to the same social group, the well-to-do.

Anti-Semitism Explained

The trouble with the Jews is that they do not listen to the agitator's advice; otherwise, he suggests, all might be well. For some inexplicable reason, they reject his sincere offers of friendship: "Why do these short-sighted Jews continue to goad us? Why don't they cultivate our friendship instead of inspiring our animosity?"[22] The agitator drives to an extreme the idea, still held by many Jews themselves, that Jewish behavior or character accounts for the hostility against them. He denounces the narrow-minded ethnocentrism of the Jews:

> If you want to arouse an anti-Jewish sentiment in America that will sweep like influenza across the fields of our nation, break down these immigration barriers. . . . Be temperate and satisfy the needs of your people instead of the racketeers within your own midst who are raising money with which to build up straw men and knock them down again.[23]

The agitator is particularly indignant at the Jewish effort to combat anti-Semitism. Such an idea is denounced as outright madness: "National Committee to Combat Anti-Semitism . . . this crazy organization should be folded up by the Jews themselves."[24] Anti-Semitism is nothing but a reaction to the Jewish persecution of anti-Semites: "These merciless programs of abuse which certain Jews and their satellites work upon people who are not in full agreement with them create terrible reactions."[25]

From the idea that the Jews promote anti-Semitism by their stupidity there is only one step to the idea that they promote it deliberately: "Kahn is one of those Jews who is devoting his life to the promoting of anti-Semitism. God save the race from such Jews."[26] Opposition to anti-Semitism is depicted as a method for escaping all criticism and for attacking innocent gentiles:

> "Anti-Semitism" is a defense mechanism. Its origin is very ancient. It is a label used by Jewish scoundrels to protect themselves against *just* as well as *unjust* criticism. No other race claims any such general immunity from criticism. The label frightens many persons with weak spines.[27]

No wonder that the agitator in exasperation accepts the label: "Inspired press constantly calls me anti-British, as well as pro-Nazi, and anti-Semitic. If following Christ's footsteps makes me 'anti-Semitic'—so be it."[28]

The persistent denial of anti-Semitism thus becomes a proud admission of it, with the suggestion that such admission is an act of courage.

Unseriousness

Obviously, the agitator has the time of his life in discussing anti-Semitism. One moment he may strike a pose as someone too frightened for words: "We cannot be specific in describing the race responsible for the hatred campaign because we Americans would lose our necks if we would dare to speak up."[29]

Or he gives a clownish display of bewilderment:

> As my followers know, I am opposed to racism in all its varied forms, but for some reason, which I cannot figure out, there is a certain clique of Jews in every community who stop at nothing short of murder itself to prevent our people from assembling. I must continue to believe, until I am convinced otherwise, that these people are financed . . . by Josef Stalin.[30]

Or he imitates the techniques of the money-back-guarantee advertisement:

> *Lie Number 12:* Gerald Smith is anti-Semitic. He answers this by saying that if any person can find a written or public utterance he has ever made against any race or any creed, he will retire from public life.[31]

He may also throw in an ambiguous reference to how efficiently he would deal with the question if he were in power: "If we will put Christ first in America and the problems of America first in our hearts, these unhappy conditions involving racial groups will be ironed out in a hurry."[32]

Or he directly combines a protestation of tolerance with a transparent threat: "I am not religiously intolerant. I don't care if the Jew stays in the synagogue all day long. Then I would know where he was."[33]

It is noteworthy that the last utterance was answered from the audience with the remark "They go in there to count their dough." In discussing the Jews the agitator knows that he can get away with anything. It does not matter whether he calls himself a friend of the Jews with reservations or an adversary without reservations. It does not matter what the Jews feel about it. The fact that Jewish helplessness can become an occasion for jokes shows how he can succeed in suppressing human feelings in the audience and in promising more substantial pleasures when the real hunting season opens. The Jew is the victim, and victims are there to be victimized. The Jew *should* be persecuted because he *is* persecuted—this is the core of the agitational theme of the Jew as victim.

It is now possible to trace the dynamics of the enemy themes. In portraying the enemy as ruthless, the agitator prepares the ground for neutralizing whatever predispositions for sympathy for the underdog his audience of underdogs may feel. If the enemy is ruthless, then there is no reason to feel sympathy for his simultaneous—if contradictory—helplessness. In this way the Jew as victim becomes legitimate prey.

Moreover, the agitator can play upon the ambivalent feelings toward the weak who even as they are objects of sympathy, are also the objects of suspicion and hatred. It is dangerous to become identified with the weak; one avoids the persecuted victim almost as a matter of course. From such distrust of the weak to joining a hunt against them is a step that implies the complete repression of altruistic motives. Such repression is not innately rooted in human character but is determined by specific social conditions, one such condition being the mob appeal that rallies citizens to hunt down a criminal. But if a more convenient quarry can be substituted for the criminal, the innocent will be persecuted as if he were a criminal, and the fact of his misfortune and weakness will be seen as proof of his guilt.

Theme 13: The Other

The theme that says the Jew should be a victim because he is a victim is developed into the notion that he would not and could not be singled out for persecution if he were like everyone else. The Jew must have done something to deserve the general hostility directed against him, and he has done this because he is by nature unassimilable.

The Jew is caught in a trap. When viewed as the Other, he is primarily accused of refusing to adjust himself, but if he shows the slightest sign of trying to be like the gentiles, he is told that he cannot change and is accused of malicious motives in wanting to change.

> Native Americans have no lasting patience with a people that stresses its *differences,* when it dares to do so, and retreats to an imaginary haven of its *likenesses,* after its differences have become a source of acute and general annoyance.[34]

The agitator uses a number of devices to suggest that it is the Jews' otherness that is the cause of their persecution.

The Jew as Anti-Christ

The most ancient explanation of anti-Jewish feeling is that the Jews rejected Christ. This explanation implies that the Jew has not been singled out by his enemies but has rather singled himself out. As a result the status of the Jew is fixed for the entire Christian era:

> Take history and go back. I could take you back 400 years ago, and the same little minority group were thrown out of Spain. Why? Because they deliberately refused to live like any other man in the country.[35]

Striving to exploit religious sentiment, the agitator consistently refers to the Jews as the "deadly enemies of Christianity itself"[36] and "the hidden anti-Christ power,"[37] and as indulging in a "ghastly assault on the Christian religion."[38] But this kind of conscious religious "argumentation" offers, especially in modern times, rather limited possibilities for the agitator, if only because—theoretically at least—the Jews can escape hostility by conversion.

The agitator therefore strives to strike deeper psychological chords in his audience by perverting the universalistic nature of Christianity into an endogamic religion that is equated with "Americanism." More important, he uses traditional religious language to stir certain ambivalent attitudes that arise from the Christian recognition that Jesus was a Jew. Images of blood and violence occur abundantly in his denunciations of Jews as anti-Christians. The Jews are absolutely ruthless, they "expect to show no mercy to Christians."[39] In fact, their persecution of Christ has never ceased. "Though He had many friends, there was no one to speak out in His defense: 'For fear of the Jews no one spoke out openly of Him.' It has always been so. It will always be thus."[40]

By vividly depicting this allegedly eternal hostility, the agitator is able to present his audience with sadistic images:

> Why is there in this world such deadly animosity for the name of Christ? . . . Pilate ordered that he be scourged, whipped—but even the show of blood upon his back did not satisfy the sadistic mob of Hell. They could be satisfied with nothing but crucifixion, death on the cross.

> So, down through the centuries, the Satanic sons and heirs of Beelzebub have continued to cry. "Crucify! Crucify!," whenever the name of Christ is mentioned.[41]

Thus the ambivalent image of the Jew persisting from childhood religious training is transformed by the agitator into an image of an unchangeable group that consistently opposes every aspect of the Western tradition. While pretending to preach Christian ideals, the agitator becomes the advocate of a radical anti-Christianity that denies the possibility of redemption to unbelievers.

For genuine believers, the condition of the unconverted can be the cause not only of disapproval but also of pity. But the agitator's "theological" explanation of the Jew's stubborn refusal to be converted cannot lead to pity; it leads, on the contrary, to the suspicion that the Jew's refusal to see the light of truth is based not on ignorance but on some secret superior knowledge. While the Christians chase the mirage of eternal salvation, the Jews grab all the material goods. The Jews do not have to worry about the restrictions imposed by Christian ethics—and as the pious Christian prays, they empty his pockets. The Jews thus enjoy all the fruit forbidden to the Christians.

As a result, the agitator's repeated charge that the Jew is a "businessman first, last and always,"[42] and that "the only God whom he worships is the calf of gold"[43] has implications contradicting the agitator's occasional excursions into theology. The agitator is here simply appealing to a strictly secular feeling: envy of unfair advantages. The Jews are so ruthless and money-mad that they exploit even their status as a persecuted minority to gain extra privileges:

> They [the Jews] are unwilling to share the common fate of their fellowmen but they are demanding *special* consideration as a "minority," a "stateless" class, a "homeless" race, a "helpless" people, a "persecuted" religion.[44]

The Jew makes a racket even out of his role of anti-Christ.

Clannishness

The Jews refuse to conform—in making this traditional accusation the agitator speaks out as a serious educator who wants each fellow to mingle with the crowd. He is disturbed by snobbishness and pretension of superiority:

> Let the Jews remember that too many Americans are conscious of some of the tenets of Judaism. Jews are so ultra-clannish that they frown upon a Jewish girl's marrying a Gentile boy because the Goyim is not good enough, either morally or intellectually, for the girl.[45]

Trying to make capital of the age-old fact of Jewish seclusion as though it were simply a manifestation of Jewish character, the agitator intimates that the Jew must be kept apart from the community, and then accuses the Jew of seclusiveness.

The charge of clannishness also helps suggest that Jews are primarily concerned with their own needs and indifferent to the welfare of the country in which they live:

> No one should expect from an American Jew the same devotion to American traditions, or to the stability of American society or even to the perpetuity of our constitutional government, as from other racial and national elements of the population.[46]

Ferment

The Jew refuses to change himself, but at the same time he constantly changes his environment. The epitome of restlessness for its own sake, he is never satisfied with his place in society.

The Jews, suggests the agitator, are troublemakers, if only becuase they try to improve their status. But the Jews are blamed for this very rebellion against the situation that produces their insecurity: their restlessness is attributed to an irrepressible will to power. The homelessness of the Jews is their own doing: "They have no country, never had one and never intend to have one. . . ."[47] In the countries where they find temporary rest, they plot to achieve dominance:

> Jews so far forget their kindly and just treatment in this Christian land as to take the lead in every subversive movement for its overthrow; when they carry on continual agitation against our economic system and our form of government in their open forums and conclaves of their rabbis.[48]

When the Jews act as troublemakers they have come out of their seclusion. Hence, the agitator's denunciation of their subversion is an implicit call to drive them back to the ghetto. But the image of the Jew as the irrepressible agent of change seems to have a still deeper psychological impact on an audience that is itself restless and insecure for in a turbulent world where others, including the agitator, are compelled to grope hesitantly and often blindly and to fall back upon such vague notions as imminent doom or conspiracy, the Jews seem to feel at home. Using their "age old tactics," [49] they have somehow managed, suggests the agitator, to preserve their identity over the ages, evil though it is; their troublemaking enterprises, whether directed toward financial control of the world or revolutions against the world or both, always show that the Jews have a clear goal. In a world of shattered and atomized personalities, the image of such an enemy as it is unconsciously conjured by the agitator seems both attractive and dangerous to his audience. By attributing these secretly desirable traits to the Jews, the agitator stirs his audience's envy, and to feel envy of the helpless, hunted foe is to increase the desire to use violence against him.

Spotting the Jew

The image of the Jew as Anti-Christ and its secular derivations of the Jew as clannish and the Jew as social ferment are the more conceptualized symptoms of Jewish otherness. But the Jew can also be detected by other, more primitive characteristics that are sometimes so elusive as to defy description. While the conceptualized traits reflect the Jews' unwillingness to conform, these other traits reflect the Jews' inability to conform because of their idiosyncrasies. The former may sometimes be concealed, but the latter show through every disguise, and are the best way to identify a Jew. The agitator plays the part of a bloodhound always hot on the scent of the Jew who cannot hide his true identiy.

Among these alleged distinctive traits, there is first of all the Jew's undefinable foreignness. The word epitomizing this trait of foreignness is *oriental* or *Asiatic*. The agitator speaks deprecatingly of "orientals who are American citizens,"[50] of oriental concepts of government, of oriental mobs that overrun the White House, of oriental aliens that invade our nation and rifle the cash register, etc., etc. Associations of the forbidden, immoral, and luscious seem to play a role in the use of the term *oriental*.

The attribute of foreignness is supplemented by a wealth of more specific references to Jewish history. The agitator can dispense with using the word *Jew* when he speaks of Pharisees, money changers, the goldmongers clan, the usurpers of Christian liberties. He can content himself with mentioning "those flagless citizens,"[51] or indulge in a kind of "guess who" test: "Every classification of decent citizens in this country—except perhaps one—has openly condemned Communism."[52] He can name the Jew without naming him: "If Churchill says it is O.K., then it is all right from Hyde Park all the way down to the East Side of New York, from which district some big names have come."[53]

He can also, just as in the case of anti-Semitism, take advantage of the official prohibition and resort to the rhetorical figure of apophasis: "There were certain over the radio unnamable naturalized persons living in America."[54]

Sometimes several attributes are merged, as in the following quotation in which the traits of anti-Christianity, anti-Americanism, control of propaganda apparatus, psychopathic behavior, and sinister business machinations all point to the Jew:

> I do not subscribe to the proposition that if we have prosperity we must have war. That is Satan's gospel. Peace is the gospel of Christ. The radio and the press are filled with the propaganda of war. Should we Americans engender an artificial hatred towards any nation to satisfy the merchandisers of murder and the owners of debt?[55]

Public censorship of broadcasts only partly accounts for the agitator's habit of designating the Jews by indirection; the device serves purposes other than mere circumvention of the law. It is a game, a rehearsal of the anticipated hunt and a verbal reproduction of the age-old hunt of the persecuted. But this game in addition to its entertainment value serves also to teach the audience to discover spontaneously what the agitator wants it to discover. The attention of the audience is concentrated on the Jews more effectively when they are not mentioned explicitly. Look into the rat holes, the agitator seems to say, I don't have to tell you whom you will find there.

At the same time the agitator seems to match the enemy's tactics by entering into a conspiracy with his followers in which he speaks to them in the anti-Semitic in-group language: he summons his followers not to reveal the esoteric knowledge he has imparted to them, thus strengthening the bonds between him and them.

The prohibition against uttering the enemy's name is an archaic heritage. By not naming the Jew, the agitator suggests that he is so powerful that the mere act of calling him "the Jew" might mean danger. But simultaneously he suggests another implication. The Jew is so despicable and wretched that even the mere mention of his name is repulsive. When the Jew is not mentioned in the same way decent people are, his character as outcast is stressed, and he seems to the audience a weak and helpless figure. In this way, again, the agitator develops the device mentioned in the previous chapter: the Jew's strength, a cause for hating him, is shown as merely a façade of his essential weakness, a reason for persecuting him.

Yet the Jew remains ubiquitous. Foreign while yet familiar, he can be encountered everywhere, hiding under every mask and always spotted by the agitator. The Jew is unable to cover up his tracks.

Jewish Names

The climax in the process of spotting the Jew occurs when Jews, still without being called Jews, are referred to by Jewish-sounding names. Now at last the quarry has been trapped and is ready for the kill. The audience reacts with laughter; in the agitator's apocalyptic oratory, such moments of triumphant detection seem to provide one of the few bits of relief: "Sidney Hillman, or more correctly Schmuel Gilman"[56] or, "Karfunkelstein, alias Leon Blum"[57] or "Meyer Genoch Moisevitch Wallach, sometimes known as Maxim Litvinov, or Max-movitch, who had at various times adopted the other revolutionary aliases of Gustave Graf, Finkelstein, Buchmann, and Harrison was a Jew."[58]

The agitator suggests that he for one cannot be cheated: he always discovers the essence behind the appearance. It is not true, he seems to say, that a name is just a name; if we look at it more closely, if we find its origin and pronounce it correctly, its true meaning is revealed. The Jewish name is a label that makes clearly visible the nature of its bearer; it is a stigma, it pins the Jew down, and he can no longer escape.

The strong emotional reaction that the mention of Jewish names always seems to produce suggests that they are not perceived as ordinary names, i.e. conventions, but that they are felt to be an integral part of Jewish personality. The fact that Jews can be recognized merely by their names seems to bear this out; and the fact that the Jews have preserved their names despite all historical vicissitudes (in the course of which they lost every other conventional sign of national identity) makes their names an important symbol of their historical continuity. But the Jewish name is also a symbol of the continuity of the persecution to which the Jews have been exposed. By bringing out this latter aspect, by forcing the Jew who actually or allegedly uses an alias to show his real name, the agitator twists the badge of pride into a badge of disgrace.

The agitator's frequent recourse to cumulations of Jewish names suggests that the device reverses the symbolic significance of such names in still another way. The repetition of Jewish family names creates the impression that they are all more or less the same, consequently that their bearers are all the same, and can be dealt with simultaneously and equally. Instead of denoting an individual, the Jewish name is made to indicate a species, a race. The name becomes a stereotype of nonindividuality: if you know one Jew you know them all.

The Jewish name is transformed into a term of abuse, and in hurling it at the enemy the agitator engages in name-calling in the literal sense of the term. As a mocking epithet, its sound is not only foreign but ridiculous. It strikes the audience as a joke: "Walter Lipshitz Winchell—I'm not joking—that's his name."[59]

The agitator sometimes engages in painstaking heraldic research:

> It is known, however, that Winchell's father used the name of Jacob Laino, and that Winchell assumed the name of "Lawrence" in his youth. "Our real name," he once wrote with a show of impatience, is "Schmaltz." *Our guess would be that Winchell's real name (if it ever comes out) is, or should be Vevele Weinschul, which is a good, honest, respectable name.*[60]

The family name, envied token of tradition and heritage for non-Jews, becomes a symbol of degradation for the Jews. What the gentiles are proud to display, the Jews seem eager to hide. Their history is made into their curse and disgrace. By evoking a past when the Jews were persecuted (or, as in the above quotation, reminding the audience that the Jew who enjoys American freedom was once a subject of an anti-Semitic country), the agitator verbally reenacts the injustice previously done to the Jews.

Mimicking

We come here to what is perhaps one of the most crucial anti-Semitic stimuli: mimicking (Cf. Max Horkheimer and Theodor W. Adorno, *Dialektik der Aufklärung* [Amsterdam: Querido, 1947], pp. 212ff.), which is not limited to the pronunciation of Jewish names. Striking examples are to be found in the agitator's way of describing Jewish complaints. He suggests that the Jews do not speak like human beings but make weird sounds; whenever they express emotions, they are loud, conspicuous, unbearable, and comical. The agitator refers to "the wailing yelps and weird wails of subversive Jews and Communist gangs"[61] or imitates sounds supposedly made by Jews among themselves: "America's Jewish Kommissars Screech, Squabble and Scrap."[62] When the Jews want to protest against Hitler, these "alien-minded super-collectivists" indulge in "loud sneers and jeers and hymns of hate";[63] on other occasions, they yell, howl, whine,[64] and so on.

What the Jews are here implicitly blamed for is that they seem to challenge both the discipline of civilization, which prescribes restraint, and the suppression of the urge to display one's own emotion. They appear free to act out their passions and desires, their demands and fears, their sympathies and above all their antipathies. Once again, the

Jews refuse to conform, this time on a deeper emotional level. They are portrayed as despicable and dangerous, for they insist on the right to be individuals. The agitator discredits such expressions of individualistic rebellion.

This condemnation of Jewish expressiveness is accompanied by its caricaturing imitation. The followers are forbidden to indulge in such expressiveness for themselves, but they are permitted to imitate manifestations of it in their alleged enemies.

The fact that the audience enjoys such caricatures and imitations of allegedly weird Jewish behavior shows that this Jewish foreignness is not as external to them as it might seem. They feel it in their own flesh, it is latent in them; the Jew is not the abstract "other," he is the other who dwells in themselves. Into him they can conveniently project everything within themselves to which they deny recognition, everything they must repress. But this projection can be effected only on condition that they hate the Jews and are permitted to realize the repressed impulse in the form of a caricature of the enemy. They find an outlet for their repressed aspirations only by simultaneously condemning them.

Theme 14: The Menace

According to the agitator, Jewish influence is behind every threat to society and every frustration of his followers' hopes. From the idea that the Jews are persecuted to the idea that they are persecutors, the transition is not too difficult; it has been made often enough in the past to become a kind of stereotype. But this stereotype is not merely the product of anti-Jewish agitation; it would seem that the history of the Jews and interpretations of this history have contributed to the creation of an idea of the Jew in which persecuted and persecutor are inextricably blended.

The fate of the Jew has always been an object of theological speculation; his survival has struck many thinkers as a mystery that could not be explained by natural causes. A well-known religious philosopher who was by no means hostile to the Jews refers to them as a "pre-eminently historical people (Nicolas Berdyaev, *The Meaning of History* [New York, 1936], pp. 86ff.) who

> according to the materialistic and positivist criterion ought long ago to have perished.... The survival of the Jews, their resistance to destruction, their endurance under absolutely peculiar conditions and the fateful role played by them in history; all these point to the particular and mysterious foundations of their destiny. . . . The Jewish destiny

> is characterized by a particular dramatic intensity which makes the purely Aryan spirit seem dull by comparison. . . . The Jewish spirit constitutes a distinct racial type. . . . It is still animated by the aspirations towards the future, by the stubborn and persistent demand that the future, should bring with it an all-resolving truth and justice on earth, in the name of which the Jewish people is prepared to declare war on all historical traditions, sacraments, and associations.

The above passage is based on an explicit rejection of a "materialist" or "naturalist" approach to history, but even on the level of the "ideal" or the "transcendent" the image of the Jews as persecuted leads almost irresistibly to the idea that they are essentially different from and opposed to the world as it is.

In the agitator's language the idea of the sacred mission of the Jew acquires a negative sign. The theologian's "mysterious foundations" are transformed into a deliberate Jewish conspiracy; the "particular dramatic intensity" of "the Jewish spirit" into Jewish ruthlessness and cunning; and the "war on all historical traditions, sacraments, and associations" into vicious aggression against the gentile world. Awe and admiration can be sublimated forms of fear and envy; and when the agitator reduces the emotions inspired by the "idealist" theological interpretation to those of his own level, he transforms the awe and admiration into fear, envy, and hatred. The sheer fact that the Jews have managed to survive through so much suffering seems to him and his followers evidence that they must have certain secret and menacing powers. Because they are and have been persecuted they can be plausibly charged with having the vindictive and cunning mentality of slaves; because they have survived all persecutions, they can be plausibly assumed to command extraordinary resources, and to be endowed with an extraordinary vitality. They alone seem to be self-sufficient, and able to preserve their individuality in a world that suppresses individuality.

Vindictiveness

During the prewar and war years one of the persistent themes of agitation in the United States was that the Jews had instigated a crusade against Hitler to revenge themselves for his persecutions:

> Day after day, and far into all these pregnant nights, we hear the ceaseless, senseless din of propaganda, all of which is for the purpose of making us war-minded enough to go to war to save World Jewry's financial, political, economic and social fortunes.

Ever since the Armistice of November, 1918, Jewry's International High Command has been making plans for the next World War—which is now-beginning in Europe.[65]

To drive home his point more effectively, the agitator may characterize Jewish machinations as a well-established and understandable reaction, only then to accuse the Jews of cowardice and selfishness:

We would not condemn the Jews so much for their culpability in declaring and prolonging this war if they would manifest sufficient intestinal fortitude to say that the war now being waged is to protect their vast international business interest.[66]

However, the audience is not allowed for one moment to think that Jewish hostility to Hitler is justified. The Jews are vindictive by nature: "It is a matter of record that Jews over the world, particularly the United States, long ago 'declared war' on Germany," created "a distorted impression of events in Central Europe." and generated "antagonisms and retaliations, until finally the flame ignited."[67] They

bristle with hate because their pride has been hurt by Adolf Hitler. They have a persecution complex and they want America to go to war . . . even if it costs the lives of ten million Americans, as long as they can have their revenge.[68]

Jewish lust for revenge is depicted as unrestrained, as directly pathological. As the war approached its climax, the agitator's line was that "Jewish leadership insists on annihilating and enslaving all people of German blood, regardless of their innocence or their guilt," and he prophesied that "they [the Jews] will likely bring down on their heads a reaction even worse than that through which they have just passed."[69]
The notion that Hitler's treatment of the Jews was a "reaction" to their vindictiveness follows a sentence in which the Jewish interest in this war is described as "understandable." The agitator speaks as though there were no distinction between the idea that the Jews are vindictive because they were wronged and the idea that he is wronged because they are vindictive. He seems to have no difficulty in blaming the persecuted for the worst actions of the persecutors. Alluding to a report that the Gestapo forced some Jews into its service, he concludes:

In view of savagery displayed in Russia, by Jewish OGPU, wherein torture carried to unmentionable extremes helped liquidate during

> past 25 years some 50,000,000 persons; and in view of *Rabbi Alstat's*
> admissions, can it be that the gruesome liquidations now attributed
> to the Gestapo were carried out by some kind of beasts?[70]

No matter how lurid the colors with which alleged Jewish power
is painted, the agitator always suggests that this power is ultimately
imaginary. The idea that the Jews are helpless is perhaps nowhere
stressed more strongly than when the agitator refers to their power.
The unserious and sometimes directly grotesque connotations in such
references do not seem to weaken the basic implication that there is
an identity between the persecutor and persecuted. Like sadist and
masochist, the two are not distinguished in the unconscious.

Persecution of the Jews even comes to be conceived as a prerequisite
of Jewish power. The idea is presented with a touch of irony.

> Space is too limited to comment on why Jews hired gangsters to
> stage pogroms against other Jews. But it IS necessary that Jews be
> persecuted. If they were not, their whole international system would
> collapse. That is why it was necessary that Hitler be made to kill so
> many before the United States would destroy Germany. By Jewish
> reports. Hitler killed every Jew in Germany about six times. It is
> hard to believe that a Jew could be killed that many times, have all
> his property confiscated, and then show up at a refugee camp with a
> fur coat and suitcases full of money, clamoring about his sacred right
> to come to the United States.[71]

The identity of the persecutor and the persecuted is explicitly
stated by an English street orator who, referring to the refugees
of the *Exodus 1947*, complained that "now Britain was a fifth-rate
nation, dictated to by four thousand Jews afloat in British ships."
(Quoted by Woodrow Wyatt, *New Statesman and Nation*, August
30, 1947.) It is difficult to believe that even a profascist audience
fails to perceive such a charge as a joke—but it is a startling joke, a
proof of the agitator's impudence or prowess and his determination
to resort to any means to attain his end. It is proof that against the
Jew everything goes; just because he is helpless he can be hit below
the belt. But the charge also sets associational trains in motion: the
refugees, after all, *are* a stubborn and troublesome lot, and if they
do not dictate to the British Empire, they certainly tried to, and they
do force the government to waste a great deal of time on them. The
idea of their power is a good joke, but it is not "dismissed" as other
jokes are—quite the contrary.

Cunning

The Jews do not satisfy their lust for revenge openly. They always act behind the scenes, and it is they who are "the power behind *all* dictators."[72] The agitational texts suggest that the most important Jewish instrument of domination is, next to money, the manipulation of public opinion.

The agitator exploits certain actual occupational facts. The relatively high percentage of Jewish participation in the motion picture and radio industries and in the press is used in two ways. First, the Jews are depicted as the absolute masters of the media of mass communication. "We recognize the tremendous influence which the sons of Jewry wield in the press, the cinema and on the radio, the three chief sources which control public opinion."[73] In fact, all "movies . . . are run by Jews";[74] the Jews "control the press . . . control the motion picture industry a hundred per cent,"[75] and "press and radio in the United States is definitely under Semitic domination."[76]

Second, this alleged position of the Jews is depicted as a consequence of their innate intellectuality. This may be stated in the form of a compliment:

> My fellow citizens, I am not ignorant of Jewish history. I know its glories. I am acquainted with its glorious sons. I am aware of the keen intellectuality which has characterized its progress in commerce, in finance and particularly in the field of communication.[77]

Resentment against the Jews as wielders of intellectual power is fed by the obscure realization that such power is basically precarious; the agitator has a way of suggesting that success spells danger for the Jews: "In the fields of publicity, finance, commerce, communications, amusement and industry, the Jews have risen to perilous heights."[78]

The Jews seem to have succeeded in using standardized products of mass culture for the pursuit of their own exploitive ends: "The Jew combines owning and controlling the movies and radio have a cheap trick in their method of Hollywood clowns using radio programs to advertise and glorify each other."[79]

The followers' own ambivalent attitude toward mass culture, the feeling that in the last analysis they are somehow betrayed by what they read and hear and see, is exploited for agitational purposes. While manipulating the others—so the agitator tells his audience—the Jews protect their own interests. Mass culture is a product of intellectuality, and intellectuality is above all seen as a means of exploitation.

The Jews are conceived as living by their wits and avoiding physical work. They achieve their goals by means of intellectual machinations, stock exchange manipulations, or revolutionary propaganda, but they never seem to toil in the sweat of their brows. This is a trait common to the banker and communist, and is one of the elements of the paradoxical image of the communist banker.

Significantly enough, the agitator rarely accuses the Jews of violent crimes. The Jews are depicted as crooks, conspirators, warmongers, revolutionists, but they never seem to do things with their hands. Compared to them, a common murderer or burglar is a laborer with tools and skills who must engage in physical work to achieve his ends. The Jews are not even such hard-working criminals. Work without hardship is identified with exploitation, and to the followers the vision of a people who enjoy life without paying for it is intolerable. Hence the accusation that the Jews aim at compelling the gentiles to perform all the "dirty" work:

> I speak of the International Organized Jewry who seeks a One World government, mongrelizing of the races (of all except their own) a world police force, world court, (again Jew-dominated) and a one world government with once free and independent Christian Americans as the slaves to till the soil, sweat in the industries, fight the wars and be the slaves.[80]

These old motives of resentment may be intensified by an obscure suspicion that the intellectual no longer fulfills his traditional function of serving the spiritual needs of the community. He is identified with the best-selling author, the movie script writer, and the successful newspaperman. He seems to make a good living by producing a content that serves merely to divert those engaged in less gratifying tasks.

Domination by intellect is experienced as usurpation because it is not backed by actual physical power and ultimately it depends on the consent of the dominated or on deception. Consistently depicted as oversophisticated, practicing debauch, enjoying forbidden things, tempting the suckers by futile entertainment, and pursuing destructive aims, the modern intellectual, as the agitator sees him, is a secular variation of the devil. But the agitator is not in the least against the principle of manipulating people by means of the entertainment industry; he merely objects to the fact that it cannot be used for his own "righteous" purposes: "The moving picture business today is largely in the hands of Satan and his emissaries. . . . Satan has things pretty much his own way in a sphere that ought to be a powerful factor for righteousness."[81]

Self-Sufficiency

Our list of traits that the agitator ascribes to the Jews includes several that supposedly define the Jews' character: for instance their freedom from the shackles of Christian morality, their readiness to help each other, their irrepressible dynamism, their expressiveness, their cunning. All these traits are denounced as despicable and hateful, yet they also lend themselves to another interpretation, for they can be viewed as desirable assets in the individual's struggle for existence. On some occasions the agitator almost explicitly indicates that he conceives the Jews as people who somehow manage to get more out of life than the gentiles:

> I am not an anti-Jew. The Jew has his place but he has it no more than you or I. He has a place where we will put him in time, and when he gets there he won't be able to spend much money, not more than we have now.[82]

But the strain of envy present in such an accusation is not confined to the stereotyped notion that the Jews possess inexhaustible financial resources. The other traits referred to above also seem worldly assets that have been appropriated by the Jews, while the non-Jews have lost or are losing them.

The very multiplicity of Jewish attributes is significant. The Jew appears as a colorful figure: he is interesting, he attracts attention, he does not have to stress his originality, he is allegedly recognized by innumerable obvious signs, by his language, manners, ideas. The very fact that he is a Jew distinguishes him from the anonymous crowd. It is true that his characteristics are contradictory. He is persecuted and privileged, strong and weak, rich and poor, religious and atheistic, clannish and promiscuous, modern and archaic. But the Jew somehow synthesizes all contradictions; despite his multiplicity he remains one, easily and clearly identifiable. A remarkably integrated personality, he gives free expression to individualistic impulses that others must repress; at the same time he has a highly developed rational faculty, and has not lost the sense of collective solidarity.

The Jew's capacity for enjoying life creates the illusion that in an era when the individual is under tremendous pressure, the Jew, by defying the trends of the day, remains an individual and profits from it. To an audience obsessed by feelings of insecurity, the agitator suggests that the Jews are a people who have succeeded in weaving a continuous historical texture of their own since the beginnings of time and who know at any given moment how to cut this material to meet any new situation. He often refers to Jews by epithets or images taken from the Bible or from their ancient and medieval history; even their most modern techniques of propaganda are nothing but a repetition of age-old devices: "technique and its [propaganda] terminology from the Sanhedrin and from the Sanhedrin's progeny."[83]

The Jew, the agitator intimates, is at home in every country, he is not fettered by linguistic, geographic, ethnographic frontiers. He is ubiquitous—everywhere on the earth and everywhere in history. He has solved the problem of belonging, and although he is an individual, he is never isolated. And he shapes his own fate; while the other peoples are never held responsible for their misery, the Jew is responsible for both his own and the other nations' fate.

His fate as an individual is also the fate of his people. The Jews always help one another, sacrifice themselves for one another, and as we have been told, even stage pogroms against themselves when this can serve their purposes. Although unique individuals, they act like a swarm of insects and invade other countries like epidemics.

The image of the Jew who escapes the heavy demands of self-discipline, whose morals are easy, who does secret and forbidden things, and who enjoys life without paying for it is all the more provoking because the Jew seems able to do all this even while his power is so precarious. For Jewish power, the agitator implies, has no solid foundations in reality; it is based solely on manipulations and machinations. It cannot withstand the exercise of brute force, and brute force is something that the Jews never have at their disposal. The very survival of the Jews can thus be felt as a challenge, for it seems to refute the idea that ultimately everything in life is based on physical power, and that those deprived of it must submit to those who wield it. The Jews symbolize the utopia of harmony that has come to be regarded as a deception. This almost automatically suggests that they can enjoy happiness only by deceiving others.

At a time when bare survival comes increasingly to be felt as the sole value, and conformism as the sole method of assuring one's survival, Jewish survival seems an intolerable challenge. If the world has borne with the Jews for centuries, it cannot bear with them any longer. They must be liquidated because they are doomed; there is no place for the individual in the world today. In the last analysis, elimination of the

Jew does not seem to be motivated by expectation of material gain but by the fact that in modern life individual happiness seems to become so exceptional that the presence of a group that seemingly continues to pursue it is felt as an affront and a menace.

It would be erroneous to represent the Jew as the ultimate enemy of the agitator. Although the agitator's invectives converge on the Jew, his attack is aimed at all forces in society that he finds reprehensible. The Jew becomes the symbol on which he centers the projections of his own important rage against the restraints of civilization.

Such sentiments are not unique to American agitation:

> I also want to talk to you, quite frankly, on a very grave matter . . . I mean the clearing out of the Jews, the extermination of the Jewish race. It's one of those things it is easy to talk about—"The Jewish race is being exterminated," says one Party member, "that's quite clear, it's in our program—elimination of the Jews, and we're doing it, exterminating them." And then they come, 80 million worthy Germans and each one has his decent Jew. Not one of all those who talk this way has witnessed it, not one of them has been through it. Most of you must know what it means when 100 corpses are lying side by side, or 500 or 1,000. To have stuck it out and at the same time—apart from exceptions caused by human weakness—to have remained decent fellows, that is what has made us hard. This is a page of glory in our history which has never been written and is never to be written, for we know how difficult we should have made it for ourselves, if—with bombing raids, the burdens and the deprivations of war—we still had Jews today in every town as secret saboteurs, agitators and troublemongers. We should now probably have reached the 1916–17 stage when the Jews were still in the German national body.

> We have taken from them what wealth they had. I have issued a strict order, which SS Obergruppenführer Pohl has carried out, that this wealth should as a matter of course be handed over to the Reich without reserve. We have taken none of it for ourselves. Individual men who have lapsed will be punished in accordance with an order issued at the beginning which gave this warning: Whoever takes so much as a mark of it is a dead man. A number of S.S. men—there are not very many of them—have fallen short, and they will die without mercy. We had the moral right, we had the duty to our people, to destroy this people which wanted to destroy us. But we have not the right to enrich ourselves with so much as a fur, a watch, a mark, or a cigarette or anything else. Because we have exterminated a bacterium we do not want, in the end, to be infected by the bacterium and die of it. I will not see so much as a small area of sepsis appear here or gain a hold. Wherever it may form, we will cauterize it. Altogether,

however, we can say that we have fulfilled this most difficult duty for the love of our people. And our spirit, our soul, our character has not suffered injury from it. [Speech of the Reichführer-SS Heinrich Himmler at the meeting of S.S. major-generals at Posen, October 4, 1943, quoted in *Nazi Conspiracy and Aggression* (Washington, 1946), p. 558.]

The use of the stereotypes of Jewish greed and sabotage, and the metaphor of the bacteria cannot obscure the fact that something more than wealth and hygiene is involved. Although the speaker uses terms such as *spirit*, *soul*, and *love of our people*, the essential point he wants to impress upon his listeners is this: under no circumstances must they succumb to human impulses. The dehumanization and killing of the Jew cannot be carried out effectively unless the killer too is dehumanized, unless he extirpates in himself every claim to human existence as an individual.

Notes

1. CF, Apr., 1945, p. 556.
2. CF, Oct., 1945, Upton Close letter in, p. 653.
3. McWilliams, New York, July 18, 1940, street corner.
4. LIB, Sept., 28, 1939, p. 10.
5. SJ, Nov. 17, 1941, p. 18.
6. SJ, Apr. 20, 1942, pp. 7 & 8.
7. LIB, June 3, 1933, Mrs. Anna B. Sloane in, p. 10.
8. DEF, Sept., 1937, p. 5.
9. AP, Feb., 1945, p. 8.
10. LIB, Apr. 21, 1940, p. 12.
11. SJ, Mar. 13, 1939, p. 11.
12. LIB, Nov. 7, 1938, p. 9.
13. AID, June 10, 1945, p. 2.
14. Smith, Cleveland, May 11, 1943, meeting.
15. LIB, Nov. 28, 1940, p. 2.
16. SJ, July 7, 1941, p. 4.
17. SJ, June 5, 1939, p. 2.
18. CF, Sept., 1945, p. 635.
19. Smith, St. Louis, Mar. 25, 1944. meeting.
20. Coughlin, Detroit, Nov. 20, 1938, radio.
21. SJ, June 5, 1939, p. 2.
22. CF, Oct., 1944, p. 452.
23. Smith, Detroit, Mar. 19, 1943, meeting.
24. CF, Mar., 1945, p. 540.
25. CF, Dec., 1943.
26. CF, Feb., 1945, p. 519.
27. AP, July, 1944, p. 1.
28. AID, May 6, 1942, p. 1.

29. Phelps, Los Angeles, October 20, 1940, radio.
30. CF, July, 1945, p. 604.
31. CF, July, 1942, p. 3.
32. CF, June, 1943, p. 215.
33. McWilliams, New York, July 25, 1940, street corner.
34. AP, Nov., 1944, p. 3.
35. McWilliams, New York, July 18, 1940, street corner.
36. Phelps, Los Angeles, Aug. 20, 1940, radio.
37. DEF, Feb., 1940, p. 4.
38. AP, Nov., 1944, p. 12.
39. PW, June 10, 1936.
40. SJ, Mar, 30. 1942, p. 16.
41. CF, May, 1942, p. 3.
42. SJ, Sept. 29, 1941, p. 19.
43. Coughlin, Speech on Jan. 22, 1939, reprinted in *Why Leave Our Own*, p. 45.
44. AP, Feb., 1945, p. 10.
45. SJ, Sept. 29, 1941, p. 19.
46. DEF, Nov., 1939, p. 22.
47. McWilliams, New York, July 18, 1940, street corner.
48. DEF, July, 1939, Lewis Valentine Ulrey in, p. 22.
49. AID, Jan. 27, 1941, p. 2.
50. SJ, Sept. 15, 1941, p. 5.
51. Coughlin, Speech on Feb. 5, 1939, reprinted in *Why Leave Our Own*, p. 73.
52. SJ, Dec. 4, 1939, p. 6.
53. Phelps, Los Angeles, Oct. 13, 1940, radio.
54. Phelps, Los Angeles, Dec. 26, 1940, radio.
55. Coughlin, Speech on Jan. 22, 1939, reprinted in *Why Leave Our Own*, p. 45.
56. Kamp, *Vote CIO . . . and Get a Soviet America*, p. 14.
57. Coughlin, Speech on Feb. 5, 1939, reprinted in *Why Leave Our Own*, p. 67.
58. Sanctuary, *Litvinoff, Foreign Commissar of U.S. S. R.*, p. 4.
59. Smith, St. Louis, Mar. 25, 1944, meeting.
60. Kamp, *With Lotions of Love . . .* p. 28.
61. X, Feb. 17, 1945, p. 3.
62. LIB, Feb. 28, 1938, p. 6.
63. Kamp, *Native Nazi Purge Plot*, p. 5.
64. Cf. CF, May, 1942; RTL, Oct., 1941.
65. LIB, Oct. 28, 1939, p. 6.
66. AID, Dec. 9, 1940.
67. DEF, Apr., 1940, p. 5.
68. Phelps, Los Angeles, Oct. 20, 1940, radio.
69. CF, May, 1945, p. 565.
70. AID, Apr. 30, 1945, p. 1.
71. *The Individualist*, Mar. 31, 1947, p. 4.
72. AID, Dec. 9, 1941, p. 2.
73. Coughlin, Speech on Jan. 29, 1939, reprinted in *Why Leave Our Own*, p. 48.
74. Mote, Cleveland, July 1, 1942, meeting.
75. Maloney, New York, July 25, 1940, street corner.

76.   DEF, June, 1941, p. 16.
77.   SJ, Nov. 28, 1938, p. 10.
78.   SJ, Sept. 29, 1941, p. 19.
79.   X, Mar. 3, 1945, p. 2.
80.   X, June 6, 1947, p. 2.
81.   DEF, Feb., 1941, p. 17.
82.   White, New York, July 18, 1940, street corner.
83.   AP, Sept., 1944, p. 3.

7

A Home for the Homeless

As a would-be leader of a popular movement, the agitator cannot content himself with articulations of malaise and denunciations of the enemy; he must offer some kind of statements about his goals and the means by which he proposes to reach them.

The "positive" statements of any advocate of social change may be discussed under four heads:

1. Descriptions of the values and ideals that are to replace the rejected values and ideals.
2. Formulations of goals that contain some assurance that the factors leading to present frustrations will be eliminated, and that a situation will be created in which frustrated needs will be fully gratified.
3. Descriptions of the methods of realizing these goals: a practical program of action.
4. References to the character of the movement's adherent as contrasted with the character of the enemy. The adherent is not merely one who is exempt from the enemy's vices; he also has positive virtues. (A prohibitionist, for instance, is not merely a teetotaler but also a man who, precisely because he does not succumb to the vice of drink, is an upright citizen, faithful husband, and a thrifty, far-sighted, self-controlled individual.)

This last group of statements will be discussed in the next chapter. In this one we shall take up the first three, dealing respectively with the agitator's values, goals, and methods of achieving them. Of all agitational themes, those that might be described as programmatic are the least well developed.

Platforms and Programs

As soon as we examine the platforms and programs of the agitator, we find that there is a considerable dearth of materials. When formulating a specific objective, he almost cynically aims to go one better than the government, his most dangerous competitor. For instance, he proposes a "Serviceman's Reconstruction Plan," which provides that "each member of the United States Armed Forces, upon his honorable discharge, be paid $7,800."[1]

When the agitator does issue a "Statement of Principles" it is as vague as the following document of the "Committee of 1,000,000, a patriotic and dynamic crusade which began with nine constituents and now has more than 3,000,000":[2]

> The foundation principles of this committee, which have been unchanged since its beginning in 1937, are as follows:
> 1. To rebuild the spirit of America.
> 2. To wipe out to the last vestige Communism, Nazism, and Fascism in all forms. (In view of the attempt now being made to join us in a political union with foreign countries, we express our bitter objection to all such schemes to compromise the sovereignty of America, such as "Union Now With Britain." "Federal Union, Inc." etc.)
> 3. To redefine the American national character.
> 4. To instill a new spirit in American youth, dedicated intellectually and physically to the maintenance of American institutions.
> 5. To issue a call to farmers and laborers to resist what is now known to be an international plot to make them part of a world revolution.
> 6. To rededicate the citizenry of America to the family altar and to the spirit of the Church.
> 7. To secure the maintenance of a well-defined standard of American living.

Some of the points in such platforms are restatements of the stereotyped images of the enemy (the communists must be wiped out); others are examples of shadowboxing; and still others are merely glittering generalities. It would be easy enough to go through such platforms and show their internal inconsistencies as well as the contradictions between what they proclaim and what the agitator says on other occasions, but such exercises would have slight value.

Reaction Patterns

The agitator seems to steer clear of the area of material needs on which liberal and democratic movements concentrate; his main concern is a sphere of frustration that is usually ignored in traditional politics. The programs that concentrate on material needs seem to overlook that area of moral uncertainties and emotional frustrations that are the immediate manifestations of malaise. It may therefore be conjectured that his followers find the agitator's statements attractive not because he occasionally promises to "maintain the American standards of living" or to provide a job for everyone but because he intimates that he will give them the emotional satisfactions that are denied them in the contemporary social and economic setup. He offers attitudes, not bread.

Actually, he fails to touch upon the roots of emotional frustration in our society. He does not present his followers with a prospect of joy or happiness but, rather, encourages a verbal discharge of emotion. Significantly, the whole meaning of the agitator's movement is represented as a reaction: "I assure you, we are aroused and your challenge is hereby met by a mightier challenge."[3] The followers are invited to hit back at those who direct history against them. Rather than a movement expressing universal aims, the agitator's movement proposes itself as a kind of protection agency that will ward off the enemy.

All the while, the audience is expected to act not because of desires or motives of its own but only out of exasperation, when it has been goaded beyond endurance by the enemy's depravity. "When enough Gentiles have been booted out of jobs, the Gentiles are reactively bound to arise and boot out Jews."[4]

Theme 15: Either-Or

The Agitator's Values

Agitation differs from both the reform and revolutionary types of social movements in that it attacks values not in open, explicit terms but surreptitiously, under the guise of a defense of existing ideals. In that way the agitator can both reject current values and avoid the task of formulating a new set of values. Nowhere does he explicitly indicate, even in the most rudimentary fashion, any adherence to universal standards or criteria that could take the place of discarded ideals and form the nucleus of a new moral, philosophical, religious, and political outlook.

It would be false, however, to imagine that his work of disintegration results in a complete vacuum. To destroy loyalties to universal beliefs, the agitator always insists that all ideals and ideas cannot be taken at face value but that they are rather mere camouflage for the enemy's will to survive. This will to survive now becomes the agitator's implicit frame of reference. As a result, his picture of the world and of the problem of man's conduct in that world are tremendously simplified. Instead of a variety of more or less complex situations that are judged in terms of a set of differentiated ideas, the agitator proposes to view the world as split between two irreconcilable camps. There is no possibility of working out a solution acceptable to all, or even a solution in which everyone will find a satisfying place. The adversary can never be won to the agitator's cause, even if and when the desired condition for which the agitator works is achieved; the only way to deal with the enemy is to exterminate him. The agitator assimilates opposing human groups to hostile biological species, and ultimately, in his view, the march of history relapses into the processes of nature.

In such a world people are neither guided nor inhibited by moral standards. All ethical problems are reduced to the single problem of choosing between the stronger and weaker camp, that is, of discovering which camp will ensure one's survival. The enemy, by his very nature, is unable to choose, but those who have the privilege of choice must adhere to the most powerful camp if they are to avoid destruction. Here, then, is a world in which values may in fact interfere with the crucial choice even if they do not already serve as tricky means of insuring the enemy's victory. It is an Either-Or world—survive, by no matter what means, or perish, with no matter what good intentions. Either-or—for or against—this fundamental dichotomy is basic to the agitator's world outlook.

In the Either-Or world constructed by the agitator, the essence of human life is violent conflict, a conflict that is unavoidable and present on all levels of human existence.

> The great masses of humanity are divided by a deep and wide chasm. On the one side of this chasm are the real producers of wealth—the underpaid farmers producing the food and fiber for all and the underpaid laborer processing the food, the fiber, the homes and all the material things of a civilization.

> On the other side of a deep wide chasm is a little group of wealthy men. Every capitalistic system under the sun is perfectly satisfied with things as they are within the state and yet not satisfied that their economic domination is enough.[5]

This economic dichotomy is transposed to the sphere of international politics. "It is a war between the 'Haves' and the 'Have-nots.'... In plainer language: because Jewish international bankers own or control the gold of the world, *it is their war*."⁶ According to the agitator the same division will continue after the war: "The Jewish Agency is the *united front* of Jewry (a kind of Jewish League of Nations impenetrable to Gentiles) against the non-Jewish world, regardless of any internal dissension in their own midst."⁷

In the field of domestic politics the motif of self-preservation is invoked directly:

> As far as I am concerned, we have been reduced to that one simple elementary problem of self-preservation. . . . Head-choppers in Washington might become so ambitious as to create an unhealable disunity by their extreme practices.⁸

More often the appeal to self-preservation is clothed in ideological garb, as in the following:

> We are coming to the crossroads where we must decide whether we are going to preserve law and order and decency or whether we are going to be sold down the river to the Red traitors who are undermining America.⁹

or

> The Talmudic philosophy of Europe-Asia-Africa and Nudeal is directly opposite that of Christian.¹⁰

The conflict, whether conceived in biological or dressed in ideological terms, is pictured as all-embracing and omnipresent; no situation or issue is outside its fatal orbit. The profoundest causalities in history— "Every serious student of world affairs today knows that the mighty conflict of the centuries is under way and must move on to its final, inevitable and devastating climax"¹¹—as well as such trivial matters as the shape of the traffic lights in New York City are alike experienced as consequences of the same Manichean struggle. To cope with such a situation requires the most drastic measures: "'We do not want the Franco way for America,' is the common theme of these editorial critiques. To be sure we don't; *neither did Spain!* But the alternative is Islam, or, in our day, Red godless Communism."¹²

The dilemma is absolute:

> God pity you blind business men who think that there is any cure for a situation thus poisoned. Unless you stand up and fight you

will wake up some night and face the knife of a revolutionist at your throat just as they did in Russia, Spain, Mexico, and elsewhere.[13]

Those who choose wrongly will suffer the consequences:

> The "bloodless revolution" phase is about over. Time will soon be, when you and others like you, will have to decide what leadership you will follow. The wrong choice means terror, rape, murder, starvation and destruction—besides which what occurred in Europe and Asia will be tame.[14]

The Either-Or dilemma seems to cut deeper than even the most fundamental political or social conflicts; it seems to be a universal characteristic of existence, a kind of predestination of human, subhuman, and superhuman conflicts. The agitator presents his vision of this Either-Or world not as the logical outcome of his deprecation of values but as a given and unquestionable existential insight. Actually the Either-Or situation is an unavoidable corollary of a world without universal values, without the hope of a final redemption that is an integral part of Western religious and philosophical thought. The agitator offers no vision of a better world, no hope that men will ever be able to live as brothers. All that is possible, he implies, is to survive in a dog's world, to band together as an elite in order to take from others what we want for ourselves. Moral values yield to a sober estimation of the problem of self-survival:

> May I say this to you, ladies and gentlemen: There are five hundred million people starving in the world today. There are five hundred million people that are paupers of the war. We face the same problem you have to face when you go down a poverty-stricken street; you have got your little payday check and you make $60 a week; you have got the boy in school, you want to be generous, you want to be a Christian, you want to do all you can, but just the moment you stop and dissipate all you have upon these people of the street, you have deserted your own, you have violated nature and you have struck suicide to your own household.[15]

Inherent in this whole attitude is the agitator's tendency to shift the emphasis of discussion from a defense of ethical values to biological self-defense. This shift involves a far-reaching change in the structure of human belief. In a liberal society the concept of loyalty involves capacity for judgment, feeling, and exercise of will; ideally speaking, a man's choice of belief is determined by his rational insight. In the

agitator's world, the ideational components of belief are largely eliminated, and one's acceptance or rejection of a creed is summoned, so to
speak, to function independently. All the agitator's listeners are supposed to raise their hands when the agitator asks them to accept an
attitude, and to shake their fists in fury when the agitator bids them to
reject it. This simple acquiescence is the result of the Either-Or choice.

Theme 16: Endogamic Community

The Agitator's Goal

In his role as a social therapist, the agitator is a strong believer in the
exogenic theory of disease: every pathological symptom is traced to a
foreign agent. But if the agitator's ideas about pathology are definite,
his concept of what is normal is remarkably vague. All he can offer is a
rededication to the established institutional and ideological framework
of the American republic as it has persisted since the founding fathers.
"I challenge Americans to reconsecrate themselves . . . to America,"[16]
he exclaims. If anything has gone wrong, it can be only because we
Americans have bothered with concerns that are not American or have
strayed from American ways.

Offhand, it might seem that just as on other occasions the agitator tries
to don the mantle of populism, he is here trying to identify himself with
the conservative tradition. Unlike his European counterparts he is always
eager to tie up his cause with respectable ideas and names; in his speeches
he frequently mentions Washington, the Founding Fathers, Lincoln, and
congressmen known for their conservative views.

Another conservative implication of the agitator's nationalism is
his insistence that every social issue involves a conflict between the
ingroup and the out-group; he consistently refrains from analyzing
social problems in terms of internal conflicts. Unemployment, for
example, he sees as due to an influx of undesirable aliens; likewise,
the problem of food distribution has nothing to do with variations of
purchasing power within the nation, but is caused by the insatiable
appetites of other countries. In the name of "Americanism" the agitator expressly denies class and social differences; "Americanism is like
pure water which tastes just as good to a ditch digger in Chicago as to
a Supreme Court judge in Washington,"[17]

The image of "pure water" is perhaps not accidental; except for
purity the agitator seems to have great difficulty in assigning any
specific content to his nationalism. In the agitator's eyes, nationalism means first of all negation of its opposite, internationalism.

He sometimes justifies this negation by debunking the liberalistic doctrines of world peace, by exposing the power politics that goes on behind the scenes of international bodies, and by sneering at the "advocates of world peace" who "don't agree among themselves."[18] But his main argument is: "We can't solve internal problems, so how can we claim to solve international problems?"[19] On the other hand, the only internal problem he stresses is the presence of foreign reds and Jews.

Even when he tries to anticipate the charge that he is always negative, and proposes a positive goal, the best he can do is to restate his essential negativism:

> If Christians are determined to establish a Christian front, let not their motives be misinterpreted. Certainly it is not an anti-Semitic front. It is a front for Christ and for His principles. It is a militant front which is not content to let the enemies of Christ, be they Gentile or Jew, dis-establish Christ in our government, our commerce, our industry, our factories, our fields or our institutions of education. Our militancy, however, may not be negative; may not be anti-Semitic. It must be positive and for Christ.[20]

At the point where the agitator gets to his fundamental notions about Americanism, he parts company from the conservative by interpreting the imperative of patriotism as a call for endogamic seclusion. All of the arguments or pseudoarguments by which he tries to buttress his extreme nationalism are overshadowed by an absolute, almost instinctive rejection of everything foreign. For the agitator, the act of joining an international body not only is equivalent to the surrender of national sovereignty but also involves the distasteful prospect of having to mingle with other people in a gathering "made up of a few Orientals and a few Russians and a few Europeans . . . and a few South Americans"[21]—a prospect he does not find pleasing.

The ancient distrust and fear of the stranger seems to be at the base of the agitator's nationalism, for when he does try occasionally to give political concreteness to his nationalism, all he can produce is a few threadbare phrases: free enterprise, individualism, protective tariffs, and simple flagwaving. "The spirit of the founding fathers is still in our midst."[22] Or: "Let American individualism function—let free enterprise produce."[23]

Can a present-day audience, no matter how low its intellectual level, be satisfied with such an arid collection of clichés? Can it be satisfied with the distinctly unpleasurable note of denial that reverberates beneath the agitator's nationalism? For instead of material and moral security the agitator offers his listeners nothing but a refurbishment of slogans that have clearly not sufficed for protection from the foreign evils against which he warns them. Only when taken against the background of the world the agitator conjures, the Either-Or world hopelessly divided into incompatible camps, does the affirmation of endogamic exclusiveness seem to hold primitive attractions that might compensate for its apparent aridity as the goal of a movement.

To disappointed and disoriented listeners, the affirmation of exclusiveness may mean the assurance that their identity will be preserved. Their sense of alienation may thereby be somewhat relieved, and replaced by a sense of belonging to something, no matter how vague. As the opponent of "the scourge of internationalism,"[24] the agitator plays the role of the head of a family who is worried about the hardships his children suffer far from home and summons them to come back. He is less concerned with complex international political problems than with such humble questions as money, material comfort, health:

> I swear to my God that not a single dime of any money I may ever get my hands on will ever be sent to Europe's afflicted as long as one single American citizen remains destitute, jobless, paralyzed and suffering from neglect.[25]

In these humble concerns food occupies a prominent place. Before giving to others, Americans must be sure that they eat their fill and eat what they want:

> We assume that treaties and agreements and understandings shall be reached with other nations, but we want no League of Nations, we want no world court and no world congress . . . any more than we want our neighbor, three houses down the street, telling us whether we're going to have coffee or milk for breakfast.[26]

As late as March 1947, the agitator, in the name of food, denounces the Truman doctrine:

> Giving our food and supplies to foreign nations or even selling them to them in credit which we will never get paid for, keeps prices high because of "shortages" and that is exactly what the New Deal International money changers have been and are imposing upon us.[27]

His solicitude goes as far as the pettiest detail. Like a stingy house-wife who frowns upon her children's extravagant habit of inviting guests for dinner, and who wants at least to save the best morsels for her own family, he advises his listeners: "I believe absolutely, when you have got one shipload of oleomargarine and one of butter, send the oleomargarine . . . and keep the butter at home!"[28]

If the agitator refrains from outlining a detailed program for abundant living, he is at least vocal in assuring his listeners that whatever is available will fall into the right hands, for—and here we find another possible element of gratification in his arid appeals to preserve what exists—his listeners are promised to play a privileged role in the nation as he conceives it. Just as with material goods, so the spiritual benefits of Americanism are to be enjoyed only by an endogamic elite of Christian Americans.

The basic implication of the agitator's "defense" of American prin-ciples is that the human rights he proclaims should be transformed into a privilege. Even this doubtful privilege is nowhere defined clearly, except in contexts where its meaning comes down to the right to persecute minorities. The agitator speaks in grandiose terms of "the final judge-and-jury of what's what in America . . . the American people." But when this final judge-and-jury that "has yet to render its decision" finally does it, the only result "will be a decline of the Jewish population in both Washington and Hollywood. No, we do not mean a pogrom! We refer to migrations."[29]

The privilege here offered to the endogamic elite includes the essential promise to implement their rights as Americans by a vague permission (made more thrilling because it is accompanied by an apparent denial—"No, we do not mean a pogrom") to participate in the coercive functions of society. The promise of beneficent depen-dence in a nation that will be like a family is supplemented by the promise to the obedient followers that they will enjoy power over their prodigal and wicked brothers.

Theme 17: Housecleaning

The Agitator's Methods

Even more vague than the agitator's statement of his goals is his defini-tion of the means by which he tends to achieve power. By virtue of his almost total silence on this matter, the agitator implicitly suggests that in this respect at least his movement is like a traditional political move-ment that intends to use orderly and democratic methods to change the government. At the same time, the agitator seems to promise his audience a more active role in the liberation. "This meeting," he reminds his audience, "is not a lecture course, it is not an open forum. . . . We are making history here today."[30] For though he has no wish other than to take power by the most peaceful and orderly means, the enemy may force him to use force; if so, "we will fight you in Franco's way."[31] Similar threats of a general uprising are to be found in his vague references to "Thirty Thousand 'Minute Men'" who are reported to be training at Lexington and Concord[32] and in his prophecies that the enemies' "days are numbered."[33] In a bolder mood, he declares that "there will be no stopping the blood running in our city streets"[34] and that "the country's due for civil war, anyway."[35]

Yet it must be emphasized that the agitator's calls to direct action are at least as vague as his definitions of his goal. It would be erroneous to believe that his programmatic silence is merely a cover for preparations for an armed uprising. In fact, the agitator takes care to make clear that his proposed uprising is not really a revolution. Throughout his remarks there runs a strong current of respect for institutionalized force. It is not accidental that the agitator who attacks the executive, legislative, and even judiciary branches of the government with indiscriminate virulence, will invariably identify himself with the forces of law and order, especially the police, and occasionally discover quite imaginative arguments to persuade them to take his side: "The Police of USA well know that the first to be liquidated in the event of a 'takeover' by the Synagogue of Satan (Organized Jewry-Intl. Finance) thru 'revolutionary' tactics, are the Police men."[36]

The agitator becomes quite lyrical when he speaks of armed forces. In 1943, while the nation was engaged in an unprecedented war effort, he demanded, as though no one else had thought of it before him,

> a line of fortifications built on land and water and in the air around the United States, that can be pierced by no alien force. It will be made up of cruisers, destroyers, gunboats, mosquito fleets, anti-aircraft guns, and airplanes, both bombers and fighters, troop transports, merchant vessels and a perfectly trained army, navy and marine force.[37]

The spontaneous rebelliousness the agitator wants to set in motion is to remain unstructured and unorganized; it is to be confined to an immediate emotional reaction. To describe this reaction, the agitator falls back upon familiar clichés: there is going to be trouble, "hell is going to pop."[38] But seldom does he suggest anything more specific or far-reaching than a march on Washington.

Even as a demagogue he never goes so far as to call upon the masses to take power into their own hands and establish their own governmental authority. Such a proposal would contradict his whole approach to his followers. As he describes it, the influence of the masses on the government must always be, at most, an indirect one; their aroused fury is to be kept in a kind of indefinite suspension, a perpetual and never fulfilled threat against the legislators and officials who might act against their wishes. The agitator never lets himself be carried away by his revolutionary élan; he knows when to stop and transform it into its opposite. This is one point at which he seems always to have himself most completely under control. Even when he does offer his followers a picture of a successful upheaval, it hardly involves any fundamental change in government:

> With a determined *MARCH* on *WASHINGTON* you could expect the guilty cowards in both House & Senate to run away, leaving the patriots, who could then go thru with the impeachment proceedings. That patriotic remnant of the Congress then could enact a law declaring who would serve as Pres., V-P, etc., until next election. That is the law![39]

The agitator takes it for granted that after the purge the people will withdraw to their homes and leave the government in the hands of the "patriotic remnant." In his eyes the masses remain essentially passive. The agitator's quarrel with the government is not at all basic, it merely involves a desire to see it manned by satisfactory personnel: "Place the Nation's affairs—every department—every agency—every job—in the hands of capable, experienced, honest experts whose loyalty to American principles of government has never been questioned."[40]

In fact, it seems that one of the objections that the agitator has to the government is that it does not govern: "The chaotic results of the bad government which has been inflicted upon us . . . point to the conclusion that some reorganization is necessary for a system of government which fails to govern."[41]

Behind the apparent contradictions between the agitator's call for rebellion and his desire merely to effect changes in the personnel of the government, is his reliance on the old European device of a *putsch*, in which there is a realignment of ruling circles without the intervention of the masses of people. It may therefore be asked why this proposal should be found attractive by the agitator's listeners. If the agitator were desirous of offering an opportunity for social action to an audience that suffers from a sense of nonparticipation in public life, the results of his *putsch* would necessarily be extremely disappointing: a brief, sensational flareup after which nothing of consequence would have been changed. The movement, on the face of it, has no goals nor does it seem to offer an appreciable field of action for its followers; it seems merely a movement for the sake of movement, a futile excitement for nothing at all.

We may find a clue to a possible answer to our question if we examine the content of the practical steps that the agitator advocates to end existing abuses, and the imagery he employs in such contexts. These steps consist almost uniformly of metaphors of discarding, throwing out, eliminating, as preparatory to extermination. "All refugees . . . should be returned to the lands from which they came";[42] "All aliens and former aliens should be deported."[43] The United States will "throw the Reds out"[44] and "kick out" the Jews.[45] Sometimes the orderliness and police character of the procedure is indicated by references to the need for "so called Refugees" to "be cataloged"[46] or for compiling lists of names[47] of the undesirables to be deported. The accompanying imagery is consistently drawn from the realm of hygiene. The word purge occurs directly: "We must purge America of every un-American organization and activity which might menace our national defense in the hour of a great crisis,"[48] and in innumerable variations. Thus the agitator talks about "cleansing America."[49] He advocates a "cleansing bath . . . of violence,"[50] a purge "of every 'ism.'"[51] the "political sterilization of the Jewish internationalists."[52] and "an internal fumigation to rid ourselves of European germs before we succumb to their diseases."[53]

The agitator's output is full of references to the present condition of the country as an ill-kept house. He complains that the enemies "have littered our fair land."[54] that "ideological and intellectual disease germs"[55] and contaminating the United States, and that it is "time to clean house."[56] He denounces "this whole smelly mess" with which this nation has become afflicted[57] and speaks of the necessity of "yanking this country from its devil of a mess!"[58]

Like the Low Animal metaphor this hygienic metaphor occurs too consistently and too profusely to be dismissed as accidental. It seems on the contrary to perform significant functions in the agitator's speeches and writings, one of which may be to make respectable his proposed political operation by presenting it in the guise of a harmless and familiar housecleaning. By comparing his rebellion with an act of elementary hygiene, he suggests that essentially everything is all right and that all we need is some more "order" or "orderliness."

The idea of a "housecleaning" seems to have a reassuring effect on both listeners and potential backers: nothing too extreme is contemplated. At the same time it serves as a substitute for genuine political activity. The great decisions are made by the heads of the family, while the rest of the family (that is, the audience) can busy itself with keeping the place clean, picking up the "mess," and protecting the house from foreign burglars. Consequently, the gruesome or bloody consequences of the agitator's purge become a mere unavoidable by-product of the community's renewed health and well-being. The agitator uses as his emblem the oversized American housewife with a fly swatter in one hand and a broom in the other: an image of the harmless and aggressive follower, of harmlessness transformed into aggression. For all his ruminations about apocalypse, for all his warnings about threatening catastrophe and for all his insistence on the Either-Or nature of the impending showdown, the agitator can summon no more glorious picture of his great act of liberation than this simultaneously ridiculous and threatening picture of a housewife doing her chores.

These remarks on the political content of the "housecleaning" theme may be supplemented by others based on psychoanalytical theory. According to this theory, education for cleanliness is one of the most difficult experiences a small child ever encounters. The child offers tremendous resistance to it, and even after he has been habituated to follow the social codes of cleanliness, the traumatic experience of cleanliness training exerts far-reaching consequences on both the conscious and unconscious layers of his personality. One of the major devices used to coerce children into cleanliness habits is threats that they will become sick and be punished for their sickness if they violate the rigid hygienic codes. As a result, they find the more obvious manifestations of uncleanliness repellent. The theory that there are significant and dynamic connections between the reorganized anal drives (as psychoanalysis describes the socially formed attitudes toward cleanliness) and such character traits as order, exactness, and pedantry is well known. So also is the notion that suppressed infantile instincts reassert themselves in later life through neurotic symptoms—among other ways, as delectations in the forbidden sphere of dirt.

The agitator is a virtuoso in manipulating such susceptibilities. In stigmatizing the enemies as people who live in the midst of the most offensive rubbish and refuse, he permits his audience to toy with verbal equivalents of the outlawed infantile pleasures. By insulting the enemy—that is, by attributing to the enemy familiarity with dirt and filth—it is possible to come into contact with forbidden materials and to perform forbidden acts. The same person who would be consciously ashamed to display even the slightest inclinations towards such infantilism grasps this occasion to indict the enemy for his own lust—and thereby finds an involuted method for expressing that lust. But simultaneously the projection of repressed desires onto the enemy reminds the audience that there is something shameful and disgusting about such desires. Projection makes possible simultaneous enjoyment and rejection.

Stereotypes utilizing the symbols of dirt, filth, and odor are used to impress the audience with the fact that all speeches and literature put out by the enemy should be discarded at once. Because the agitator counts upon the willingness of people to listen and to read, he must make the reaction of refusing to hear the views of his competitors quasi-automatic. This automatism cannot be achieved merely by discrediting the competitor's wares as fraudulent. It requires an immediate negative emotional reaction, which is obtained by the warning that the enemy's material should not be touched because it is filthy.

Perhaps the deepest layer of personality that can be psychologically organized or manipulated is the complex human reaction toward odors. When people smell a bad odor, they quite often do not turn away from it; instead they eagerly breathe the polluted air, pretending to identify it while complaining of its repulsiveness. One does not have to be a psychoanalyst to suspect that in such instances the bad smell is unconsciously enjoyed in a way somewhat similar to that in which scandal stories are enjoyed. We probably here touch upon phenomena quite successfully repressed in the collective unconscious of mankind, a last faint reminder of animal prehistory, of the way animals walk face downward while using their nose as a means of orienting themselves. The idiosyncratic violence with which various disgusting odors are rejected, and on which the agitator speculates, points to a repressed and forgotten origin. What the agitator does here, as in so many other instances, is to encourage these atavistic predispositions. The dark and forbidden things the listener enjoys with such insistent indignation are the very same things he would like to indulge in. Whether the agitator is conscious of his manipulation of these susceptibilities or is subject to them himself, is a moot point; what is important is that he does manipulate them in a sustained and patterned way.

It is no accident that metaphors of stench and slime are prominently represented among the agitator's hygienic metaphors. He speaks of the "cesspools of Europe,"[59] he likens capitalism to "a stinking corpse,"[60] and he refers to enemy propaganda as "malodorous." He does not hesitate to compare himself to a sniffling dog: "Well, I didn't have to sniffle him very long to find out he had the Willkie smell all over him."[61] But this evil smell is combated by a pleasant smell: "I resolved in 1940 when I got nipped by that financial smell that came down from Wall Street and rolled on to the flats of Indiana to get the smell of horse and cow—I vowed never again would I fall for such a trick."[62]

The audience, it is interesting to note, applauded the reference to the good smell, while laughing at the reference to the bad one.

In the agitator's view of the world, the atmosphere is permeated with foulness. When the audience reacts to his portrait of this world in terms of its socially conditioned response and prejudices, the image of the dirty and evil-smelling enemy solicits reactions that range from moral indignation to outright fury against those who create such an atmosphere. The prevalence of moral and material rubbish demands the most thorough sanitary measure. Such legitimate catharsis purifies the enjoyment that accompanies the delight of fantasies about forbidden dirt.

Those of his followers who expected to move into a new home are given only the same old shack—thoroughly housecleaned.

Notes

1.   McWilliams, *The Serviceman's Reconstruction Plan*, p. 1.
2.   CF, June 1942, p. 2.
3.   Coughlin, Newark, N.J., July 30, 1939, radio.
4.   LIB, Jan. 14, 1939, p. 9.
5.   SJ, Jan. 1, 1940, p. 7.
6.   SJ, Aug. 11, 1941, p. 3.
7.   AID, June 9, 1942, p. 4.
8.   CF, Oct.–Nov., 1942, p. 10.

9.   CF, Feb., 1946, p. 714.
10. AID, May 14, 1941, p. 1.
11. LIB, Apr. 7, 1940, p. 1.
12. SJ, Feb. 12, 1940, p. 2.
13. Smith, *"Mice or Men,"* radio address, p. 3.
14. AID, July 10, 1939, p. 4.
15. Smith, Detroit, March 19, 1943, meeting.
16. Smith, *"Mice or Men,"* radio address, p. 4.
17. CF, Sept., 1942, p. 12.
18. Smith, Detroit, Mar. 22, 1943, meeting.
19. Smith, *ibid.*
20. Coughlin, speech on Feb. 19, 1939, reprinted in *Why Leave Our Own,*
     pp. 98–99.
21. CF, Oct.–Nov., 1942, p. 8.
22. Coughlin, Speech on Mar. 26, 1939, reprinted in *Why Leave Our Own,* p. 161.
23. Kamp, *Famine in America,* p. 50.
24. DEF, Aug., 1939, p. 4.
25. Phelps, Los Angeles, Sept. 8, 1940, radio.
26. CF, Oct.–Nov., 1942, p. 8.
27. X, Mar. 22, 1947, p. 2.
28. Smith, Detroit, Mar. 19, 1943, meeting.
29. LIB, Mar. 14, 1940, p. 5.
30. Smith, Detroit, Feb. 7, 1943, meeting.
31. Coughlin, Newark, N.J., July 30, 1939, radio.
32. SJ, Dec. 25, 1939.
33. Maloney, New York,, July 25, 1940, street corner.
34. AID, July 24, 1939, p. 1.
35. LIB, Mar. 28, 1938.
36. AID, June 15, 1942, p. 3.
37. Smith, Detroit, Mar. 22, 1943, meeting.
38. Smith, New York, Oct. 20, 1936, meeting.
39. AID, Oct. 7, 1941, p. 1.
40. Kamp, *Famine in America,* p. 50.
41. SJ, Apr. 4, 1938, p. 10.
42. Smith, *The Plan,* p. 4.
43. Phelps, Los Angeles, Oct. 2, 1940, radio.
44. SJ, Nov. 27, 1939, p. 6.
45. Maloney, New York, Aug. 3, 1940, street corner.
46. X, April 28, 1945, p. 2.
47. Cf. PW, Sept. 23, 1936, p. 2.
48. Smith, *Enemies Within Our Gates.*
49. McWilliams, New York, July 29, 1940, street corner.
50. LIB, Dec. 30, 1933, p. 12.
51. DEF, Sept., 1939, p. 6.
52. LIB, July 28, 1940, p. 6.
53. Phelps, Los Angeles, July 28, 1941, radio.
54. SJ, Feb. 20, 1939, p. 20.
55. Smith, *Enemies Within Our Gates.*

56.   Kamp, *How To Win The War,* p. 2.
57.   CF, July, 1942, p. 13.
58.   LIB, Feb. 14, 1938, p. 5.
59.   Phelps, Los Angeles, July 28, 1941, radio.
60.   SJ, June 7, 1937, p. 2.
61.   Smith, Detroit, Oct. 21, 1942, meeting.
62.   Smith, *ibid.*

8

The Follower

In the movements of all traditional advocates of social change one can find incipient versions of their hopes for the future. The movement embodies the advocate's goal in embryo, the new world within the shell of the old. The harmonious and friendly relations that flourish or are supposed to flourish among the adherents anticipate the society they are trying to build.

Agitation is distinguised by a remarkable lack of such positive symbols. Nazi propaganda tried to conceal the essentially negative and reactive nature of the "Aryan" by developing the notions of the biological race and the hemmed-in nation. But these notions, obviously irrelevant to American life, are of little help to the American agitator when he attempts to portray his adherent. Yet, as the advocate of the endogamic community, he can hardly define his followers in terms of a social class. The American agitator falls back on the clichés of professional patriotism, Fourth of July Americanism.

The invention of the Aryan race and the agitator's glorification of the Simple American are symptomatic of similar efforts to strengthen social coercion. Both the *Volksgemeinschaft* of the Nazis and the community of pure Americans proposed by the agitator are actually pseudo-*Gemeinschaften,* or pseudocommunities. Such notions are deceptive solutions of the problem created by the disintegration of individualism. The agitator seems aware of this disintegration, but he conceives it as caused by an external force rather than as inherent in the structure of contemporary society: "There are forces at work which . . . would destroy the individuality of Americans and make of them automatons."[1]

The agitator bars the way toward understanding those forces. His normative image of the follower, built simply as a reactive response to the image of the enemy, is as ambivalent as that of the enemy: deceptive strength and real impotence. In the face of the formidable threat represented by the enemy, the adherents are made to believe that they can survive only by huddling together in an exclusive community and by obeying the orders of the leader. But if the enemy must be exterminated, the adherent can just be saved from extermination. In the last analysis, both are equally contemptible: the enemy as the projected target of the adherent's fury, and the adherent because he can do nothing but resort to such projections.

Theme 18: Simple Americans

Striving to recruit the largest possible number of people to his banner, the agitator tries to transcend traditional political or social divisions and to appeal directly to

> the great common body of the American people, who are deacons of churches, trustees of churches, who go to High Mass on Sunday morning, who build the fires and keep the doors of the synagogues, who grub the stumps and husk the corn and chop the cane, and do the work.[2]

The majority of Americans, he intimates, support his cause. His estimates vary: "these seventy-five to one hundred million real, plain, simple American folks,"[3] or "75% of the American people."[4] In more expansive moments he is certain [that] more than eighty percent of the American people are getting sick and tired of being misled by foreign fraud."[5] "Everybody who is against war and communism is called an anti-semite. 85% of America followed Nye, Smith and Coughlin."[6] And finally reaching a rhapsodic climax, he proclaims that "mine is not the cry of just one American citizen. It is the plea and the prayer of millions of Americans."[7]

The most obvious purpose of such assertions is to instill in the listeners the feeling that, just as they cannot be wrong when they buy a nationally advertised product, so they cannot be wrong when they represent a general political trend. In addition to this reassuring function, these claims to mass following help to emphasize the basic weakness of the helplessly outnumbered enemy.

Friends and allies are equipped with seemingly unmistakable identification marks. The agitator makes his followers feel that they are something special. They must be convinced that they belong to an elite even if the elite presumes to include the vast majority of the people.

As soon as the agitator tries to define this elite, he apparently encounters insuperable obstacles. The poverty of the characteristics attributed to the follower is in striking contrast with the richness of characteristics assigned to the enemy. When the agitator tries to characterize this elite socially, he only borrows various stereotypes. When he predicts that "some day Gentile Americans are going to wake up to what is being done to the 'forgotten man'"[8] or denounces any offenses against "the common man" and his "welfare."[9] he is borrowing from the arsenal of progressive clichés. When he refers to his adherents as "we old-fashioned Americans"[10] or as "individualists who still believe in Constitutional government and the American way of life,"[11] he is using the language of conservatism. And when he speaks of the "poor stockholders . . . the forgotten men."[12] he is using the middle-of-the-road stereotype designed to impress prospective middle-class adherents.

The inadequacy of such symbols is obvious: they are not sufficiently distinctive to become the exclusive property of the agitator. Still trying to construct a portrait of his followers, the agitator resorts to nationalism described as the exclusive property of Christians, the "Christian Nationalists."[13]

The Christian is defined in negative terms: he is the non-Jew, who can remain a Christian only by never mingling with Jews. The mark of purity, by which the adherent can remain faithful, is a refusal to mix with the contaminating Jews. A Christian who associates with Jews is contemptuously referred to as "Shabes-goy";[14] such people are condemned as "those Gentiles to whom Christ referred as being 'two-fold more the child of hell' than the Jewish leaders of that Synagogue of Satan."[15]

To complement his notion of the Christian follower as one who is not a Jew. the agitator tries to adapt the Nazi notion of a pure Nordic race. The results are pathetically poor; all he can produce is a vague biological intimation in "Americans of the original species."[16] In the characterization "real Americans"[17] the abstract adjective *real* barely conceals the negative meaning of *non-nonreal*. What the agitator implies is that his adherents are all those who do not fall under any of the categories of the enemy. His elite or in-group is essentially negative; it depends for definition on those in the out-group. It is what the "other" is not, a pure residue. The very leveling of class differentiations and cultural distinctions involved in this image makes impossible any kind of specific or positive identification of his followers.

The agitator makes no genuine appeal to solidarity. Even when he addresses himself to the vast majority of "American Americans,"[18] he suggests that what unites them is the common danger they face in the Jew. By making their precarious situation their major sign of identification, he retains his manipulative power over them. Under the guise of granting his followers identity, the agitator denies it to them. He says in effect: If you belong to the common people you need not ask for something else because it is quite enough to be considered one of the common people rather than an enemy of the people. Anything else might expose you. Both he and his audience feel that the cement of our social structure is not love, solidarity, or friendship but the drive to survive, and in his appeal to his followers, as well as in his portrait of their characters, there is no room for solidarity. There is only fear.

Grassroots Anti-Intellectuals

That the agitator refers to his followers as common folk, a kind of "proletarian elite," might seem offhand to suggest that he seeks to disavow the antidemocratic implications of his discriminatory statements by the use of a well-tested device. But this is also a device that by its very nature often tends to transform democratic psychological patterns into totalitarian ones. Closely related to the common resentment against anyone who dares be different and hence implicitly directed against minority groups, it establishes conformism as a moral principle, a good in itself.

Seizing on the "simple folk" theme as a pretext for fostering an aggressively anti-intellectual attitude, the agitator describes his American Americans as a people of sound instincts and, he is happy to say, little sophistication. He suggests that, on one level, the conflict between his followers and the enemy is nothing but a clash between simple minds and wise guys, level-headed realists, and crazy sophisticates. He delights his followers by proclaiming his own lack of intellectuality:

> I do not understand political science, as an authority from an academic viewpoint. I am not familiar with the artistic masterpieces of Europe, but I do say this tonight: I understand the hearts of the American people.[19]

Implying that intellectual pursuits are inherently depraved, he refers contemptuously to "the parlors of the sophisticated, the intellectuals, the so-called academic minds."[20] Heavy is the responsibility of the "Scribes and Pharisees of the Twentieth Century . . . [who] provide a nation with its dominant propaganda including seasonal fashions in politics, religious attitudes, sub-standard ethics and half-caste morals."[21]

Here the agitator is, first of all, playing on the resentment of uneducated people against the educated, a resentment he often transforms into sneering anti-intellectualism. But in addition to this attitude, which the agitator can expect to find ready-made in his audience and merely inflates, he exploits another and at the moment perhaps more significant attitude: the modern disappointment with rationality. All the symbols of liberalistic enlightenment are the targets of his attack. Psychology, especially psychoanalysis, is singled out for vehement and sarcastic denunciation, for among other crimes, "by uncovering secrets of rich men and women," it wields " 'control' over the subject."[22] Offering typical patient "resistance" to psychoanalysis, the agitator scorns any suggestion that his audience of simple Americans might be frustrated. "'Frustration'? No wonder Freud is worshipped in certain quarters. Did he not invent a label that enables any suspect to take the offensive against his accusers?"[23] No, not frustration but sound, healthy instincts and common sense characterize his followers. They are not taken in by

> that old city-slick, tweedle-dee, tweedle-dum stuff.... We will come out with a crusading, militant America First Party and we are going to take this government out of the hands of these city-slickers and give it back to the people that still believe two plus two is four. God is in his Heaven, and the Bible is the Word.[24]

Theory, discussion, interchange of opinion—all this is futile, an impediment to the struggle for self-preservation. The situation is too urgent to permit the luxury of thought. Having discovered that "actions are more realistic than hypocritical catchwords,"[25] the agitator tells his followers that there is no point in wasting time in talk. As the result of anti-intellectualism, the speech-maker denounces speeches: his group "is not 'another organization.' We hold no banquets. We waste small time in speech making. *The Silver Legion* comes to Christian citizens who want ACTION."[26]

The agitator's doctrine of aggressive intolerance is represented as the "natural reactions of plain people to [having heard] the truth."[27] He hardly bothers to veil his function of releasing the emotions of those simple Americans who are his followers:

> Our people frequently do not express themselves because there are only a few of us who speak with abandon in times like this, but in the hearts of our people are pent-up emotions which go unexpressed because they fear their vocabularies are insufficient.[28]

The agitator, in praising the simple folk, praises only their humble and folky ways, in which the latent savagery and brutality that is both repressed and generated by modern culture, still manifests itself. He offers them little else.

Attracted by the promise of a new spiritual home, the audience actually gets the tautological assurance that Americans are Americans, and Christians Christians. The simple American is a member of an elite by virue of birth but in the last analysis, he can be defined only in negatives: he is a Christian because he is not a Jew; he is an American because he is not a foreigner; he is a simple fellow because he is not an intellectual. The only positive means the agitator has of identifying the Simple American is as a follower. The adherent who turned to the agitator in the vague hope of finding identity and status ends as more than ever an anonymous member of a characterless mass, a lonely cipher in an army of regimented ciphers.

Theme 19: Watchdogs of Order

Hypnotic Alertness

For all their strength, the Simple Americans are apathetic and lethargic, they are like a "slow, muscular, sleeping giant."[29] This fact fills the agitator with a kind of despair; he argues, implores, cajoles, shouts himself hoarse to arouse them to awareness of their danger: "O God! When will the American people awaken and snap out of their lethargy? When will they arouse themselves to the dangers which confront them internally as well as externally?"[30] He summons them to alertness: "Wake up, Americans! It is later than you think! ACT BEFORE IT IS TOO LATE!"[31]

Offhand, this call to alertness may seem like that of all other proponents of social change who also excoriate apathy and indifference. But the agitator's warnings and admonitions seem hardly to have any genuine relationship to a situation. Even the most trivial of occasions elicits the call to alertness: that "character assassins have smeared our two greatest heroes—Lindbergh and Rickenbacker—should be enough to wake up America."[32]

Significantly, the agitator never tries to justify his call to alertness by subsequent explanation, even of the most rudimentary kind. Although it is possible to detect signs of similarity between the agitator's call and religious revivalism, their actual functions are quite different. In a sermon the call to awareness is addressed to the soul of the individual, with the aim of strengthening his conscience or superego; likewise, the reformer as a rule endeavors to inculcate a stronger social sense among his adherents by lifting their concerns from the private to the general level. But the agitator, under the guise of pursuing a similar purpose, actually invites his listeners not to change themselves spiritually or socially but simply to place all blame, all sin, on the external enemy. He asks them not to become more conscious of the causes of their difficulties but simply to give vent to their feelings: "I challenge all true Americans today to come out from your place of hiding, express yourselves, give vent to your opinions, stand squarely upon your feet. . . . America awake!"[33]

In such direct appeals to the people to cease being "very patient and good-natured,"[34] in such warnings that "long enough we have been apathetic,"[35] and in such direct statements as "That's the way I like my people to be, angry,"[36] the agitator defines the alertness of his Simple Americans as something that is the opposite of alertness. They are invited, not to organize rational responses but to act out their impulses. The agitator plays on his audience's predisposition to seek escape from rigid psychological controls. People want unconsciously to "give in," to cease being individuals in the traditional sense of self-sustaining and self-controlled units. The ability to control oneself reflects a more basic ability to compete with others and thereby determine one's economic and spiritual fate. But today the social pressures to which each individual is subjected are so overwhelming that he must yield to them both economically and psychologically. He must act according to the pattern of conformist social behavior rather than according to the needs of his individual personality. The social and cultural pressures to which he is subjected become the determining factors in molding his personality. As a result, the very diminution of his "ego" decreases his ability and his willingness to exercise self-control. Hysteria, an extreme expression of this lack of self-control and a psychological trait that is rapidly spreading through all of society, is the audience reaction on which the agitator banks when he calls for displays of anger and emotion. When the agitator so insistently demands such outbreaks, he lifts an already tottering taboo from the conscience of his audience and suggests to its members that an abandonment of self-control has by now become the socially correct mode of behavior.

Because he was the one who released the instinctual urges of his listeners, the agitator is in an especially favorable position to control and manipulate them. The alerted Simple Folk rush hysterically in obedience to the agitator's call. Where do they go? Responding constantly, they are kept in a perpetual state of mobilization and are not given an opportunity to collect their thoughts. What takes place is not an awakening but rather a kind of hypnotic trance that is perpetuated by constant admonitions to alertness.

Just as the enemy never rests—"certain Jewish organizations are working day and night to open America's borders to five million Jewish refugees"[37]—so the Simple Americans are asked to be on guard constantly and indefatigably. The audience is driven to submit to the agitator's incessant harangues until it is ready to accept everything he says in order to gain a moment's rest. Once aroused, the simple folk "are known to be *pure hell!*"[38] but the very way in which they have been aroused merely perpetuates their inferior status.

"Let's Go"

In designating his followers as Simple Americans, the agitator no doubt seeks to give them a sense of superiority and strength, yet, as we have seen, the image of the adherent that he constructs is singularly lacking in positive gratification. Themes like the "Endogamic Community" and "Housecleaning" suggest some sort of spiritual gratification, but even these indulgences and gratifications prove to be essentially negative. At no point does the agitator promise any substantial improvement in his adherent's status. Perhaps, then, we might infer that the agitator is appealing to the notion that the poor man should be content with his lot on the dubious grounds that he is somehow morally superior to both the rich and those who rebel against the rich. Such an inference is only partly correct.

When the agitator appeals nostalgically to the "good old times," he can at most be vaguely sentimental—hardly an attitude by means of which to solidify his followers in his movement or to present them with a satisfactory image of themselves. It is difficult to believe that "dreams of little white houses with blue roofs, built near singing streams, with sheep and cattle grazing in quiet pasture land"[39] or the maudlin account of a party where "the women baked yummy cakes, sold refreshments, etc. We all sang and had a jolly, sociable and inspiring time besides. . . . Rich people are noticeable by their absence in this cause"[40] represent the sole positive stimulus available to the agitator. For somewhere, somehow the agitator must give his followers the feeling that his calls to alertness have some reality basis and that by heeding his appeals they will get something worthwhile.

One possible clue may be found in the extreme aridity of the agitator's statements. Although he does not explicitly advocate a dangerous and frugal life, as the Fascists did to some extent, his dubious and often directly negative attitude toward material benefits and pleasures suggests that what he does dangle before his followers' eyes is the prospect of participating in a Spartan elite—an elite without special happiness or privileges but with greater access to the centers of social power. The American American is always seen as surrounded by dangerous and cunning enemies, and all that he can do is to use social power as a means of self-preservation. The agitator intimates to his audience that the thing that matters is not so much possession of goods as social control; once you are "in," you are likely to get a share of what can be had. Such a promise of a share in actual social control may serve as a very powerful antidote to the pervasive and frustrating sense of exclusion from which his audience suffers. The agitator, unlike all traditional advocates of social change, does not promise a good society, he does not tell his followers that there will be delicious fruits to be had once power is attained. All he tells them is that power in itself is worthwhile.

Not the traditional "gravy" promised by politicans, but power construed as the right directly to exercise violence is what the agitator offers his followers. And here again the agitator is perhaps less unrealistic than might appear offhand. By permitting his followers to indulge in acts of violence against the enemy group, the agitator offers them the prospect of serving as semiprivileged agents of a social domination actually exercised by others. But the followers nonetheless do share in the reality of power, for power ultimately is grounded on force, and they are to be the dispensers of brute force. True, the followers are to get only the dregs of power, the dirty part of the game—but this they will get. And hence their feeling that "it's the right of Christian Americans to be the master in the United States of America,"[41] has some psychological justification. Though they have only the prospect of becoming watchdogs of order in the service of other, more powerful groups, the watchdogs do exert a kind of subsidiary power over the helpless enemy.

This promise of sadistic gratification is relayed through linguistic stimuli. Intimating that the act of venting pent-up emotions on a scrapegoat is, if not quite desirable, something natural and hence unavoidable, the agitator says that "good Americans are boiling inside and some of them, unfortunately, are looking about for something, perhaps a group on which to focus their attention, on which to lay the blame for conditions."[42]

He clearly indicates the direction in which they are supposed to look: "Liquidate the millions of burocrats . . . kick out the top heavy

Jew majority, many foreign born that NOW dictate and direct our domestic and foreign policies."[43]

The outbreak of violence is justified by the agitator in legal terms by being implicitly compared to a police action: "The rank and file of sober, sincere, and peaceable citizens [should] pull them [New-Dealers] out of power and lock them up, pronto, as their crimes may be proven."[44]

As justification for such calls to violence, the agitator paints vivid pictures of the enemy's brutality, for though the group is seen as inhuman, its members are allowed one all too human characteristic: enjoyment of cruelty. They "would actually and physically crucify Father Coughlin . . . there is in their hearts a sadistic thirst for blood."[45] They have an apparently unquenchable thirst for blood; they would like "to drink the blood of every German"[46] and "with their own foul tongues, they would lap up the blood of their own critics."[47]

Blood and Death

Perhaps the most effective though indirect method by which the agitator encourages violence is his consistent use of images that condition the audience to accept violence as "natural" and respectable. In his world murder and death are invariable parts of the landscape. His threats are couched in the language of brutal action, of explosions of anger that sweep everything aside. He predicts that the enemy's activity will "dynamite a Boulder Dam of public reaction which will create a domestic crisis unequaled in the history of our people."[48] The people ought to march on Washington "with monkey wrenches and lead pipe"[49] once his ideas have begun to "ignite in the public mind."[50] He complains that he is

> smeared in the press, boycotted, liquidated, described as a menace, fired from his job, relieved of his command, viewed with suspicion, editorialized against, hounded with gossip, preyed on by character assassins, ripped from gut to nose, he must be socially disemboweled, economically wrecked, burned out with the sulphur of editorial excoriation, banished if possible, exiled wherever practical, scorned, branded as psychopathic, isolated as one of the lunatic fringe.[51]

This torrent of words exemplifies a basic function of modern agitation: rehearsal. The verbal fury of the agitator is only a rehearsal of real fury.

Can his followers then have any qualms about the retaliatory methods they use against the enemy? For against such a background of enemy ruthlessness, in an atmosphere that reeks of cruelty and murder, the sadistic urges of both agitator and follower are unloosed. Perhaps unconsciously and perhaps not, the agitator slips in an anticipatory description of his followers' cruelty: "We pushed you out of Coney Island, Rockaway, Long Beach and we will push you outta here—out into the ocean."[52] He loves to imagine how fearful and cowardly the enemy is: "Winchell is perhaps best known for his physical cowardice . . . afraid to pass an undertaking parlor by himself . . . terrified at the smell of embalming fluid."[53]

Indulging in verbal equivalents of the violence he evokes, the agitator wishes he "could write messages that would burn the trousers off the brazen intolerants who have the unmitigated gall to criticize us."[54] Or he gloats at the thought that "many Americans of the original species would like to see the Hon. Hans von Kaltenborn broadcast with his bare feet on a hot brick."[55] And he promises that "there'll be some fat, greasy scalps hanging on the wall."[56]

In the guise of a warning that the destruction of the enemy will not be fun, he promises fun, and while urging restraint he spurs his followers to violence: "Hanging hordes of Jews in apple orchards, or even watching the cracking of their Communist front with satisfaction, has nothing to do with yanking this country from its devil of a MESS!"[57] Or in the guise of a little joke, he continues to urge violence: "Next time, let's plow under the international bankers instead of the pigs and cotton."[58]

A favorite symbol of sadism, the delighted description of whipping, also occurs in agitation:

> Christ, we recall, took the cord of his garment and physically lashed the money changers out of the portico of the sacred Temple in Jerusalem. Was Christ precipitate? Are we to be more "Christian" than Christ? . . . Let's go![59]

> Reaching macabre depths of perversity and sadism, he adds: "So you might as well start adjusting your thinking to the inhuman orgasm that's ahead, before America singes her Locust-Swarm savagely."[60]

The Elder Brother

By encouraging such sadistic fantasies the agitator does not, like most political leaders, appear in the role of the restraining or moralizing father but rather as the elder brother who leads the small-fry gang in its juvenile escapades. Yet it would be erroneous to infer that he preaches free and wild joy in aggression, for with every gesture that urges his audience to indulge in violence, he reminds his followers, no matter how indirectly, that their aggression involves the forbidden, that they are still weak and can free themselves from the enemy's tyranny only by submitting unconditionally to his leadership. In the anticipated hunt, the followers can expect no spoils: they must be satisfied with the hunt itself.

Though they are destined to be the watchdogs of order tomorrow, today they are still weak: "Do not think for a moment that it will be easy—or fun."[61] The blending of strength and weakness that characterizes the agitator's image of the enemy also holds for his followers. Like the enemy conspirators, the followers must shun the light of day, for they are always in danger of attack by the enemy. Here, as in so many other instances, the image of the adherent is merely an inversion of the image of the enemy. The agitator confesses to this weakness:

> A man said to me, "Come to Houston and talk to my friends." I went over there and there were about one hundred of them, and when I got over there I was supposed to have a meeting at a public place, but they said, "We are going to have it out in one of the houses because we are afraid of the reprisals of the New Deal if we held it in a place where our names are known."[62]

So the agitator, for all his claims to the support of the overwhelming majority of the people, has no recourse but to turn to conspiracies. He urges his followers to form "platoons of 25 persons that are pliable. They can be suddenly thrown into action in their respective districts in the work of teaching the principles of social justice to others."[63]

The agitator's gift to his audience—his permission to indulge in violence—is a Trojan horse. Even the promised violence is hard to deliver, even that one last shred that might give some measure of positive personality to the image of the adherent turns out to be illusory. All that remains is the immediate condition of constantly renewed excitement and terror; the followers are allowed no rest, they must constantly ward off enemy attacks that never occur, they are called to the most heroic and self-sacrificing acts of violence that never take place. In the end the follower again becomes an "innocent bystander" who is the most deeply involved accomplice.

The adherent is nothing but an inverted reflection of the enemy. He remains a frustrated underdog, and all the agitator does is to mobilize his aggressive impulses against the enemy. The underdog becomes watchdog and bloodhound, while yet remaining essentially an underdog, for the most he can do is to react to external threats. The image of the adherent thus serves indirectly to condition the audience to authoritarian discipline.

Notes

1. SJ, Mar. 4, 1940, p. 19
2. Smith, New York, Oct. 20, 1936, meeting.
3. Smith, New York, Oct. 20, 1936, meeting.
4. CF, June, 1942, p. 14.
5. Phelps, Los Angeles, Aug. 14, 1941, radio.
6. Smith, Cleveland, May 11, 1943, meeting.
7. Phelps, Los Angeles, Aug. 18, 1940, radio.
8. AID, July 24, 1939, p. 1.
9. AP, Feb., 1944, p. 9.
10. Smith, *"Stop Treason,"* radio address, p. 3.
11. Kamp, *With Lotions of Love . . .* p. 4.
12. Phelps, Los Angeles, Aug. 3, 1941, radio.
13. CF, Feb., 1946, p. 714.
14. BR, Feb. 26, 1945, p. 4.
15. AID, June 2, 1942, p. 3.
16. AP, Feb., 1945, p. 3.
17. Smith, *"Mice or Men,"* radio address, p. 1.
18. Kamp, *Vote CIO . . . and Get a Soviet America,* p. 6.
19. Smith, New York, Oct. 20, 1936, meeting.
20. Smith, St. Louis, Mar. 25, 1944, meeting.
21. AP, Aug., 1944, p. 1.
22. AID, May 5, 1941, p. 2.
23. AP, Feb., 1944, p. 13.
24. Smith, Detroit, Mar. 19, 1943, meeting.
25. Coughlin, Speech on Mar. 26, 1939, reprinted in *Why Leave Our Own,* p. 161.
26. LIB, Oct. 14, 1933, p. 11.
27. CF, Jan., 1948.
28. Smith, Detroit, Mar. 22, 1943, meeting.
29. Smith, *"The Next President of the U.S.,"* radio address, p. 4.
30. Phelps, *An Appeal to Americans,* p. 22.
31. Sanctuary, *New Deal is Marxian Sabotage,* p. 2.
32. CF, Feb., 1943, p. 152.
33. Smith, *"Which Way, America?"* radio address, p. 1.
34. Smith, *"Labor on the Cross,"* radio address, p. 1.
35. Coughlin, Newark, N.J., July 30, 1939, radio.
36. Smith in an interview with the New York Post, quoted in E. A. Piller, *Time Bomb,* New York, 1945, p. 124.
37. CF, Mar., 1945, p. 530.
38. LIB, Dec. 30, 1933, p. 12.
39. Phelps, Los Angeles, July 30, 1941, radio.
40. PRB, Oct. 8, 1942, p. 4.

41.   McWilliams, New York, Aug. 3, 1940, street corner.
42.   Phelps, Los Angeles, Aug. 14, 1941, radio.
43.   X, Nov. 21, 1947, p. 2.
44.   RC, Apr. 21, 1941, p. 16.
45.   CF, May, 1942, p. 4.
46.   CF, Nov., 1944, p. 475.
47.   AP, Aug., 1944, p. 1.
48.   Smith, Detroit, Mar. 22, 1943, meeting.
49.   Mote, *Testimony Before Senate Military Committee*, p. 3.
50.   AID, Jan. 13, 1941, p. 1.
51.   CF, Feb., 1946, p. 710.
52.   SJ, Nov. 24, 1941, p. 14.
53.   Kamp, *With Lotions of Love . . .* p. 29.
54.   Phelps, Los Angeles, Aug. 10, 1941.
55.   AP, Feb., 1945, p. 3.
56.   Coughlin, quoted in A. B. Magil, *l.c.*, p. 15.
57.   LIB, Feb. 14, 1938, p. 5.
58.   Smith, Los Angeles, Nov. 3, 1945, meeting.
59.   SJ, Dec. 4, 1939, p. 6.
60.   LIB, Jan. 14, 1939, p. 9.
61.   SJ, Nov. 27, 1939, p. 6.
62.   Smith, New York, Oct. 20, 1936, meeting.
63.   SJ, June 13, 1938, p. 23.

9

Self-Portrait of the Agitator

The democratic leader usually tries to present himself as both similar to and different from his followers: similar in that he has common interests with them; different in that he has special talents for representing those interests. The agitator tries to maintain the same sort of relationship to his audiences, but instead of emphasizing the identity of his interests with those of his followers, he depicts himself as one of the plain folk, who thinks, lives, and feels like them. In agitation this suggestion of proximity and intimacy takes the place of identification of interests.

The nature of the difference between leader and follower is similarly changed. Although the agitator intimates that he is intellectually and morally superior to his audience, he rests his claim to leadership primarily on the suggestion of his innate predestination. He does resort to such traditional American symbols of leadership as the indefatigable businessman and the rugged frontiersman, but these are overshadowed by the image he constructs of himself as a suffering martyr who, as a reward for his sacrifices, deserves special privileges and unlimited ascendancy over his followers. The agitator is not chosen by his followers but presents himself as their prechosen leader—prechosen by himself on the basis of a mysterious inner call, and prechosen as well by the enemy as a favorite target of persecution. One of the plain folk, he is yet far above them; reassuringly close, he is yet infinitely aloof.

Although spokesmen for liberal and radical causes refrain, for a variety of reasons, from thrusting their own personalities into the foreground of their public appeals, the agitator does not hesitate to advertise himself. He does not depend on a buildup manufactured by subordinates and press agents, but does the job himself. He could hardly trust anyone else to paint his self-image in such glowing colors. As the good fellow who has nothing to hide, whose effusiveness and garrulousness know no limit, he does not seem to be inhibited by considerations of good taste from openly displaying his private life and his opinions about himself.

This directness of self-expression is particularly suitable for one who aspires to be the spokesman for those suffering from social malaise. The agitator seems to realize almost intuitively that objective argumentation and impersonal discourse would only intensify the feelings of despair, isolation, and distrust from which his listeners suffer and from which they long to escape. Such a gleeful display of his personality serves as an ersatz assertion of individuality. Part of the secret of his charisma as a leader is that he presents the image of a self-sufficient personality to his followers. If they are deprived of such a blessing, then at least they can enjoy it at second remove in their leader.

Those who suffer from malaise always want to pour their hearts out, but because of their inhibitions and lack of opportunities they seldom succeed. Conceiving their troubles as individual and inner maladjustments, they want only a chance to be "understood," to clear up the "misunderstandings" that others have about them. On this need the agitator bases his own outpouring of personal troubles. When he talks about himself the agitator vicariously gratifies his followers' wish to tell the world of their troubles. He lends an aura of sanction and validity to the desire of his followers endlessly to complain, and thus his seemingly sincere loquacity strengthens his rapport with them. His trials are theirs, his successes also theirs. Through him they live.

By seemingly taking his listeners into his confidence and talking "man to man" to them, the agitator achieves still another purpose: he dispels any fear they may have that he is talking above their heads or against their institutionalized ways of life. He is the elder brother straightening things out for them, not a subversive who would destroy the basic patterns of their lives. The enemy of all established values, the spokesman of the apocalypse, and the carrier of disaffection creates the atmosphere of a family party in order to spread his doctrine the more effectively. Blending protestations of his weakness with intimations of his strength, he whines and boasts at the same time. Cannot one who is so frank about his humility also afford to be equally frank about his superiority?

The agitator's references to himself thus fall into two groups or themes: one covering his familiarity and the other his aloofness, one in a minor key establishing him as a "great little man," and the other in a major key as a bullet-proof martyr who despite his extraordinary sufferings always emerges victorious over his enemies.

Theme 20: Great Little Man

Unlike those idealists who, sacrificing comfort in behalf of a lofty social goal, "go to the people," the agitator comes from the people; in fact, he is always eager to show that socially he is almost indistinguishable from the great mass of American citizens. "I am an underdog who has suffered through the depression like most of the people."[1] Like millions of other Americans, he is "one of [those] plain old time, stump grubbing, liberty loving, apple cider men and women."[2] Yet he is always careful to make it clear that he is one of the endogamic elite, "an American-born citizen whose parents were American born and whose parents' parents were American born. I think that's far enough back."[3] There is no danger that anyone will discover he had an impure grandmother.

Not only is he one of the people, but his most ardent wish is always to remain one and enjoy the pleasures of private existence. He hates to be in the limelight, for he is "an old-fashioned American" who, he cheerfully admits, does not even know his "way around in the circles of high society at Washington."[4] If it were really up to him and if his conscience didn't tell him otherwise, he'd spend all his time on his favorite hobby: "If we had a *free* press in America I doubt if Gerald Smith would publish *The Cross and the Flag*. I am sure I wouldn't publish AMERICA PREFERRED. In my spare time I'd play golf."[5] Even when he finally does seek office, it is only after a heart-rending conflict and after he has received the permission of his parents: "First, I would have to get the consent of my Christian mother and father, because years ago I had promised them that I would not seek office."[6] And on those rare occasions when he can escape from his duties for a few minutes of relaxation, he proudly tells his listeners about it: "Well, friends, Lulu and I managed to get time out to attend the annual carnival and bazaar of the Huntington Park Chapter of the Indoor Sports Club."[7]

Even at this rather uncomplicated level of identification the agitator is ambiguous. By his very protestations that he is quite the same as the mass of Americans he smuggles in hints of his exceptional status. Public life, he intimates, is a bother, and whoever deserts his private pleasures in its behalf must have some good reason for doing so. By constantly apologizing for his abandonment of private life and his absorption in public life, the agitator suggests that there are special provinces and unusual responsibilities that are limited to the uniquely endowed. If one of the plain people, such as he, gains access to such privileges and burdens, then it must surely be because of his unusual talents. He has embarked on a difficult task for which he is specially qualified, and therefore his followers owe him gratitude, admiration, and obedience.

A Gentle Soul

Although he is, by virtue of his special talents, a man who has risen out of the common people, the agitator remains a kindly, gentle soul— folksy, good-natured, golden-hearted. Far be it from him to hold any malice against any fellow human being, for "if we must hate, let us hate hate."[8] Nor is he "the kind of person who carries hatred or bitterness for any length of time . . . In spite of all I have gone through . . . I have never lost my sense of humor, my ability to laugh, even right into the face of seeming disaster."[9]

Like all other Americans, he is a good and solicitous father to his children, and in a moment of difficulty appeals touchingly to his friends for help: "My son, 9½ years old, is pestering me, wanting a bicycle. Get in touch with me, please, if anyone knows where I could obtain a second-hand bicycle very cheap."[10] But his virtues come out most clearly in his role as model husband. He regales his audience with bits of intimate family dialogue: "I said one day to my sweet wife."[11] And even he, the would-be dictator, does not hesitate to admit that the little, or not so little, wife is the boss at home: "If I don't look out I'll be looking for a boss' lap on which to sit and chew gum. Well, Lulu's the boss and, having gained about 25 pounds during the past six months, she has plenty of lap on which to sit."[12]

As he makes the rounds of his meetings, his faithful wife accompanies him: "A few weeks ago found Mrs. Winrod and me spending Sunday at Sioux City, Iowa, holding meetings in the Billy Sunday Memorial Tabernacle."[13] And when he wishes to express his gratitude to his followers, it is again as the gentle soul, the faithful family man: "The wife and I are very grateful for the prayerful letters, kind words, and sums remitted so far."[14] So sweet and lovable are both his personality and his family life that he offers family pictures for sale: "How many have received 1. Calendar of Mrs. Smith, me and Jerry? 2. A copy of my 'undelivered speech'?"[15]

Troubles Shared

One of the agitator's favorite themes is his economic troubles, about which he speaks to complete strangers with perfect ease:

> I must confide to you without reservation . . . I have spent everything I have; I have surrendered every possession I had in this world in

order to carry on this fight. I will not be able to borrow any more money; I have nothing left to sell.[16]

Another agitator complains that by engaging in political activity he has embarked on "a gamble with the security of my wife and children at stake."[17] And still another offers the audience a detailed financial statement:

> The taxes on my Kenilworth home are unpaid and there are some $1800 in outstanding bills accrued since I stopped depleting my few remaining securities, although I have paid light, phone and groceries . . . his [her husband's] refusal to give us any of the milk check income from my farm, his continuing to spend this income while associating with the woman he brought to sleep in my own bed at my farm, finally made it necessary to take some legal steps to protect the family.[18]

The agitator is just as frank about the condition of his health as about his financial or marital contretemps. We find him making great sacrifices that cause him to commiserate with himself: "I come home and say to Mrs. Smith. 'How does this old heart of mine keep up?' . . . But I know how men like that go—they go all of a sudden."[19] And even when his heart does not bother him, his teeth do: "The last time I saw Charlie Hudson, he still had been unable to afford to get needed dental work done. His wife takes roomers."[20] His afflications threatened to handicap his political work:

> My dentist informed me I must have four teeth removed at once. I don't mind that so much as I do the fact that I may come on the air tomorrow, after the teeth have been extracted, and sound like a dear old gentleman who has been drawing old-age pension for forty years or more.[21]

By multiplying references to his family, his health, and his finances, the agitator tries to create an atmosphere of homey intimacy. This device has immediate, gratifying implications. The personal touch, the similarity between agitator and audience, and the intimate revelations of "human interest" provide emotional compensation for those whose life is cold and dreary, especially for those who must live a routinized and atomized existence.

Equally gratifying to listeners may be the fact that such revelations help satisfy their curiosity, a universal feature of contemporary mass culture. It may be due to the prevalent feeling that one has to have "inside information" that comes "from the horse's mouth" in order to get along in modern society. Perhaps, too, this curiosity is derived from an unconscious infantile desire to glimpse the forbidden life of the grown-ups—a desire closely related to that of revealing and enjoying scandals. When the listener is treated as an insider his libido is gratified, and it matters little to him whether he hears revelations about crimes and orgies supposedly indulged in by the enemy or about the increase in weight of the agitator's wife. He has been allowed to become one of those "in the know."

Public Privacy

When the agitator indulges in his uninhibited displays of domesticity and intimacy, he does so not as a private person but as a public figure. This fact endows his behavior with considerable ambivalence. His lyrical paeans in praise of the pleasures of private existence imply *ipso facto* a degrading of this privacy when he exposes it to public inspection. This gesture has the double meaning of an invasion of the agitator's private life by his public life and of his public life by his private life. In this way the traditional liberal differentiation between the two is made to seem obsolete and in any case untenable. Privacy is no longer possible in this harsh social world, except as a topic of public discussion.

Finally, these revelations of private life serve to enhance the agitator's stature as a public figure, who, it has already been suggested, vicariously symbolizes the repressed individualities of his adherents. He establishes his identity with the audience by telling it of his financial troubles and other kinds of failures, but he also underlines the fact of his success. He has risen from the depths in which the followers still find themselves; in contrast to them, he has managed to integrate his public and private personalities. The proof of this is simple enough: is he not talking to the followers and are they not listening to him? As a symbol of his followers' longings, the agitator centers all attention on himself, and soon his listeners may forget that he is discussing not public issues but his qualifications for leadership.

That the agitator simultaneously stresses his own weakness, that he pictures himself as all too human, does not impair the effectiveness of his attempt at self-exaltation. By the very fact that he admits his weaknesses while stressing his powers, he implies that the followers too can, if to a lesser extent, become strong once they surrender their private existence to the public movement. They need but follow the path of the great little man.

Theme 21: Bullet-Proof Martyr

Aside from his remarkable readiness to share his troubles with his fellow men, what are the qualities that distinguish the great little man from the rest of the plain folk and make him fit to be one of "those ... who lead"?[22] Here again the agitator is ready to answer the question. Although the agitator calls himself an old-fashioned Christian American, Christian humility is hardly one of his outstanding virtues. For all his insistence that he is one of the common folk, he does not hesitate to declare that he is an exceptionally gifted man who knows and even admires his own talent.

That he has no difficulty in overcoming conventional reticence about such matters is due not merely to his quite human readiness to talk about himself but also to the fact that his prominence is not merely his own doing. As he has emphasized, his natural inclination is not to lead humanity; he would rather play golf. But he cannot help it—forces stronger and more imperious than his own will push him to leadership. Both because of his innate dynamism and because he has been singled out by the enemy, the mantle of leadership, like it or not, falls on his shoulders.

The Inner Call

Suggesting that his activity is prompted by sacred command, the agitator speaks of himself as the "voice of the great unorganized and helpless masses."[23] He is "giving vocal expression to the thoughts that you have been talking about around your family tables."[24] But it also comes from holier regions: "Like John the Baptist." the agitator is "living just for the sweet privilege of being a voice in the wilderness."[25] As such, the agitator does not hesitate to compare himself to Christ: "Put down the Crown of Thorns on me."[26] He sees himself continuing the work of the "Divine Savior."[27]

But for all his suggestions that he has a divine responsibility, the agitator does not pretend to bring any startling new revelation. He does not claim to make his audience aware of a reality that they see only partially; he does not claim to raise the level of their consciousness. All he does is to "say what you all want to say and haven't got the guts to say it."[28] What "others think ... privately," the agitator says "publicly."[29] And for this purpose he is specially talented: as one agitator says of another, he delivered what was "perhaps the greatest address we have ever had on Christian statesmanship."[30]

Like a new Luther, he bellows defiance of established powers without regard to consequences: "I am going to say some things this afternoon that some people won't like, but I cannot help it, I must speak the truth."[31] Nothing can "halt and undo the innermost convictions of stalwart sons of Aryan blood,"[32] not even the ingratitude of those who spurn him: "Nevertheless, there I will stand demanding social justice for all even though some of the ill-advised whom I am endeavoring to defend will take a pot-shot at me from the rear."[33]

Nor is the agitator's courage purely spiritual:

> If the Gentiles of the nation back up Pelley now in his challenge to the usurpers of American liberties, they are going to get a "break" that they have never dreamed possible till Pelley showed the spunk to defy the nepotists.[34]

The agitator, aware of both his qualifications and his courage, knows that

> when the history of America is written . . . concerning the preservation of the American way of life. I am going to be thankful that in the day when men were cowardly and overcautious and crawled under the bed and allowed themselves to be bulldozed by a bunch of wire-whiskered Communists and atheists and anti-God politicians, that there was one man by the name of Gerald L. K. Smith that had the courage to be an old-fashioned, honest to God, Christian American![35]

And the agitator knows too that his courage extends to somewhat smaller matters as well:

> When I went to the Auditorium, although it was very cold, probably five degrees below zero—twenty degrees the first time, five degrees the second time—the place was packed and every inch of standing room was taken. I had to pass through a picket line, one of those vicious picket lines organized by Reds and enemies of our meeting there.[36]

It is this blending of seriousness and unseriousness, of the sublime crown of thorns and the toothache that characterizes the agitator's approach to composing his self-portrait as well as to the other themes of his speeches and writings. He is both the little man suffering the usual hardships and the prophet of truth: Walter Mitty and Jeremiah rolled up into one.

Such an indiscriminate mixture of trivial and sublime symbols might appear blasphemous or simply disgusting, but the agitator seems to count on a different kind of reaction. Instead of imposing on his listeners the difficult task of following a saint, a task that might after all cause them to feel that they too must assume some of the traits of sainthood, he gratifies them by dragging the lofty notions of sainthood down to a humdrum, *kleinbürgerlich* level. The followers thereby are offered an object of admiration, the image of the desanctified saint, that is closer to their own level of feeling and perception. The agitator imposes no strain on them.

There is still another gratification for the audience in the agitator's narcissistic outbursts of self-praise. A courageous and self-reliant man might be disgusted with the spectacle of someone celebrating himself as the repository of all the manly virtues, but people who are acclimated to self-denial and self-hatred are paradoxically attracted by the selfish narcissist. As a leading psychoanalyst puts it: "This narcissistic behavior which gives the dependent persons no hope for any real love arouses their readiness for identification" (O. Fenichel, *The Psychoanalytical Theory of Neurosis* [New York: Norton, 1945], p. 510). Accordingly, the agitator does not count on the support of people capable of self-criticism or self-reliance; he turns to those who constantly yearn for magical aids to buttress their personalities.

Persecuted Innocence

Like any advocate of social change the agitator appeals to social frustration and suffering, but in his output there is a striking contrast between the vagueness with which he refers to the sufferings of his listeners as a social group and the vividness with which he documents his personal trials. He speaks as though the malaise resulted in tangible hardship in him and him alone. His trials and ordeals are truly extraordinary, almost superhuman, and by comparison the complaints of his followers seem merely to refer to minor nuisances, insignificant reflections of his glorious misfortunes. He is the chosen martyr of a great cause: himself. As they compare their lot to his, the followers cannot but feel that they are almost like safe spectators watching a battle between the forces of evil and their own champion of virtue.

In building up this image of persecuted innocence, the agitator uses religious symbols. He "has come through the most heart-rending Gethsemane, I believe, of any living man in America today,"[37] and he does not hesitate to compare himself to the early Christian martyrs: "Many leaders . . . sneered at Father Coughlin and turned thumbs down on the Christian Fronters. as did the Patrician population of Rome turn their thumbs down on the Christian slave martyrs."[38]

But these religious associations are only decorations for ordeals that are strictly secular; the agitator's sufferings are of this world. Here he runs into a difficulty. In actual fact, he has met with little interference from the public authorities. (Except for those involved in the war-time sedition trial and one agitator convicted as an enemy agent, the American agitators have suffered only from exposures and criticism.) Yet he realizes that as a man with a mission, he must be persecuted. If the past will yield no evidence, perhaps the future will, for who is to deny him the right to premonitions:

> I don't know what is going to happen to me. All I ask you to do is, don't be surprised at anything. If I am thrown in jail, if I am indicted, if I am smeared, if I am hurt physically, no matter what it might be, don't be surprised at anything, because everything in the calendar is now being attempted. . . . I am glad to make that sacrifice.[39]

One reason that the agitator has difficulty in specifying the persecutions to which he is subjected is that his enemies work in secret. They force him to the most surreptitious behavior: "I, an American, must sneak in darkness to the printer to have him print my booklet and to get it out to the people like a bootlegger."[40] He is beset by vague dangers that are difficult to pin down: "One of these newspapermen, according to another newspaperman, is said to have predicted somewhat as follows: 'Two Jews from England were over here to see that Hudson does not get home alive.'"[41]

But when the agitator gets down to bedrock, it becomes clear that what he most resents is public criticism, which he describes as "smearing" and "intimidation." He complains that "Jewish New-Dealers in the Congress . . . started a mighty ball rolling to smear Pelley from the scene."[42] And "because I dare to raise my voice foreigners are intimidating me and trying to get me off the air."[43] Nor does he feel happy that "frequently we have heard it prophesied over the radio by such noble patriots as Walter Winchell and others, that we were about to be incarcerated in concentration camps."[44]

A Slight Case of Murder

However insubstantial the evidence he can summon for his martyrdom, the agitator, it must be admitted, works it for all it is worth. He continually suggests that he has embarked on a dangerous career and that he is actually risking his life. The threat never abates, as we shall see in tracing it during the course of one agitator's statements over a period of twelve years.

As early as October 1936. he realized that his death warrant had been signed. Like his political boss, who was assassinated, "it may cost my life."[45] And not without reason: "Ten threats came to me within twenty-four hours here in New York City."[46]

Three years later these threats of murder were still harassing him: "I continued to receive all sorts of threats against my life."[47]

By 1942 the rather slow-working murderers had a definite objective: to keep him out of the Senate. "I am convinced that there are men in America who would rather commit murder than see me in the United States Senate."[48] Other murderers, or perhaps the same ones, found his literary output more objectionable than the possibility of his becoming a senator: "I have been warned that I will not live to complete this series of articles."[49]

Half a year passes, and the enemy is still intent on murder. "A certain set of ruthless men in this nation have actually called for my assassination."[50] The murderers seem finally to have worked up enough energy or courage to come within striking distance:

> I held a meeting down in Akron, Ohio, one time and my Committee resigned the afternoon of the meeting. . . . I had to walk into that armory alone. . . . I walked from the hotel over to this place which seated about 6,000 people alone, and when I got over there, the place was packed. . . . I walked down the center aisle, walked right up to the microphone and the first thing I said was this, "There are men in this room who would like to see me killed tonight."[51]

Yet even then there is no record of the murderers doing anything. Two more years went by and by the spring of 1945 the still-healthy agitator noted that the threat to his life had become so real that it was even confirmed by police authorities: "Shortly before the end of the meeting I received a message from the police detectives to the effect that they were convinced that there was a definite plot to do me great injury, perhaps kill me."[52] Nothing seems to have come of that danger, but by the summer of the same year the agitator reported that "people who know what is going on are convinced that a plan is on foot to actually get me killed at the earliest possible moment."[53] As of the moment of writing, the agitator remains alive and unharmed, never having once been the victim of assault or assassination. As late as April 29, 1948, he still maintained that he was the object of an attempt on his life, this time by means of "arsenic poisoning."[54]

That he has no genuine factual data to support his charges does not seem to disturb the agitator: he persists in believing that an evil force is out to get him. His recital of fears, smearing, premonitions, anonymous letters—all this adds up to the familiar picture of paranoia. The paranoiac's conviction that he is persecuted cannot be logically refuted because it is itself extralogical. In agitation the leader acts out, as it were, a complete case history of persecution mania before his listeners, whose own inclinations to regard themselves as the target of persecution by mysterious forces is thus sanctioned and encouraged. Nevertheless it is the agitator who remains at the center of the stage; it is on him that all the imaginary enemy blows fall. By symbolically taking upon himself all the burdens of social suffering, he creates unconscious guilt feelings among his followers, which he can later exploit by demanding their absolute devotion as recompense for his self-sacrifice. And because the enemy exacts the heaviest penalty from him, he has the implicit right to claim the highest benefits once the enemy is defeated. Similarly, because the enemy singles him out for persecution, he has the right to engage in terroristic reprisals. All of these consequences follow from the agitator's self-portrait as martyr.

But simultaneously the agitator, for all the dangers to which he is exposed, does manage to survive and continue his work. He is not merely the martyr but also the remarkably efficient leader, and on both counts he deserves special obedience. Because he is both more exposed and better equipped than his followers, his claims to leadership are doubly vindicated.

The Money-Minded Martyr

There are many indications that, at its present stage at least, American agitation is a racket as well as a political movement. To what extent the agitator actually depends on his followers' financial contributions it is difficult to say with any degree of certainty. In any event, he does not account for the use of the money he collects. It seems probable that at least some agitators have been heavily subsidized by anonymous wealthy donors, and it is known that some of the smaller fry make a living by selling their literature.

When the agitator appeals to his followers for money, he strengthens their devotion to the cause by leading them to make financial sacrifices. In agitation such psychological factors are probably of greater importance than in other movements, for it must be remembered that in agitation the follower has no precise idea what his cause is, that the whole background of the agitator's appeal is one of destruction and violence, with a meager minimum of positive stimuli. What remains then is the agitator himself—his inflated personality and his pressing needs. The agitator does not hesitate to act the insistent beggar. He begs meekly: "Oh, I'm just a common American citizen, friends, poor in the world's gifts, depending on the quarters and dollars of friends and radio listeners."[55] But he also begs for himself as the agent of history: "It is a long grind to get the thousands of dollars absolutely necessary as a minimum in this way. But it must be done if the fight is to go on."[56] "Why hold back your financial aid NOW—when revolution itself is being shouted from our public rostrums?"[57]

He begs for aid, but he also warns that those who do not come through now may live to regret it: "If any of you don't agree with the principles of America First and don't care to contribute to our cause, this is the time for you to get up and walk out."[58] Those who do not comply face the dreaded penalty of exclusion: they have to walk out and be alone with themselves.

Magic of Survival

That he has managed to survive under terrible financial handicaps and political persecution arouses the agitator's self-admiration. "How could he emerge unscathed with such colossal forces arrayed to smash him?"[59] His invulnerability is remarkable and is only slightly short of miraculous. His safety is, in fact, adduced as proof that he has gone through dangers, and as he concludes his report of the plot hatched against him by English Jews, he remarks with a note of defiance in his voice: "I arrived safely Sunday night."[60] His life seems to him protected by an anonymous providence: *"Pelley is an absolute fatalist . . . he believes that nothing can harm him until he has done the work which he came into life at this particular period to do!"*[61] And he always returns to the fight: "I intend to . . . toss off the shackles that have been thrown around me . . . to spread my wings again . . . and to soar to new heights to carry on the battle."[62] His powers of exertion are tremendous: "I speak two hours here and two hours there, and write all night and talk all day to people and write letters and work . . . and everything else, and still I always seem to have the strength to do what lies before me."[63]

Seen from one perspective, all this bragging is rather harmless. A narcissist naturally believes himself invulnerable and omnipotent, and his slightly ridiculous posturings only endear him to his audience. He is reduced to a level that is within their vision. Like the extraordinary exploits of the hero of a movie or a cheap novel, the agitator's adventure ends on an ultimately happy note: the hero is saved. From this harmless relapse into an adolescent atmosphere, the followers, together with the agitator himself, draw a certain simple gratification. They have been in the company of a hero who is not too heroic to be akin to them.

And yet somewhere in the interstices of this harmless braggadocio there lurk the grimmer notes of violence and destruction. The agitator's self-portrait of miraculous survival has a solid reality basis; he really does enjoy a high degree of impunity. He is safe and sound, magically immune, secretly protected, and this despite his verbal violence and scurrilous denunciations of the powers that be or of some of the powers that be. If his enemies do not carry out their threats of murder, it is not because they would not want to but because they do not dare. Their power, the agitator thereby suggests, is rather less impressive than it appears; they have only the façade of power. Real power is on his side.

Behind this defiance of the enemy's threats lurks another suggestion: when the hour strikes and the seemingly strong enemy is revealed in his true weakness, the agitator will take revenge for the torments of fear that have been imposed on him. Perhaps it is not too bold to conjecture that as the agitator continually stresses his own bodily vigor, he is implicitly developing a complementary image to his leading metaphor of the enemy as a Low Animal. His own body is indestructible, but the helpless bodies of the enemy—those parasitical and disease-breeding low animals—are doomed to destruction. Behind the whining complaints and the triumphant self-admiration of this indestructible martyr looms the vision of the eugenic storm troops. The agitator is a good little guy, to be sure; he is a martyr who suffers endlessly; he survives by virtue of superior destinies; but in the long run he makes sure to protect himself.

Tough Guy

The agitator knows that sometimes he must bare his teeth. Often he does it with the air of a youthful gang leader testing his hoodlums:

> I am going to test my people. I am going to see if the fathers that left their bones on the desert had real sons. I am going to find out if the children of the men that rebuilt San Francisco after the earthquake are real men.[64]

Such vague anticipations of the agitator's future role are supplemented with more direct hints about his present strength. He means business, even if he is a great little man. "I am a tough guy. I am tough because I have got the goods on them."[65] The easygoing braggart is also a brutal swashbuckler. "They can threaten me all they want to. I am not a damned bit afraid to walk the streets of New York all by myself. I don't have to. I have the toughest men in New York with me."[66] Nor does he always have to sneak in the dark to his printer: "Huskies of my 'American Group' protect me when I take my printed booklets from the printer's plant."[67]

The bodyguard, however, is used not merely against the enemy. The same bodyguard that protects the leader from the enemy also protects him from any interference from his listeners; their role is to listen, not to participate. When he speaks, you had better listen—or else. In this way the agitator already establishes himself as a constituted authority. The agitator brags about this:

> So as we moved down through the middle of the meeting I said. "Now, we are not going to have any disturbance, we are not going to be heckled and the first man who attempts that, we will throw him out through the nearest window." So one fellow like this boy, way up in the balcony said something and somebody didn't understand what he said and he was almost pitched out of the window.[68]

It is in this atmosphere, in which even the followers are threatened with manhandling if they step out of line, that the agitator tests out a future device: the totalitarian plebiscite. "Do you authorize me to send a telegram to Senator Reynolds . . . put up your hands. . . . All right, that is number one."[69] He feeds them cues: "I bid for the American vote under that flag. Give that a hand."[70] Such presentiments of the plebiscite are in themselves trivial enough, but they serve to emphasize the agitator's role as the sole legitimate voice to which everyone must listen in silence except when told to speak up in unison.

Inside Knowledge

Not only is the agitator physically powerful and something of a terrorist to boot but he also has access to secret and highly important information, the source of which he is most careful not to reveal. He quotes mysterious "sources" that enabled him "to correctly diagnose 3 years ago that the 1940 presidential election would not be bonafide."[71] He asserts that "there has fallen into my hands a copy of these confidential instructions which came out from New York City concerning the underground science."[72] By miraculous but unspecified means he manages to penetrate into the heart of the enemy fortress where his sharp ears hear the confidences that "Zionists in America whispered with secret circles."[73]

On other occasions the agitator can offer only promises of revelations to come: "I shall try to keep you posted concerning the diabolical conspiracy."[74] Or his information is too horrible to disclose: "I personally have had some experiences in the last year that would make your blood run cold, if I could tell you what they were."[75] Or he is bound by professional secrecy:

> Two contacts, best unnamed on account of nature of information divulged, inform: ". . . believes that he has discovered the hdqtrs. of what seems to be Grand Orient Masonry . . . uptown in New York City. A building in the middle of a large block, surrounded by apartment houses; in a sort of courtyard, with a high barbed wire fence around it. No one is ever seen to enter this place, altho access could be had underground from one or more of the surrounding houses. A large telephone cable, sufficient for over 100 lines, goes to the place which is guarded night and day by armed guards."[76]

The agitator uses the language of an adolescent gang leader. He seeks to ingratiate himself with his listeners by promising them some highly important information. Some day the listeners will be "let in." But the agitator uses this technique of innuendo in ways other than the relatively harmless promise to divulge secrets. He withholds information in the very gesture by which he seems to give it out. He reveals not secrets but the existence of secrets; the secrets themselves are another variety of "forbidden fruit." Those affected by the promise to be "let in" are even more affected by the fact that the agitator has access to information inaccessible to them. To listen to innuendo and to rely on deliberately vague statements requires a certain readiness to believe, which the agitator directs toward his own person. So long as he does not reveal the "sources" of his knowledge, the agitator can continue to command the dependence of his followers. Unlike the educator, he never makes himself superfluous by revealing his methods of gaining knowledge. He remains the magical master.

This secret knowledge, like his toughness, is a two-edged weapon. It implies an ever-present threat from which no one is quite safe: "Some day that thing is really going to come out, and when it comes out it is going to smell so high that any man that is connected with them, with that outfit, will be ashamed to say that he ever knew them."[77] Or: "I have written a letter containing some mighty important information which I have placed in the hands of attorneys in this city.... The letter will not be printed ... if we arrive home safely at the end of our campaign."[78]

Behind such statements there is the suggestion that he knows more than he says, and that nothing can ultimately remain hidden from him. If his self-portrait as a tough guy anticipates the storm trooper, then his insistence on his "inside knowledge" anticipates the secret files of the totalitarian police, which are used less against the political enemy, known in any case, than as a means to keep the followers in line. Sternly the agitator indicates this to his followers: get used to the idea now, if you want a share in this racket, you have to obey its rules—and I make the rules.

The Charismatic Leader

The self-portrait of the agitator may seem a little ridiculous. Such an absurd creature—at once one of the plain folk and the sanctified leader; the head of a bedraggled family and a man above all material considerations; a helpless victim of persecution and a dreaded avenger with fists of iron! Yet contemporary history teaches us that this apparently ridiculous braggart cannot be merely laughed away.

In establishing this ambivalent image of himself the agitator achieves an extremely effective psychological result. In him, the martyr ultimately triumphant over his detractors and persecutors, the adherents see all their own frustrations magically metamorphosed into grandiose gratifications. They who are marginal suddenly have a prospect of sharing in the exceptional; their suffering now can appear to them as a glorious trial, their anonymity and servitude as stations on the road to fame and mastery. The agitator finds the promise of all these glories in that humdrum existence of his followers that had driven them to listen sympathetically to his appeals; he shows them how all the accumulated stuff of repression and frustration can be lit up into a magnificent fireworks, how the refuse of daily drudgery can be converted into a high explosive of pervasive destruction.

The self-portrait of the agitator is thus a culmination of all his other themes, which prepare the audience for the spectacle of the great little man acting as leader. Taking advantage of all the weaknesses of the present social order, the agitator intensifies his listeners' sense of bewilderment and helplessness, terrifies them with the specter of innumerable dangerous enemies and reduces their already crumbling individualities to bundles of reactive responses. He drives them into a moral void in which their inner voice of conscience is replaced by an externalized conscience: the agitator himself. He becomes the indispensable guide in a confused world, the center around which the faithful can gather and find safety. He comforts the sufferers of malaise, takes the responsibility of history and becomes the exterior replacement of their disintegrated individuality. They live through him.

Notes

1. Phelps, Los Angeles, Sept. 26, 1940, radio.
2. Smith, New York, Oct. 20, 1936, meeting.
3. Phelps, Los Angeles, Aug. 7, 1941.
4. Smith, *The Hoop of Steel,* p. 23.
5. AP, May, 1945, p. 8.
6. CF, May, 1942, p. 8.
7. Phelps, Los Angeles, July 28, 1941, radio.
8. Coughlin, Speech on Jan. 29, 1939, reprinted in *Why Leave Our Own,* p. 57.
9. Phelps, Los Angeles, July 21, 1941, radio.
10. Phelps, Los Angeles, Sept. 19, 1940, radio.
11. Smith, New York, Oct. 20, 1936, meeting.
12. Phelps, Los Angeles, Aug. 1, 1941.
13. Winrod, *Letter,* Feb. 1943, p. 3.
14. Hudson, letter to subscribers of his Bulletin, July, 1942.
15. Smith, Detroit, Apr. 9, 1942, meeting.
16. Smith, *Why is America Afraid?*
17. Phelps, Los Angeles, Aug. 18, 1940, radio.
18. RTL, Feb. 28, 1942, p. 3.
19. Smith, Detroit, Mar. 19, 1943, meeting.
20. PRB, Apr. 8, 1942, p. 1.
21. Phelps, Los Angeles, Jan. 14, 1941, radio.
22. CF, July, 1945, p. 604.
23. CF, May, 1942, p. 9.
24. Stewart, New York, July 13, 1940, street corner.
25. Smith, Cleveland, May 11, 1943, meeting.
26. Smith, Detroit, Apr. 9, 1942, meeting.
27. DEF, Oct., 1942, p. 11.
28. Smith, St. Louis, Mar. 25, 1944, meeting.
29. SJ, July 7, 1941, p. 4.
30. CF, Aug., 1945, p. 616.
31. Smith, *Why Is America Afraid?*
32. LIB, Sept. 21, 1939, p. 7.
33. SJ, June 5, 1939, p. 2.
34. RC, Oct. 20, 1941, p. 16.
35. Smith, Detroit, Mar. 19, 1943, meeting.
36. Smith, *ibid.*
37. DEF, Nov., 1940, p. 5.
38. SJ, July 7, 1941, p. 4.
39. Smith, Detroit, Mar. 19, 1943, meeting.

40. Phelps, Los Angeles, Nov. 20, 1940, radio.
41. AID, June 23, 1942, p. 4.
42. Pelley, *What You Should Know About The Pelley Publications*, p. 4.
43. Phelps, Los Angeles, Sept. 29, 1940, radio.
44. Smith, Detroit, Mar. 22, 1943, meeting.
45. Smith, New York, Oct. 20, 1936, meeting.
46. Smith, *ibid.*
47. Smith, *"Reds On The Run,"* radio, p. 2.
48. CF, May, 1942, p. 9.
49. CF, Oct.–Nov., 1942, p. 3.
50. CF, Feb., 1943, p. 154.
51. Smith, Detroit, Feb. 7, 1943, meeting.
52. CF, Apr., 1945, p. 557.
53. Smith, *Letter,* "The Battle of Babylon," July, 1945, p. 1.
54. Smth, St. Louis, April 29, 1948, meeting.
55. Phelps, Los Angeles, Sept. 8, 1940, radio.
56. PRB, Aug. 10, 1942, p. 5.
57. SJ, Nov. 27, 1939, p. 19.
58. Smith, St. Louis, Mar. 25, 1944, meeting.
59. Pelley, *What You Should Know About The Pelley Publications,* p. 5.
60. AID, June 23, 1942, p. 4.
61. Pelley, *Official Despatch,* p. 4.
62. Phelps, Los Angeles, Dec. 31, 1940, radio.
63. Smith, Detroit, Mar. 19, 1943, meeting.
64. Smith, New York, Oct. 20, 1936, meeting.
65. Phelps, Los Angeles, Oct. 8, 1940, radio.
66. McWilliams, New York, July 29, 1940, street corner.
67. Phelps, Los Angeles, Nov. 12, 1940, radio.
68. Smith, Detroit, Feb. 7, 1943, meeting.
69. Smith, Detroit, Mar. 19, 1943, meeting.
70. Smith, New York, Oct. 20, 1936, meeting.
71. AID, Jan. 19, 1942, p. 4.
72. Smith, *"Dictatorship Comes with War,"* radio, p. 3.
73. SJ, July 14, 1941, p. 7.
74. Smith, *Letter,* Mar., 1943.
75. CF, Feb., 1943, p. 154.
76. AID, Nov. 26, 1941, p. 2.
77. Smith, New York, Oct. 20, 1936, meeting.
78. Phelps, Los Angeles, Feb. 7, 1941, radio.

10

What the Listener Heard

In Europe, Hitler and Mussolini openly advocated a radical break with contemporary society. They explicitly repudiated capitalism and liberalism, and negated the democratic way of life in favor of a system based on charismatic leadership. To make their ideas attractive they resorted both to a glorified evocation of the preliberalistic past and to a distorted version of contemporary revolutionary ideologies. The very name National Socialist shows how the Hitler movement tried to incorporate elements of ideologies that appealed both to the past and the future.

These preliberalistic and revolutionary elements of the fascist appeal in Europe served to mask the actual meaning of the movement. In practice Nazi totalitarianism was no more feudal than it was socialist. Its break with contemporary society took place only on the cultural and ideological level; the old liberalistic values were ruthlessly pushed aside for the needs of an industrial war machine. Old forms of economic and social coercion were perpetuated and strengthened.

The American agitator, however, has no preliberalistic tradition on which to fall back; he does not find it expedient to pose as a socialist, and he dares not explicitly repudiate established morality and democratic values. He only indirectly and implicitly assumes the mantle of charismatic leadership. He works, by necessity rather than choice, within the framework of liberalism.

Study of our themes shows that this limitation does not prevent him from conveying the principal social tenets of totalitarianism to his audience. The themes point to the disintegration of existing institutions, the perversion and destruction of democracy, the rejection of Western values, the exaltation of the leader, the reduction of the people to regimented robots, and the solution of social problems by terroristic violence. The American agitator shows that manipulation of people with a view to obtaining their conscious or unconscious adherence to his movement need not take the detour of preliberalism or perverted socialism; that the psychological attitudes and social concerns that flow from the crisis of liberal society provide a sufficiently fertile soil for the growth of anti-democratic tendencies. It is as though the American agitator had evolved a method of directly converting the poisons generated by contemporary society into the quack remedies of totalitarianism; he does not need to resort to pseudofeudal or pseudosocialist labels. His themes could be transplanted to another country, much more easily than corresponding Nazi slogans could be transplanted to the United States. The mythical notion of the pure-blooded Nordic Aryan German superman would have to undergo many profound changes before becoming an effective appeal in this country, but the agitator's Simple Americans could be used in other countries as Simple Germans, or Simple French, or Simple Britishers, and so on. One is tempted to say that the American agitation is a standardized and simplified version of the original Nazi or fascist appeals.

Because the American agitator dispenses with such secondary labels, his methods of appeal are also more universal in scope, and are not bound to any specific national tradition or political situation. Despite his professions of Americanism, not a single one of his appeals refers to concerns of situations specific to the United States. The feelings that he stirs are in no sense limited to this country, for the social abscesses on which his invectives thrive can be found in any modern industrialized society.

The agitator seems aware of this when he declares that "I stand before you tonight, as I have stood before similar groups all over America, as a symbol of a state of mind that exists in America."[1] He does not tell us what this state of mind is, but on the basis of a study of his themes we can construct a portrait of the state of mind of his most susceptible kind of listener. This listener does not directly participate in the major fields of social production and is therefore always fearful that, given the slightest social maladjustment, his insignificant little job will vanish and with it will vanish his social status. He senses that in some way he cannot quite fathom life has cheated him. And yet he wonders why his fate should have been so unhappy. He abided by the rules, he never rebelled, he did what was expected of him. Bound and circumscribed by a series of uncontrollable circumstances, he becomes increasingly aware of how futile and desperately aimless his life is. And worst of all, he can no longer believe in any miraculous salvations, for no matter how much he hopes for them he is far too much the modern man really to place his faith in miracles. He is on the bottom, on the outside, and he fears that there is nothing he can do about it. Yet there are others, the intellectuals who talk about ideals and values and morals, and who make a living—a clean, comfortable living—by manipulating words. They are smart alecks who paint pictures of wonderful societies in the future and who live so comfortably in this one. Most of them are Jews, of course, who seem to have beaten the racket. And even more so, there is that secret and inaccessible gang that lives in air-conditioned penthouses, enjoys the favors of movie stars, and luxuriates on yachts, the lucky few, who tempt him with the possibility of success and the dream of escape from his own grimy and dreary life.

Sometimes openly, more often in the veiled areas of his daydreams, our listener admits to himself that in this world—and who can imagine any other?—all that counts is success. Only the successful are to be admired. It is a deadly struggle, and those who fall must be discarded. These standards are inculcated in him by every medium of mass amusement. The very places to which he goes for relaxation—the movies, the comics, the radio—provide him not with spiritual refreshment but with an exacerbated feeling that success is the all-essential fact of modern life, and that he is not successful.

And so the listener grumbles. He grumbles against bureaucrats, Jews, congressmen, plutocrats, communists—whatever political stereotype he can find to suggest to him concentrations of power. He grumbles against the foreigners who come to this country and get good jobs. He grumbles against the party in power, votes for the one out of power and then grumbles against it. But he knows no other means of venting his social dissatisfaction, and at one point or another he begins to become suspicious of the efficacy of his grumbling. And what is more, even grumbling has its dangers. One must be careful where one grumbles. A lot of it has to be kept inside one, repressed, barely touching the rims of consciousness.

The listener would like to do something about it, something drastic and decisive that will do away with the whole mess. Imagine—strike one blow on the table and everything is changed.

Rehearsal of Violence

How prevalent is the type that has been briefly sketched above? There is reason to believe that at least strands or aspects of this "ideal" personality type are widespread in modern life. The voluminous literature on psychic discontent, ranging from advice on how to keep friends and influence people to prescriptions for peace of mind, testifies to this fact. For a variety of historical circumstances, social and economic, the American agitator has not succeeded in gaining any large masses of adherents. Except for the early years of the New Deal and those preceding Pearl Harbor, the agitator's audience has been limited to a hard core of followers: disgruntled old people, cranks, toughies, unemployables, and certain undefined groups. Such audiences are often unkindly identified as the lunatic fringe.

The agitator must know that he can hardly expect to achieve significant results without reaching a wider audience; his ambitions are certainly not confined to his present groups, but he seems to sense that such initial audiences reflect on a small scale what might under certain social conditions characterize large masses of people. The beginnings of European fascism were equally modest, its original followers recruited from similar strata of the population. The American agitator tends to behave as if his present performance were merely a rehearsal and his audience merely paradigmatic. He can afford to be "unserious."

In an economic crisis the distinction between unemployables and unemployed merges, the middle class loses its security, and the youth its confidence in the future. The possibility that a situation will arise in which large numbers of people would be susceptible to his psychological manipulation seems to provide the agitator with the impetus to continue his present small-scale operations at the head of his legion of misfits and malcontents.

The Social Basis of Agitation

It is the deep and pervasive presence of the social malaise that we sketched in an earlier chapter that is both the origin of agitation and the field in which agitation flourishes. Malaise gives rise to agitation, and agitation battens on malaise. In some dim nook of his consciousness, the agitator seems aware of this; he has a keener sense of history than those of his critics who think he can be banished from history by showing that he is inconsistent. He claims to be issuing the "most important challenge that could be made to a bankrupt, blood-drenched, war-torn, hate-filled. Satan-run world,"[2] and he predicts that "unreasonable force will hold sway"[3] if the present intolerable situation persists. This prediction, it must be granted, is not entirely fantastic, and it is precisely because the agitator does refer to pressing realities, because he does touch on the most exposed and painful sores of our social body that he is able to meet with a response.

The agitator's themes are distorted versions of genuine social problems. When he encourages disaffection from all current loyalties, he takes advantage of a contemporary tendency to doubt either the sufficiency of efficacy of Western values. When he takes advantage of the anxiety and fears of his listeners, he is playing on very real anxieties and fears; there is something to be anxious and fearful about. When he offers them a sense of belonging, no matter how counterfeit it is, and a sense of participation in a worthy cause, his words find response only because men today feel homeless and need a new belief in the possibility of social harmony and well-being. And when he calls upon them to depend on him, he capitalizes on both their revolt against the restraints of civilization and their longing for some new symbol of authority. That which they utter under their breaths, the sub rosa thoughts that they are hardly ready to acknowledge to themselves become the themes flaunted in agitation.

What the agitator does, then, is to activate the most primitive and immediate, the most inchoate and dispersed reactions of his followers to the general trends of contemporary society.

After he has subtly awakened his adherents to a realization that in some inexplicable way they are being crushed, the agitator diverts them from a true consciousness of their troubles and from any possible solution to their problems by the following "reasoning": The forces that threaten to crush them are irresistible, inexorable, and uncontrollable by rational means. To oppose them with the "bare bodkin" of ideals would be sheer folly, a kind of utopian quixotism. Therefore the best thing to do is to join them, to become one of the policemen, one of the destroyers in the service of destruction. This proposal is essentially tantamount to a suggestion that the adherents destroy themselves. Because the forces against you are so overwhelming, join with them . . . and be overwhelmed. Like a cheater in solitaire, the adherent is to become a conqueror by defeating himself.

To recognize and play upon those disturbing sicknesses of modern life that the run-of-the-mill politicians ignore, and then to divert his followers from any rational attempt to regain health—this is the essential objective role of the agitator in society. The basic implication of his appeals is that submission to social coercion is to be more ready and unquestioning. Hence the basic implications of the themes—the charismatic glorification of the leader, the extinction of civil liberties, the police state, the unleashing of terror against helpless minority groups. For all his emphasis on and expression of discontent, the agitator functions objectively to perpetuate the conditions that give rise to that discontent.

A Dictionary of Agitation

The themes cannot be understood in terms of their manifest content. They rather constitute a kind of secret psychological language. The unimpressed listener may wave it aside as a kind of mania or a mere tissue of lies and nonsense. Yet some people succumbed to it: in the United States a few, but in Europe millions. Were there no other evidence at hand, this one fact would be sufficient to establish the conclusion that there are powerful psychological magnets within agitation that draw groups of people to the leader's orbit. But we now also have at our disposal the classification of agitational themes that has appeared in these pages—our attempt to translate the secret code of agitation into language accessible to all. As we analyze this material, we find that its essential meaning—that which attracts the followers—cannot be reached by means of the usual methods of logical inquiry but that it is a psychological Morse code tapped out by the agitator and picked up by the followers. How conscious the agitator is of the genuine meaning of his message is a moot question that we have not attempted to answer here; it is a job for another investigation. But for the purpose of finding the inner meaning and the recurrent patterns of agitation, the presence or absence of consciousness on the part of the agitator is ultimately of secondary importance.

In any case, the distinction between the manifest and latent meaning of an agitational text must be seen as crucial. Taken at their face value, agitational texts seem merely as indulgence in futile furies about vague disturbances. Translated into their psychological equivalents, agitational texts are seen as consistent, meaningful, and significantly related to the social world.

In all his output the agitator engages in an essentially ambiguous activity. He never merely says; he always hints. His suggestions manage to slip through the nets of rational meaning, those nets that seem unable to contain so many contemporary utterances. To know what he is and what he says, we have to follow him into the underground of meaning, the unexpressed or half-expressed content of his hints, allusions, doubletalk.

Always, then, the agitator appeals to those elements of the contemporary malaise that involve a rejection of traditional Western values. As we have seen in the previous chapter, he directs all of his themes to one ultimate aim: his followers are to place all their faith in his person, a new, externalized, and brutal superego. Except through translation into their psychological referents, it is impossible to understand modern agitational themes.

If we strip the agitator's message of its mystical grandiloquence and rhetoric, and present it in a rationally formulated version, we are in a position to understand the role and the basis of appeal of agitation. Such a translation lays bare the objective social consequences of agitation and the potential relationship between leader and follower. It does not in itself destroy the appeal of agitation for the followers or give a blueprint for opposing the agitator politically. But it does at the very least expose the true social and psychological content of agitation—the essential prerequisite for its prophylaxis.

The Agitator Means

My friends, we live in a world of inequity and injustice. But whoever believes that this state of affairs will ever be or can ever be changed is a fool or a liar. Oppression and injustice, as war and famine, are eternal accompaniments of human life. The idealists who claim otherwise are merely fooling themselves—and worse still, are merely fooling you. To indulge in gestures of human brotherhood is merely bait for suckers, the kind of thing that will prevent you from getting the share of loot available to you today. Doesn't your own experience tell you that whenever you were idealistic you had to pay for it? Be practical. The world is an arena of a grim struggle for survival. You might as well get your share of the gravy.

Instead of joining with the oppressed and suffering with them, come with me. I offer you no promise of peace or security or happiness. I hold before you no chimera of individuality—whatever that word may mean. I scorn even the catchwords that I use when convenient.

If you follow me, you will ally yourself with force, with might and power—the weapons that ultimately decide all disagreements. We will offer you scapegoats—Jews, radicals, plutocrats, and other creatures conjured by our imagination. These you will be able to berate and eventually persecute. What difference will it make whether they are your real enemies so long as you can plunder them and vent your spleen on them?

Not utopia but a realistic struggle to grab the bone from the other dog—that is our program. Not peace but incessant struggle for survival; not abundance but the lion's share of scarcity. Can you realistically expect more?

To win this much you will have to follow me. We will form an iron-bound movement of terror. We will ally ourselves with the powerful in order to gain part of their privilege. We will be the policemen rather than the prisoners. And I will be the leader. I will think for you, I will tell you what to do and when to do it. I will act out your lives for you in my public role as leader. But I will also protect you. In the shadow of my venom you will find a home.

Notes

1. Smith, New York, Oct. 20, 1938, meeting.
2. CF, Feb., 1946, p. 702.
3. SJ, Mar. 21, 1938, p. 10.

Appendix I

Samples of Profascist or Anti-Semitic Statements by the Agitators Quoted in This Study

As we mentioned in the preface, in selecting a given agitator as object of this study we have been guided by his professed sympathy for European totalitarianism or avowed anti-Semitism. Below is a complete list of the agitators whose written or oral texts have served as the basis of our interpretations. Each name is accompanied by a sample anti-Semitic statement and in some cases by a profascist statement.

Profascist Statements

Court Asher

"In Germany reigns unity of will and effort. In this country reigns disunity, approaching chaos and civil war.... The Germans are a people with a leader. We are a people without a leader." (*X-Ray*, December 6, 1941, p. 3)

Father Coughlin

"The ordinary citizen has neither time nor means at his disposal to correlate these things.

"If he suspects that a secret alliance exists between the so-called democracies of the world—America, France, Great Britain and Russia—is he sure that they are democracies?

Anti-Semitic Statements

But how, I pray you, can any intelligent person condemn the actions of the Nazis against the Jews in Europe and endorse the colossal crimes of the Communist-Jew controlled Russia who murdered millions of Christians. The Nazis murdered Jews. Surely, killing kikes is no worse than killing Gentiles." (*X-Ray*, September 1, 1946)

"It is time for Americans to recognize that Washington, D.C. is being dominated by a Jewish concept of life and that our people are being regimented into a totalitarianism which is best described as a 'Jewish democracy.'" (*Social Justice*, July 28, 1941, p. 4)

Profascist Statements

"Is he informed that the so-called totalitarian states, against which this alliance has been established, have rebelled against the dictators of money, the controllers of gold?

"Or, is this a fabulous assertion?" (*Why Leave Our Own*, "Foreign Relations—In Three Acts," February 5, 1939, pp. 61–62)

Leon De Aryan

"Democracy is mob rule. Do you want mob rule? Do you want to bring it to all the world and supplant orderly governments?

"Hitler said he did not want it. Mussolini said he did not want it. . . . Now if we all agree we do not want it, please, tell me, what is this war about?" (*The Broom*, June 16, 1941, p. 1)

Elizabeth Dilling

"The Germans were the best-fed, best-housed, most powerful, pinkcheeked, united and hopeful people in Europe while we were being told they were starving and ready to revolt. But now that they are holding down half the world, they menace the *British* empire but are less of a menace to us than ever before . . ." (*Round Table Letter*, February 1942, p. 1)

Charles Bartlett Hudson

"'Hate-Hitler' *CAMPAIGN* being used to prepare us for another World War. . . . Why the constant raps at 'fascism,' and the condoning by silence or excuses, the activities and threat of Anti-Christ Communism?" (*America in Danger!* July 24, 1938, p. 1)

Joseph P. Kamp

Anti-Semitic Statements

"Now these Jews don't like it that there are Americans who are Americans and really believe in what the Bill of Rights stands for. . . . They consider themselves a privileged superrace who may persecute those of a different mind and religion." (*The Broom*, December 4, 1944, p. 2)

"Instead of living and letting Gentiles live, organized Jewry continues to browbeat and extort from Jews huge funds 'to fight anti-Semitism' which they use to persecute Gentiles, to hire armies of snoopers, commit every sort of illegal conspiracy, terrorize, bully and engender indignation and anti-Semitism." (*Patriotic Research Bureau*, December 1944, p. 13)

"How would you like to have the bloodstream of your baby, or son, or husband, or daughter, or wife, polluted by dried blood collected from Jews, Negroes, and criminals?" (*America in Danger!* February 3, 1942, p. 2)

"Despite the smears, persecutions and libels, impugning my loyalty and patriotism, that I have suffered and endured at its hands, I have, up to now,

Profascist Statements	Anti-Semitic Statements
	been reluctant to name the Jewish Gestapo, not in fear of the consequences, not because it would be used to falsely brand me an anti-Semite, but for the very simple reason that such a truthful identification might be misunderstood and might unjustly reflect on good Americans of the Jewish Faith who, if they could know the truth, would be the first to condemn the vicious activities of this Gestapo, which presumes to act in their name and in their alleged interest. . . . It will not be an easy job to investigate and expose the Jewish Gestapo and the Smear Bund and their campaign. But Congress can succeed if it fully realizes the magnitude of the task and the difficulties involved." (*Open Letter to Congress*, 1948, p. 12)

Joseph E. McWilliams, and lieutenants

"Whatever man has destroyed Communism and Internationalism, if it is Mussolini, I stand with him. If it is Hitler in Germany, I stand with him, and again, if it is Franco in Spain." (New York street corner speech, July 29, 1940)	"I am Joseph E. McWilliams, the anti-Jewish candidate for Congress from this district." (New York street corner speech, July 13, 1940)

(Corresponding quotations are available from McWilliams' lieutenants at that time, Louis Helmond, Thomas Maloney, James Stewart, and Charles White.)

Carl H. Mote

"Is Hitler's barter system so objectionable to the money changers that we are fighting a global war to destroy it?..." (quoted in *Propaganda Battlefront*, February 28, 1945, p. 2)	"The Jews . . . are unwilling to share the fate of their fellowmen but they are demanding special consideration as a 'minority,' a 'stateless' class, a 'homeless' race, a helpless people, a 'persecuted' religion. ." (*America Preferred*, February, 1945, p. 10)

William Dudley Pelley

"It is a fact which posterity will attest, that Chief Pelley of The Silvershirts was the first man in the United States to step out openly in support of Adolph Hitler and his German Nazi program." (*Liberation*, July 28, 1938)	"Every student of international affairs knows that the economic conflicts and wars are caused by Jews." (*Liberation*, November 14, 1939, p. 5)

Profascist Statements	Anti-Semitic Statements
George Allison Phelps	"If you get them to talk, you'll find that they virtually bristle with hate because their pride has been hurt by Adolph Hitler. They have a persecution complex and they want America to go to war so that they can have their revenge . . . one racial group which Hitler doesn't like and which has a persecution complex. The latter group wants war even if it costs the lives of 10 million Americans, as long as they can have their revenge." (Speech, local radio station, Los Angeles, October 20, 1940)
E. N. Sanctuary "He testified that he was opposed to democracy (s.m.p. 367,370) and that 'democracy has never succeeded and never will.' He testified that he did not feel either Fascism or Nazism was a threat to our government (s.m.p. 697) and was unable to point to a single place in which he criticized either Nazism or Fascism in all his voluminous writings (s.m.p. 405). (Respondent's brief, *E. N. Sanctuary Against D. S. and T. O. Thackerey,* Appellate Division, First Judicial Department, Supreme Court, 1947, p. 8)	"Yet the Jew, who is a product of the Talmud, is a liability rather than an asset." (Letter reprinted in *The Defender,* April 1947, p. 22)
Gerald L. K. Smith	"Communism is mainly a Jewish plot. It was thought up by Jews, originated by Jews. Its revolutions have been promoted by Jews and they have even been financed by Jewish bankers. This does not mean that all Jews are Communists, but it does mean that no one can understand the Communist problem unless he understands the plot of the Jewish extremist and the international Jews. (*Newsletter,* October 1947, p. 2)

Profascist Statements	**Anti-Semitic Statements**

Gerald B. Winrod

"With the rise of Hitlerism a new consciousness has developed in Germany and the hopes of its 67 million people have been revived." (*The Revealer*, February 15, 1935)

"International Jews are making the same mistake in the United States that they have made in Europe and Asia—namely the abuse of power possessed through the secret systems of control which they have invented." (*The Defender*, March 1940, p. 3)

Appendix II

Bibliography of Printed Source Material

Court Asher (editor and publisher) — *The X-Ray.* Muncie, Indiana (Weekly)

Charles E. Coughlin (publisher) — *Social Justice.* Royal Oak, Michigan (Weekly)

Charles E. Coughlin — *Father Couglin's Radio Discourses.* 1931–1932, Royal Oak, Mich.

Charles E. Couglin — *Why Leave Our Own?* Thirteen Addresses on Christianity and Americanism. January 8–April 2, 1939.

Leon de Aryan (editor) — *The Broom.* San Diego, California (Weekly)

Elizabeth Dilling — *Round Table Letter.* (Monthly)

Elizabeth Dilling (director) — *Patriotic Research Bureau.* For the Defense of Christianity and Americanism, Chicago, Ill. (Monthly)

Charles Bartlett Hudson (editor and distributor) — *America in Danger.* Newcastle, Wyoming (Weekly)

Joseph P. Kamp — *How to Win the War . . . and Lose What We Are Fighting For.* 1942 (Pamphlet)

Joseph P. Kamp — *Native Nazi Purge Plot.* 1942 (Pamphlet)

Joseph P. Kamp — *Famine in America, Home Grown by the Farmers from Union Square.* 1943 (Pamphlet)

Joseph P. Kamp — *Vote CIO . . . and Get a Soviet America.* 1944 (Pamphlet)

Joseph P. Kamp — *With Lotions of Love.* 1944 (Pamphlet)

Joseph E. McWilliams — *The Servicemen's Reconstruction Plan.* Barrington, Ill., 1942.

Carl H. Mote (editor and publisher)	*America Preferred—A Journal of Opinion.* A Monthly Journal of Opinion on Politics, Government, Finance, History, Current Affairs, Education, Agriculture, Labor, Religion, Business and Taxation. Indianapolis, Indiana.
Carl H. Mote	*Testimony Before the U.S. Senate Committee on Military Affairs of the United States.* June 30, 1941 on S. 1579 "The Property Seizure Bill."
Carl H. Mote	Address Before the Meeting of "The American Charter." Cleveland, Ohio, July 1, 1942
William Dudley Pelley (editor)	*Liberation.* (Irregular)
William Dudley Pelley	*Pelley's Weekly.* Asheville, North Carolina (Weekly)
William Dudley Pelley	*Roll-Call.* Indianapolis, Indiana (Weekly)
William Dudley Pelley	*What You Should Know About The Pelley Publications.* (Prospectus)
William Dudley Pelley	*Official Despatch*, "Silver Shirts of America are Mobilizing to Protect Your Life" Silver Shirts of America, Asheville, N.C. (Pamphlet)
George Allison Phelps	*An Appeal to Americans.* (Pamphlet)
George Allison Phelps	*An American's History of Hollywood.* 1940 (Pamphlet)
E. N. Sanctuary	*The New Deal is Marxian Sabotage.* (Leaflet)
E. N. Sanctuary	*Litvinoff, Foreign Commissar of U.S.S.R.* 1935 (Pamphlet)
E. N. Sanctuary (translator and publisher)	*Tearing Away the Veils.* 1940 (Pamphlet)
Gerald L. K. Smith (editor and publisher)	*The Cross and The Flag.* St. Louis, Missouri (Monthly)
Gerald L. K. Smith	Printed radio speeches: *Which Way, America; Why is America Afraid?; Dictatorship Comes With War; Labor on the Cross; Americans! Stop. Look. Listen; Mice or Men?; The Next President of the U.S.*, Aug., 1939; *Enemies Within Our Gates*, Sept., 1939; *Stop Treason!*, 1939. *Reds On The Run*, Nov., 1939.

Gerald L. K. Smith	*The Hoop of Steel*; An American's Definition of Victory. Published by the Committee of One Million. Detroit, Mich., 1942.
Gerald L. K. Smith	*The Plan*, as Prepared by the Post-War Recovery Commission, 1945.
Gerald L. K. Smith	*Letters*. (Irregular)
Guy C. Stephens	*The Individualist.* Danville, Virginia (Monthly)
Gerald B. Winrod (editor)	*The Defender.* Wichita, Kansas (Monthly)
Gerald B. Winrod (editor)	*The Defender.* Wichita, Kansas (Monthly)
Gerald B. Winrod	Radio speeches on War and Peace 1939 (Pamphlet)

The text of the unpublished speeches quoted in this book were recorded either by skilled court stenographers or trained reporters.